complete
well-being

A guide TO symptoms AND cures

complete
well-being

A guide TO symptoms AND cures

DR CAROLINE SHREEVE

p

Created and produced for Parragon by

THE BRIDGEWATER BOOK COMPANY LIMITED

CREATIVE DIRECTOR Stephen Knowlden

ART DIRECTOR Colin Fielder

EDITORIAL DIRECTOR Fiona Biggs

EDITORS Sarah Yelling, Sarah Doughty

DESIGNER Nicola Liddiard

PHOTOGRAPHY Mike Hemsley at Walter Gardiner

PICTURE RESEARCH Lynda Marshall

INDEX Indexing Specialists

ISBN:1-40541-505-3   (Hardback)
ISBN:1-40541-147-3   (Paperback)

Printed in China

PICTURE ACKNOWLEDGEMENTS

A-Z Botanical Collection: pp: 15R, 51B; Corbis: pp: 46B, 59R, 63R, 90T, 122B, 178B,
180T, 187T, 202B, 239B, 247; Garden Picture Library: p. 112B; GettyOneStone:
pp. 41R, 75T, 77B, 83T, 99, 126T, 127T, 159T, 163T, 170T, 174T,179T, 185T, 217T,
233T; Image Bank: pp: 29T, 53T,124B, 207T, 243, 249; Oxford Scientific Films:
p. 40B; Science Photo Library: pp: 19R, 67T, 98T, 118B, 245T; Telegraph Colour
library: pp. 121C, 124T, 141B, 176T, 181T.

contents

introduction

Complementary medicines are more popular than ever before, and many people are beginning to take an active role in improving and maintaining their own health and well-being. There are many reasons for this, but prominent among them is the realisation that conventional medicine does have its limitations and is not infallible.

Complete Well-Being: A Guide to Symptoms and Cures takes the reader through the most common ailments and introduces a range of well-known alternative therapies that can be used to treat them. The nine ailment sections cover the usual range of problems, and present the information clearly and attractively. The second part of the book goes into more detail on the therapies themselves, describing the history, theory and consultation methods associated with them.

Complementary medicine not only offers you the opportunity to fight the symptoms of illness but also to look beneath the surface to its possible origins. One of the most important principles of complementary medicine is that it focuses

primarily on the individual, rather than on the symptoms or the underlying disease. This approach is referred to as 'holistic' – it looks at illness and its prevention and treatment in terms of you as a unique individual rather than in terms of a specific disease or collection of symptoms.

Most complementary medicines, such as homeopathy and aromatherapy, are very safe to self-administer and are also good to use on frail or elderly people, and on children. (If you are in doubt you must always consult a qualified practitioner.) One thing that must always be borne in mind, however, when using complementary medicines, is that they must not be used to replace conventional treatment if you or a family member is seriously ill. As long as you remember this you can be sure that there is a range of therapies that may help and, in some cases, make you less prone to recurrence.

Complete Well-Being: A Guide to Symptoms and Cures contains many practical tips that will empower you to take what you personally need from complementary medicine.

one: ailments

Looking after our digestive systems is an important part of our body maintenance. Stress, poor diet and not drinking enough water can all lead to disorders of the digestive tract. Ailments of the digestive system range from relatively minor problems such as mouth ulcers and indigestion, to more serious conditions such as colitis, diarrhoea or peptic ulcers.

the **digestive** system

Common mouth ulcers are small, grey sores with an inflamed mucous membrane. They vary from match-head-size to ⅕ in (0.5 cm) across and are found on the gums, roof of the mouth, under the tongue and inside the lips and cheeks. They are triggered by infections, poor immunity, stress, accidental damage from broken teeth and scalding foods.

mouth ulcers

SYMPTOMS

- Small, grey saucer-shaped sores
- A surrounding red tender halo
- Pain on talking and eating
- Large ulcers cause pain in the underlying muscle and enlarged lymph glands

Aloe vera can be used to make a soothing mouthwash to combat sore mouth ulcers. Mix the juice with boiled water and gargle.

THE CURES

VITAMINS AND MINERALS

Cabbage juice speeds the healing of mouth and peptic ulcers. Sip 7–10 fl oz (200–300 ml) daily, freshly juiced with a handful of mint leaves for added healing and improved flavour. Hold each mouthful in contact with the ulcers for as long as you can before swallowing.

Three major antioxidant vitamins – A, C and E – work together to boost immunity and strengthen mucous membranes. Beta-carotene, from which the body manufactures vitamin A, is found in brightly coloured fruit and vegetables, and one carrot, for instance, yields almost twice the recommended daily amount (RDA) of beta-carotene (1000 mcg). As much as 10–40 per cent of beta-carotene is lost in cooking (depending on the method) so eat fruit and vegetables raw, or juice them. Vitamin C (RDA 60 mg) is found in citrus fruit, but the acid can aggravate mouth ulcers. Broccoli, cauliflower, kiwi fruit and peppers are other good sources of vitamin C. Vitamin E (RDA 10 mg) heals mouth ulcers: take a 100–200 mg daily supplement and dab pure oil on ulcers as well. Found in vegetable oils, whole wheat, red cabbage, broccoli and nuts, vitamin E works best when coupled with selenium (RDA 50–100 mcg), which is present in bran, offal, seafood, wheatgerm, egg yolk and garlic.

HERBALISM

Boil a handful of carrot leaves in 10 fl oz (300 ml) of water for 5 minutes; cool slightly and use as a gargle and mouthwash. Or rinse the mouth with

4 tsp (20 ml) aloe vera juice mixed with boiled water 3 times a day.

AROMATHERAPY
Dip a cotton bud in pure clove or tea tree oil and apply neat to ulcers several times a day. Add a single drop of essential oil of rose, clary sage, geranium or savory to a tumbler of tepid water and use as a mouthwash.

HOMEOPATHY
Take 4 times a day for up to 5 days: Arsenicum 6c for a dry and burning mouth, and ulcers soothed by warm water; Mercurius 6c for stinging ulcers chiefly on the tongue, a coated tongue, bad breath, and loose, decaying teeth; and Nitric ac. 6c for painful ulcers on the soft palate (back of the roof of the mouth), with excessive saliva and bad breath.

MEDICAL TREATMENT
Antiseptic mouthwashes and gels can be used to help relieve ulcer pain and promote healing. Some mouthwashes and gels may even contain a small amount of local anaesthetic. In more serious outbreaks or in recurring cases, your doctor may also prescribe a course of vitamins, painkillers and nonsteroidal anti-inflammatory drugs (NSAIDs), and/or a short course of a steroid such as prednisone.

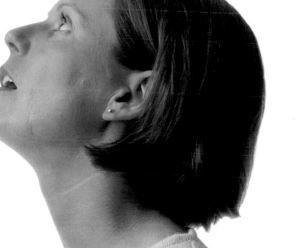

One way of preventing mouth ulcers is by regularly gargling with an antiseptic mouthwash. This will also help relieve pain from existing ulcers.

PREVENTION

Treat colds, flu and feverish illnesses as soon as they appear
Boost your immune defence system with lots of fruit and vegetables and extra vitamin C
Avoid acidic, spicy or scalding foods, smoking, careless brushing and ill-fitting dentures
Combat stress with yoga, relaxation, meditation and extra B vitamins
Use a mouthwash twice daily

Eating plenty of fresh vegetables and fruit will give your immune system a much-needed boost of vitamin C.

CAUTION

• *Seek medical advice to rule out more serious causes such as blood disorders, shingles (see page 112), or side effects of drugs*
• *Very large or painful ulcers, or ulcers that persist despite treatment, require medical attention*

mouth ulcers

Toothache results from pressure upon a dental nerve at the tooth's centre. Bacteria trapped as plaque on the teeth react with sugar in the mouth and break down the calcium salts in the tooth's substance. Chalky tartar around the base of the teeth causes numerous problems, including bad breath (halitosis), inflamed, bleeding gums, infection and dental loss.

toothache & bad breath

SYMPTOMS

- Tooth sensitive to hot or cold foods or drinks
- Ache in base of tooth
- Yellow, chalky substance (tartar) around base of teeth
- Gums bleed when you floss, brush or bite into something firm
- Bad taste in the mouth

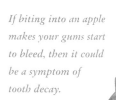

If biting into an apple makes your gums start to bleed, then it could be a symptom of tooth decay.

THE CURES

VITAMINS AND MINERALS

Reduce sugary foods to combat mouth acid and reduce decay. Chewing nuts, apples and raw vegetables cleanses and strengthens the teeth. Teeth also need calcium (RDA 800–1000 mg), found in milk and its products, mineral water, green vegetables, nuts, tinned salmon, sardines and other bony fish. Calcium absorption into the bloodstream is aided by vitamin D (RDA 10 mcg), made in the skin when exposed to sunlight and found in fish liver oil, mackerel, salmon and sardines. Dark-skinned people form vitamin D less readily, and children, especially, may need a vitamin D supplement.

HERBAL MEDICINE

A mouthwash made by infusing half a handful of rose petals, blueberry leaves, violet petals and/or sage in a litre of water, used daily, eases gum inflammation and helps to protect and strengthen teeth. Sweeten bad breath by chewing a small handful of fresh parsley.

AROMATHERAPY

Cloves' powerful antiseptic, eugenol, fights bad breath and eases sore gums. Dab the base of the tooth with clove oil or chew cloves for the same effect. Add 1 drop of essential oil of myrrh, a precious resin with powerful antiseptic and analgesic properties, to a tumbler of water and use as a mouthwash. Its bitterness can be offset by adding a drop of mint and/or cardamom oil, which also relieve toothache and gum soreness.

HOMEOPATHY

One dose every 4–8 hours, or 3–4 times per day: Mercurius 6c for tender, spongy gums which bleed easily, loose teeth and bad breath; Chamomilla 6c for unbearable toothache, aggravated by cold air and warm food and drink, and coffee at night; or Coffea 6c for toothache aggravated by heat and hot food, relieved by applying ice.

MEDICAL TREATMENT

Painkillers such as paracetamol, aspirin and NSAIDs all ease toothache. Antibiotics are prescribed to combat an abscess or gum infection. Mouthwashes containing benzoic acid, eucalyptol, methyl salicylate, thymol and sodium benzoate (among other ingredients) are clinically proven to

Oily fish such as mackerel is a good source of vitamin D, which enables the body to absorb calcium effectively into the bloodstream.

reduce plaque and tartar, and to kill bacteria. Dental treatment is required to deal with more serious problems such as the removal of decay and filling eroded teeth. Fluoride in drinking water and dental preparations combats the destructive effects of acids produced during plaque formation by binding with the calcium present in dental tissue.

Milk is a good source of calcium, but in order for the body to process it properly, children may need to supplement their diet with vitamin D.

Cutting down on our intake of sugary foods such as cakes and sweets can help prevent tooth decay.

PREVENTION
Cut down on sugary foods
Brush and floss teeth after meals
Use toothpaste and mouthwash containing fluoride
Cleanse and strengthen teeth by chewing crisp, raw vegetables
Use disclosing tablets to reveal tartar build-up
To check for bad breath, lick your inner wrist and sniff after 30 seconds

CAUTION
Use pain relief methods as temporary measures only and seek prompt dental advice for persistent tooth and gum problems
• Throbbing dental pain may indicate an abscess – seek dental or medical advice without delay

toothache & bad breath

Indigestion (discomfort felt as a burning pain in the chest and lower throat) is a symptom of an inflamed oesophagus. Causes include hot or spicy foods, and acid flowing back from the stomach. A hiatus hernia, in which part of the stomach passes into the chest cavity through the hole for the oesophagus, is often responsible, causing belching, bloating, nausea, vomiting and abdominal pain.

indigestion

SYMPTOMS

- Pain in the chest, throat and jaw
- Partially digested food that returns to the mouth on bending or lying down
- Pain between the ribs suggests a peptic ulcer
- Water brash – whereby the mouth suddenly fills with watery saliva – is also typical of a peptic ulcer

For peptic ulcers, try some cabbage juice blended with basil, marjoram and oregano leaves.

THE CURES

VITAMINS AND MINERALS
Cabbage juice has long been taken to help heal peptic ulcers. Sip 10–13 fl oz (300–400 ml) daily on an empty stomach, freshly juiced with a handful of fresh basil, marjoram and/or oregano leaves to improve the flavour and boost the effect. Small, regular meals taken 2–3 hours apart help to reduce stomach acid and soothe painful inflammation. Sip reduced-fat milk and milk beverages, and chew liquorice, which has potent ulcer-healing properties. Follow a daily vitamin/mineral regimen and take 2 kelp (seaweed) tablets daily, because large quantities of raw cabbage (or juice) can affect thyroid gland function in people with an iodine deficiency. Take additional A, C and E vitamins (see Mouth Ulcers, page 10);

B-complex vitamins for stress reduction; and a zinc supplement, 40 mg twice daily, to boost the healing process.

HERBALISM
Aloe vera juice or gel taken orally before your three main meals and at bedtime has been clinically shown to combat peptic ulceration. A herbal practitioner might prescribe an infusion of marshmallow leaves, or medications containing ginger, bay leaves, thyme, caraway, marjoram, mint or savory. Follow recipes containing these herbs to increase ulcer healing. Chew slices of dried or candied root of angelica.

AROMATHERAPY
Add a couple of drops of essential oils of cardamom, laurel, basil, cinnamon and/or lavender to a carrier oil and heat in a burner, or add sparingly to bathwater.

HOMEOPATHY

For acute attacks of indigestion, take every 10–15 minutes for up to 7 doses: Carbo veg. 30c for a stomach full of wind, relieved by belching, a burning sensation in the stomach felt through to the back, and a craving for fresh air; Nux 6c for heartburn half an hour after eating, painful retching leaving a bad taste in the mouth, irritability, and attacks triggered by stress or too much food or alcohol; and Capsicum 6c for indigestion during pregnancy, with a burning sensation behind the breastbone, great thirst, and drinking that causes flatulence and shuddering.

MEDICAL TREATMENT

Reflux (acid flowing back from the stomach) suppressant mixtures containing sodium alginate and potassium bicarbonate are suitable both for heartburn and for reflux episodes due to hiatus hernia. Antacids/antiflatulents (taken to combat wind) and antispasmodic medications may also be prescribed

Gentle exercise, such as walking on the spot, can ease stress and help move trapped wind.

to control spasm triggered by gastric irritation. Medications used to control the acid concentration of the stomach contents may also be prescribed as a course accompanied by amoxycillin and clarithromycin (antibiotics) to overcome bacterial infection of the stomach, which is now recognised as an important contributory cause of peptic ulcers.

Liquorice is known to have ulcer-healing properties. Try chewing a stick of liquorice to ease ulcer pain.

Medications containing ginger are often recommended by herbal practitioners for peptic ulcers.

indigestion

Nausea and vomiting occur after a binge on alcohol or fatty foods and during food poisoning. Hiatus hernia and peptic ulcer, migraine attacks (see page 94), motion sickness and other inner-ear disturbances also trigger nausea and vomiting. They are also common features of early pregnancy, certain cancer treatments and other medications, emotional upsets and disorders affecting the brain.

nausea & vomiting

SYMPTOMS

• Sweating, pallor, churning stomach, pressure in the throat
• Fever, stomach pains, diarrhoea suggest food poisoning
• Upper right stomach pain through to the back may mean gall bladder inflammation
• Streaks of blood after vomiting usually come from an inflamed stomach lining
• Projectile vomiting can indicate a bowel obstruction

Washing salads and fruit well reduces the risk of contracting stomach bugs.

THE CURES

VITAMINS AND MINERALS

Avoid fatty foods and alcohol, and black coffee and tea on an empty stomach. After vomiting, drink clear fluids only for up to 24 hours, depending upon the severity of the attack. Suck an ice cube, then try small sips of water until you can keep down more. Glucose sweets reduce nausea, as does ginger. Make your own electrolyte replacement drink with 1 pt (570 ml) cool, boiled water, 1 tsp (5 ml) of salt, 2 tsp (10 ml) of glucose, and lemon, orange or lime juice. A plain baked potato combats hangovers and bad migraine nausea.

HERBALISM

Ginger, fennel and anise teas all combat nausea, while lime-flower or melissa teas ease upsets caused by shock. Mint calms the stomach and removes the aftertaste of vomiting. Powdered ginger capsules can prevent and treat motion and morning sickness. Extract of milk thistle can help to ease hangover nausea, and evening primrose oil capsules taken an hour before a drinking session cut the risks of vomiting.

AROMATHERAPY

Essential oil of marjoram, lemon or thyme inhaled from a burner, or added to bathwater or plain massage oil, combats nausea and vomiting.

BACH FLOWER REMEDIES

A few drops of Rescue Remedy may allay the nausea and vomiting that can follow an emotional shock or an accident.

HOMEOPATHY

Take at 15-minute intervals or less frequently, for up to 10 doses: Ipecac. 6c for persistent nausea, griping abdominal pains, mucousy vomit, all aggravated by car travel and looking at moving objects; or Arsenicum 6c for nausea and vomiting due to peptic ulcer or food poisoning (when diarrhoea is also present), when stomach pain is eased by warm drinks, and when symptoms are worse between midnight and 2 am.

Acupressure applied to the wrist combats nausea.

ACUPRESSURE

This is applied to points on the inner surface of the wrist, quells nausea and motion sickness. Bracelet devices for applying this pressure are available from some high street chemists and mail order companies.

MEDICAL TREATMENT

Anti-emetic drugs such as prochlorperazine and metoclopramide may be prescribed for nausea and vomiting, and more serious causes may need to be investigated for prolonged attacks.

After an emotional shock, or being in an accident, you may experience a wave of nausea. A few drops of Rescue Remedy will help.

PREVENTION

Avoid fatty foods, and alcohol on an empty stomach
Wash salads and fruit, and your hands after visiting the lavatory, to reduce food-poisoning risks
Fresh air, glucose sweets, and looking away from fast-moving objects, reduce motion sickness
A dry biscuit before rising can quell pregnancy queasiness

CAUTION

• *Bad-smelling vomit and belching, and a distended stomach, may indicate an obstruction – seek medical advice at once*
• *See your doctor for prolonged or frequent vomiting, with or without abdominal pain*
• *Prolonged vomiting causes dehydration, which can be fatal, especially in children and the elderly. Signs include a dry mouth and tongue, pallor, exhaustion and loss of skin elasticity. Seek medical help urgently*
• *Large spots of bright red blood or 'coffee grounds' vomit (see Indigestion, page 14) suggest active bleeding – seek medical advice at once*

nausea & vomiting

Stomach ache varies from spasmodic bursts of infantile colic and burning peptic indigestion to a 'nagging' inflamed gall bladder (cholecystitis) and painful appendicitis. The pain's location, its nature and other symptoms usually indicate the diagnosis. Further investigations include endoscopy, biopsy, blood tests, X-rays and ultrasound.

stomach ache

SYMPTOMS

- Pain below the right ribs and into the back, with vomiting and fever: inflamed gall bladder or gallstones
- Sudden stomach pain, vomiting, diarrhoea: food poisoning
- Pain around navel, vomiting, fever or constipation: appendicitis
- Stomach ache with vomiting, fever, feeling unwell and pain on passing small, frequent dribbles of urine: urinary tract infection (see pages 68–71)

To avoid stomach ache, always sit down to eat meals and keep well hydrated.

THE CURES

NATUROPATHY
Naturopathic practitioners often recommend a fruit juice fast for gallstone sufferers, sometimes in conjunction with herbal enemas and poultices over the painful area.

VITAMINS AND MINERALS
For general advice on relieving the main upper digestive tract disorders, see Indigestion, page 14. A low-fat wholefood diet with lots of fibre and nutrients will help relieve gall bladder disorders. Cholesterol is a major component of gallstones, and vitamin C is reputed to lower the bile's concentration of this lipid, reducing further stone formation. One gram daily is recommended. Magnesium also discourages stone build-up: try 300–400 mg daily in its 'chelated' form or as a dolomite, which contains magnesium and calcium in proportions to optimise absorption by the body. Lipotropic nutrients such as choline, inositol and betaine also beneficially influence cholesterol metabolism by accelerating the transport and use of fatty acids. They are available individually, and vitamin B supplements often contain 50–100 mg of the first two. The recommended doses (usually prescribed by a qualified nutritional practitioner) are 500–1000 mg choline and 250–500 mg inositol.

HERBALISM
A hot poultice to reduce biliary colic – the strangulating pain experienced from stones wedged in the bile duct –

can be made from a handful each of artichoke leaves, grated dog's tooth roots, and poppy petals and seed capsules, mixed with half-handfuls of chicory roots and leaves and dandelion leaves.

AROMATHERAPY
Scotch pine oil can help to relieve biliary colic. Add 5 drops to your bathwater, or mix with 4 tsp (20 ml) of soya or almond oil and, after warming slightly, use it to massage the tender areas of the abdomen.

HOMEOPATHY
Give one dose every 1–2 hours: Nux 6c when there is a sensation of weight in the stomach; Dioscorea 6c for colic in babies who arch their backs and extend their legs with the pain; Mag. phos 6c for spasms, cramps in the stomach and if the pain is not relieved by belching.

An inflamed stomach can be the result of a stressful lifestyle. Sensible eating habits and avoiding stress are an important part of maintaining a healthy stomach.

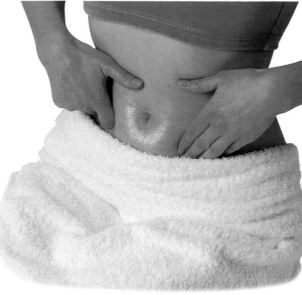

An aromatherapy massage will sometimes give relief from stomach pain.

MEDICAL TREATMENT
Appendicitis, bowel obstruction and an inflamed gall bladder require urgent surgery. Gallstones can be eliminated by laser. Medical causes of stomach ache are treated with bed-rest, fluids and dietary measures, and drugs to relieve spasm and pain.

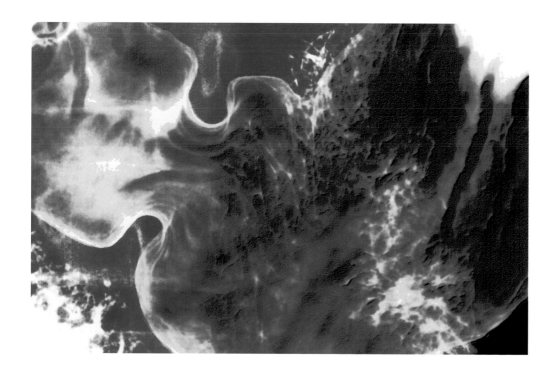

PREVENTION

Sit down to eat, and chew food thoroughly before swallowing, to aid normal digestion
For pain due to stomach and small bowel disturbance, see Indigestion, page 14
Avoid swallowing grape pips and similar debris to reduce the risk of appendicitis
Avoid dehydration and fatty foods to help maintain a healthy gall bladder

CAUTION

• *Seek medical advice for pain that persists despite treatment*
• *Make a note of how the pain started, and any accompanying symptoms*
• *Do not assume that a child with stomach ache and a cold or sore throat has mesenteric adenitis. The underlying cause for any persistent pain needs to be established by a doctor*

stomach ache

Colic here refers to pain resulting from the powerful contractions of the muscular walls of the colon (large bowel). The cause is generally either inflammation arising from an irritant such as unsuitable food or drink, harmful bacteria and their toxins, wind (especially in babies), or an emotional upset causing fear, rage or anxiety. Less often, a blockage impeding the passage of waste to the rectum may be responsible.

colic

SYMPTOMS

- Usually of sudden onset
- Pain in the centre and lower abdomen and/or along one or both sides
- Stomach feels distended and 'full'
- Flatulence (wind) passed through the rectum
- May be accompanied by diarrhoea or constipation

Rosehip extract provides extra vitamin C, which is necessary when taking steroid treatments.

THE CURES

NATUROPATHY

After diagnosis, a naturopathic practitioner will work alongside the patient's GP to promote healing for common colitis (inflamed colon), Crohn's disease and ulcerative colitis. These autoimmune disorders (see glossary) affect the upper and lower intestines respectively, blood and pus are passed with the diarrhoea, food absorption is hindered and grave weight loss may occur. Treatments include herbal enemas, sitz baths, nutritional advice, poultices and recommendations for stress relief, including acupuncture or yoga and meditation, for example. Nutritional advice for common colitis should be heeded. The other two conditions may benefit from a brief fast followed by a bland wholefood diet, low in roughage initially to promote healing, and high in protein and other vital nutrients. In addition to a basic multivitamin/mineral supplement, extra vitamins C (from rosehip extract, or acerola cherry preparations) and B$_6$ (pyridoxine – found in avocados, rice, soya products, bananas and seafood) are needed when steroid medication is being taken. Useful additional supplements to fight inflammation and promote healing include those mentioned for mouth and peptic ulceration (see page 10 and page 14); and iron and potassium.

HERBALISM

Cabbage juice and aloe vera juice or gel can be taken. A medical herbalist may prescribe 2 cupfuls daily of a hot infusion of lime-flowers, lavender, mallow and marjoram – two pinches each to 1¾ pt (1 litre) of water.

colic

AROMATHERAPY

Sip chamomile or mint tea; massage the painful area with 1 tsp (5 ml) soya oil mixed with 1 drop of chamomile or antispasmodic calendula essential oil, or add 2–3 drops of either oil to a bath. A warm poultice – a towel rung out in very warm water containing a few drops of thyme, melissa or oregano oil – applied to a tender abdomen may relieve painful colic and combat diarrhoea. Massage gently afterwards in a clockwise direction.

HOMEOPATHY

Give at 30-minute intervals for up to 10 doses or until pain ceases: Belladonna 30c for severe colic, starting and stopping abruptly, with the person sensitive to the slightest jarring; Chamomilla 6c for severe colonic spasms, especially when triggered by an angry outburst, when breathing is shallow and pain prohibits talk and movement; Aloe 6c for diarrhoea after a summer chill, an angry outburst, flatulence and greenish-yellow stools; or Pulsatilla 6c for diarrhoea that is worse at night after cold drinks and fatty foods.

MEDICAL TREATMENT

Normally bed-rest and clear fluids only, to cope with a severe episode. Medications that contain anti-cholinergic compounds and opiates ease painful bowel spasms. Antibiotics may be prescribed for bacterial diarrhoea.

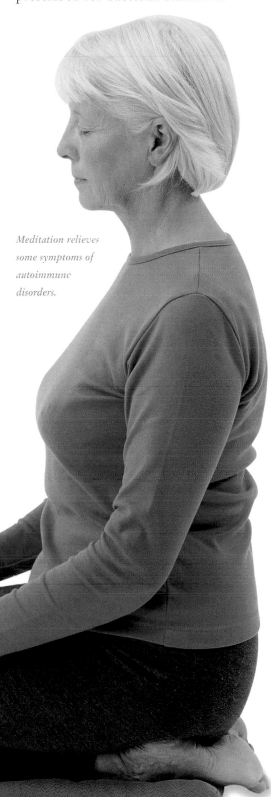

Meditation relieves some symptoms of autoimmune disorders.

Ensure your fridge is kept at the correct temperature.

colic

Bowel habits are highly individual, and constipation simply means opening your bowels less often then usual. It also refers to difficulty in passing motions. Irritable bowel syndrome (IBS) usually involves constipation alternating with diarrhoea, with bloating, flatulence and abdominal pain. Dietary factors, an inherited tendency and low mood are believed to help account for IBS.

constipation & irritable bowel syndrome

SYMPTOMS

- Passing fewer motions than usual
- Hard, painful stools
- Diarrhoea and constipation often alternate in IBS
- A tender, bloated abdomen during IBS bouts
- Colicky pains, often aggravated by food

THE CURES

NATUROPATHY
A regime of gentle exercise to get the body working, abdominal massage, herbal poultices, colonic irrigation and dietary advice may all be prescribed.

Regular exercise such as cycling stimulates a sluggish bowel.

VITAMINS AND MINERALS
Constipation caused by an unhealthy diet often responds dramatically to fibre-rich wholefoods such as wholemeal flour and its products, raw and lightly cooked fruit and vegetables, nuts, grains and pulses, freshly squeezed juices, and around 3½ pt (2 litres) of water to drink daily, together with a reduced intake of processed, refined foods containing additives. Liquorice has potent laxative properties if eaten sparingly, as have figs and prunes.

Dietary supplements useful to irritable bowel syndrome sufferers include the whole B-complex range to combat stress, in addition to a basic multivitamin/mineral supplement.

HERBALISM
Ispaghula husks are often recommended for constipation, as are oat or wheat bran, or 1 tbsp (15 ml) of extra virgin olive oil every

morning. Carrot, fennel and tarragon are all mild laxatives – an infusion of any of these may be prescribed occasionally. Senna extract has been used for centuries to ease constipation.

AROMATHERAPY

Mix 4–5 drops of rosemary oil with 2 tsp (10 ml) of grapeseed oil and massage into the abdomen for 10 minutes, using circular, clockwise strokes (this is easiest while lying down) to sooth a bloated stomach and encourage the passage of stools.

HOMEOPATHY

Take every 2 hours for up to 10 doses: Nux 6c for a strong urge to open the bowels, but nothing happens – or the feeling that there is more to come – with irritability and chilliness, particularly for elderly and inactive people who may misuse laxatives; or Opium 6c for sharp pains, straining that produces rabbit pellet stools, a sluggish bowel and poor appetite. The following specific remedies for IBS can be taken 4 times daily for up to 14 days: Argentum nit. 6c

Keep a note of your mood and emotional state in a mood diary.

for extreme flatulence, constipation alternating with diarrhoea, mucus in stools, and fluttery, tense sensations in the stomach; Colchicum 6c for watery stools, searing abdominal pains and nausea aggravated by the smell of food; Cantharis 6c for nausea and vomiting, thirst, burning pains, and when the patient also has cystitis; or Colocynth 6c for an attack triggered by anger, causing griping pains relieved by pressure on the abdomen.

MEDICAL TREATMENT

Constipation is treated with dietary and exercise advice. A bulking agent such as sterculia or ispaghula husks may be prescribed to break the constipation cycle. Enemas and suppositories may be prescribed in certain cases. Osmotic laxatives work by forming a solution in the intestines, which then attracts fluid into itself, stimulating the bowel walls to function. For the treatment of depression as part of irritable bowel syndrome, see pages 100–101. Treatment of constipation due to a sore rectum is aimed at the underlying cause.

Make sure you include enough fibre in your diet.

constipation & irritable bowel syndrome

Piles – haemorrhoids – are a type of varicose vein at the lower end of the digestive tract, around the anus or rectum. The veins dilate and stretch under pressure. Piles often run in families, and increases in abdominal pressure trigger them. Pregnancy, constipation, a chronic cough, being overweight, heavy lifting and too little exercise and dietary fibre can all be responsible.

piles (haemorrhoids)

SYMPTOMS

- Small painful swellings around the anus (external piles)
- Small, grape-like swellings on straining that retreat into the anus between attacks (internal piles)
- Bright red blood on lavatory paper and sometimes underclothing
- Itchy, prickling discomfort
- Pain on passing motions and on sitting on hard surfaces

A chronic, persistent cough may be a trigger for the development of haemorrhoids.

THE CURES

HYDROTHERAPY
Cold sitz baths are recommended for the treatment of piles.

VITAMINS AND MINERALS
Follow a wholefood diet with the recommended daily quantities of fresh fruit and vegetables, pulses, grains, nuts and wholegrain products, to increase fibre intake and combat constipation. Drink at least 8–10 fl oz (300 ml) glasses of water daily to help keep stools soft. Coffee, chocolate and cocoa, and cola drinks, can aggravate anal irritation so may be best avoided. Take extra vitamin C with bioflavonoids to improve the health of veins throughout the body, including haemorrhoids. Lacto-bacillus acidophilus culture in liquid or capsule form will also help to keep the bowels regular.

HERBALISM
Make an infusion of a handful of fresh chervil added to 1¾ pt (1 litre) of water. When the infusion is cool, use it to bathe the anal area twice each day. Make ice cubes of water in which leeks (only) have been boiled, and apply the ice to stinging piles for immediate relief. Dab piles with a solution of witch hazel, or apply witch hazel cream in the morning and at night, and also after each bowel motion.

AROMATHERAPY
Geranium cream soothes and combats anal inflammation. Add 1 drop of the essential oil to 1 tsp (5 ml) of sweet almond oil, or mix with 2 oz (60 g) of unscented cold cream.

HOMEOPATHY

Take 4 times a day for up to 10 days: Aesculus 6c for internal piles that are linked to constipation and pain, the the lower back area, spiking pain in the rectum, and lumpy stools causing sharp, tearing pain when passed; Aloe 6c for piles protruding from the anus like a cluster of grapes, when bleeding is relieved by cold applications, and when there is spattery diarrhoea and burning sensation in the rectum and anus; Nitric ac. 6c for burning, cutting pains before, during and after passing a stool, with anal fissure (unhealed anal tear) present; or Capsicum 6c for protruding piles accompanied by a burning sensation.

EXERCISE THERAPY

Dance therapy will aid return to fitness. Yoga helps piles, especially the asanas (postures) Plough, Fish and Shoulderstand.

MEDICAL TREATMENT

This focuses on treatment of the underlying cause of the problem. Haemorrhoids can be treated directly with topical solutions, and severe ones need to be removed surgically.

Witch hazel can be used in solution or as a cream to soothe piles.

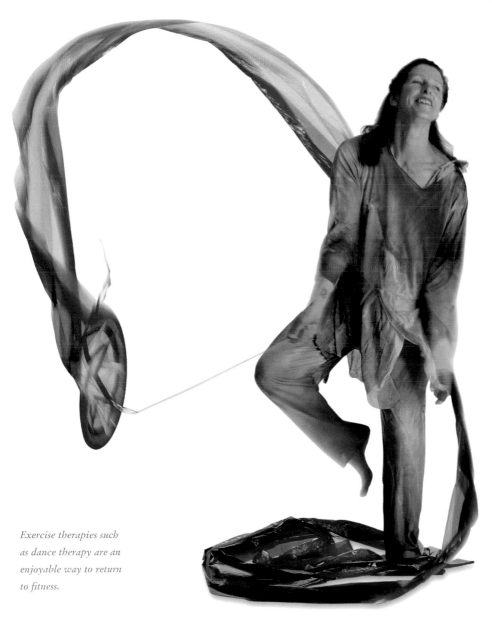

Exercise therapies such as dance therapy are an enjoyable way to return to fitness.

piles (haemorrhoids)

Blocked airways can be particularly disruptive, causing difficulty in breathing and disrupting sleeping patterns. Smoking, poor diet and gaining excess weight can all lead to blockages of the airways and lungs and cause restricted breathing. Ailments of the respiratory system include common colds and flu, hayfever, persistent coughs, nosebleeds, snoring and sinusitis.

the **airways and lungs**

Several hundred varieties of virus cause the common cold. The infection is passed by sneezing or coughing infected droplets into the atmosphere, and the strongest link with winter seems to be the more crowded conditions people endure during cold weather spells. Examples include public transport, cinemas, watching indoor sports and centrally heated work environments.

common cold

SYMPTOMS

- Prickling sensation in the nose
- Sore throat
- Sneezing
- Fever
- Running, and later blocked, nose

Colds tell us when we're run down. A mustard powder footbath helps detox the body.

THE CURES

NATUROPATHY

Inhale friar's balsam to clear thick nasal catarrh. A hot bath relaxes the muscles and produces steam to relax taut airway muscles. Gargle with warm water to relieve a painful throat. Hot footbaths containing 2 tsp (10 ml) of mustard powder to 1¾ pt (1 litre) of water enhance the body's ability to rid itself of toxins.

VITAMINS AND MINERALS

Eat plenty of fresh fruit and vegetables, and their juices, as a supply of antioxidant nutrients. To help build cold-fighting antibodies and enzymes consume 4–6 oz (120–180 g) of fresh protein daily. To ward off or treat a head cold take 2–3 g of vitamin C with bioflavonoids daily. Drink extra fluids (water or freshly squeezed juice) to avoid becoming dehydrated. Zinc gluconate lozenges – sucked rather than swallowed whole or chewed – relieve pain and irritation in the upper airways.

HERBALISM

For a streaming cold, take a finely sliced large garlic clove mashed with 3–4 tsp (15–20 ml) runny organic honey (acacia honey is especially effective). Hot elderflower tea relieves most common cold symptoms – place 1 tsp (5 ml) dried

A crowded, stuffy train is the ideal place to catch someone else's cold.

flowers or 1 tbsp (15 ml) fresh in a cup; add boiling water. Steep for 20 minutes, then strain. Add 1 tsp (5 ml) runny acacia honey and a slice of lemon. Echinacea extracts also help to prevent and relieve cold symptoms.

AROMATHERAPY

Add 4 drops of pine needle essence, 3 drops of eucalyptus essence, 2 drops of clary sage and 1 drop of thyme to a pint (570 ml) of boiling water. Inhale for sore nasal passages and throat.

HOMEOPATHY

Take every 4 hours for up to 4 doses: Aconite 30c for a cold that comes on suddenly, especially after exposure to cold, sneezing, a burning throat, restlessness, and symptoms worse at night; Belladonna 30c for a cold that starts suddenly, with a sore throat worse on the right side, a high temperature, skin that is hot and dry, a tickly cough, eyes sensitive to light, and great thirst; or Gelsemium 6c for

a cold when the person feels sluggish and shivery, and limbs are chilly, aching and feel very heavy.

MEDICAL TREATMENT

Recommendations include bed-rest, fluids, throat lozenges, aspirin or paracetamol.

Echinacea extracts can be bought as medicine, tablets or throat lozenges.

common cold

Flu symptoms can include severe pain within the eyeballs; muscular pain and tenderness; and a high temperature. Patients feel ill all over, and can collapse unexpectedly due to the toxicity of the virus, and dehydration. Flu claims lives among the frail and elderly who are more prone to secondary bacterial infections, causing pneumonia and bronchitis.

flu (influenza)

SYMPTOMS

- Sore throat, cough, cold
- 'Toxic' feeling all over
- Muscular aches and pains
- High fever alternating with normal temperature
- Painful, aching eyeballs

THE CURES

NATUROPATHY
Bed-rest and fluids are essential. Warm baths can reduce muscular pain and bring refreshment after copious sweating. Warm water gargles can relieve a sore throat, and steam inhalation is also comforting.

VITAMINS AND MINERALS
Avoid solids, and take plain water and freshly squeezed fruit and vegetables juices. Apricots, carrots and cantaloupe melons are especially rich in beta-carotene. Chicken or vegetable broth are suitable after the illness has peaked. Specific dietary supplements include vitamin C with bioflavonoids, and zinc lozenges (see also Common Cold, page 28). Beta-carotene (vitamin A) in doses up to 3 or 4 times the RDA (5000 IU or 1000 mcg) actively boosts immunity, as do vitamin E and selenium (see Mouth Ulcers, page 10).

HERBALISM
Medical herbalists may prescribe a red sage gargle for a sore throat, and an infusion of white horehound and marshmallow for a heavy, chesty cough. Try a mustard footbath to relieve 'toxic' feelings, throat and head cold-type symptoms. Place a heaped tablespoon (20ml) of dry mustard powder in a bowl (and 1tbsp (15ml) of baking soda if the water is hard). Place your feet in the

Take plenty of vitamin C and inhale lavender essence from a burner.

bowl and fill with comfortably hot water to cover feet and ankles. Keep feet immersed for 10–15 minutes, topping up with hot water as required. Then dry and keep your feet warm in bed, or wear slipper-socks. (Relief is thought to be due to the antibiotic properties of the mustard entering the bloodstream through the blood vessels of the feet.) Take echinacea preparations (see Common Cold, page 28).

AROMATHERAPY
Add 2–3 drops of pure lavender or lemon essence to a warm bath, or to the oil in a burner. Inhale essence of eucalyptus, naiouli and/or hyssop to help reduce fever and general discomfort in the upper airways.

HOMEOPATHY
Take 2 hourly for up to 10 doses: Gelsemium 6c for chills up and down the spine, feeling tired, weak and shaky, a bursting headache, and when passing urine seems to relieve symptoms; Rhus tox. 6c for restlessness and stiff, painful muscles; or Eupatorium 6c for severe pains in limbs, shivering, a bursting headache and aching eyeballs. To prevent flu take a 'nosode', a homeopathic prescription, such as Flu 30c, or a combination of this and Bacillinum 30c, once every three weeks during winter months.

MEDICAL TREATMENT
Bed-rest, fluids, and prophylactic (preventative) antibiotics will be prescribed for high-risk patients such as the elderly or those with depleted immunity and/or heart or lung disorders.

Postviral depression is a common complaint, and usually responds to nutritional therapy and counselling.

A steam inhalation with some eucalyptus oil clears the airways and eases breathing.

Eating plenty of fresh fruit and vegetables may help stave off a bout of flu.

PREVENTION

Stay away from others with the infection
Eat extra healthily to boost your immune system
Have a flu vaccination before the start of the flu and cold season
Avoid smoky, crowded places where possible, and deep-breathe fresh air several times daily

CAUTION

• *Go to bed sooner rather than later to help avoid complications (for example, chest infection)*
• *Keep up your fluid intake to around 3½ pt (2 litres) a day*
• *Don't ignore chest pains – pleurisy (see Persistant Cough, page 40) is a sign that the lungs are affected*
• *Seek medical advice for persistent symptoms, and if you have heart or lung problems*

flu (influenza)

Hayfever (seasonal rhinitis, or nasal membrane inflammation) is more common in certain ethnic groups, such as West Indians, and in people with personal or family histories of allergic eczema and asthma. Symptoms are triggered by tree pollen in late winter and early spring, flower and grass pollen in early summer, and moulds or fungal spores in late summer and early autumn.

hayfever

SYMPTOMS

• Sneezing, watery nasal discharge
• Nasal stuffiness
• Red, watering, itchy eyes
• Prickling irritation in the ears and on the roof of the mouth

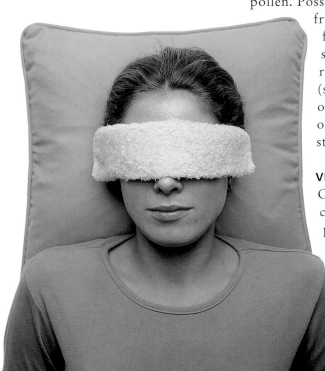

A compress with 2 drops of chamomile oil soothes itchy eyes.

THE CURES

NATUROPATHY
Practitioners seek to rebalance the body's homeostasis (inner balancing) mechanism which – in hayfever sufferers – manufactures antibodies against harmless substances such as pollen. Possible approaches include a fruit juice fast (2–3 days) for an acute attack, a strictly wholefood diet, relaxation to combat stress (see page 236), and osteopathic normalisation of spinal and cranial structures (see page 214).

VITAMINS AND MINERALS
Organic honey – especially comb honey – contains pollen granules which, contrary to expectations, help to relieve the symptoms. Avoid milk and other dairy products during attacks, as they encourage mucus formation in the airways and bowels.

Specific dietary supplements include high potency vitamin B for its anti-stress potential, with extra calcium pantothenate (100 mg daily) and pyridoxine (vitamin B_6) for badly affected people. Vitamin C (naturally occurring, with bioflavonoids), 500 mg every 6 hours, is helpful because of its antihistamine effects. Pollen capsules and royal jelly (a bee product) are also helpful.

HERBALISM
To relieve catarrh, sip 3–4 hot cups daily of an infusion of 2 pinches each of wild thyme and garden thyme to 1¾ pt (1 litre) of water. Rosehip tea (or wine) is a traditional hayfever remedy. Eucalyptus eases nasal discomfort: boil a handful of fresh or dried leaves in water, strain and spray round the house, and in the bedroom at night.

AROMATHERAPY

Add a couple of drops of chamomile oil to very cold water, and make a compress for your forehead and to cover your eyes when itchy. Inhalations of eucalyptus, tea tree, cajuput or naiouli combat the nasal symptoms. A few drops on a handkerchief in your pocket or under your pillow gives you constant access to them.

HOMEOPATHY

Nosodes of pollen and other allergens may be prescribed by a practitioner. Specific remedies can be taken as often as necessary for up to 10 doses: Arsenicum 6c for someone who is slightly feverish and exhausted but feels better for warmth, when sniffing warm water up the nose partly relieves the symptoms, a restless, burning throat, eyes irritated by light,

Wearing sunglasses can protect the eyes from becoming sore and itchy.

wheezy and tight in chest; Gelsemium 6c for ceaseless sneezing, eyes heavy and watery, and when the person is lethargic, dizzy and shaky; and Arundo 6c for symptoms early in hayfever season, a tickly nose, sneezing, no discharge, and when the ears and roof of the mouth are itchy.

MEDICAL TREATMENT

Histamine gives rise to the full range of hayfever symptoms. Antihistamines are prescribed to combat the histamine released in the body as part of the allergic response. Nasal sprays that contain sodium cromoglicate block the allergy or nasal decongestants can relieve the symptoms. Oral antihistamines can be used. Desensitising injections can minimise attacks in many sufferers.

Avoid going to places where you know the pollen count is going to be high.

Bees produce royal jelly, a useful supplement in preventing hayfever symptoms.

hayfever

Most nosebleeds happen following a fall or blow to the face. They also occur from pressure applied to delicate vessels in the nasal lining, by picking or blowing, when weakened by a cold or other inflammation. Nasal polyps are non-cancerous swellings in the nasal lining common in hayfever sufferers, which may also cause nosebleeds, as can high blood pressure and stress.

nosebleeds & nasal polyps

SYMPTOMS

- Bright red blood trickles from one or both nostrils
- Apart from a blow or fall, no pain is felt
- Nausea and occasionally vomiting if the person is frightened or swallows blood
- When polyps are present, difficulty in breathing through the nose
- Polyps can interfere with your sense of smell

Rock rose is one of the main ingredients of Rescue Remedy.

THE CURES

NATUROPATHY
Apply cold compresses or ice cubes to the bridge of the nose.

VITAMINS AND MINERALS
Follow a general wholefood diet rich in mucous membrane-strengthening nutrients. Specific dietary supplements are as for mouth ulcers (see page 10) and tonsillitis (see page 172). Some studies suggest that nasal polyps may be partly due to a deficiency of zinc and/or vitamin B_6 (pyridoxine). You could take a multivitamin/mineral supplement containing these, or add them to such a baseline supplement. The RDA of zinc (found in oysters, beef, egg yolk, fish and maple syrup) is 15mg and you can safely double this dose for a week or so to see whether the condition improves. Pyridoxine, found in rice, seafood, avocados and bananas, has an RDA of 2 mg for an adult. Take at least double this amount for a week or so to test any benefits.

HERBALISM
Cotton wool moistened with an infusion or decoction of yarrow can be packed gently into the affected nostril(s).

AROMATHERAPY
To soothe a person in pain following a blow or fall where injury does not warrant medical attention, heat a little carrier oil in a burner and add 2–3 drops of ylang-ylang, orange, basil, lavender or melissa essence. Or place a couple of drops of any of these in a basin of cold water, and ring out a clean flannel in it before wiping the person's face, once bleeding has ceased.

BACH FLOWER REMEDIES

To counteract effects of panic or fright following a fall, or the sight of blood, use the Star of Bethlehem remedy, or Rescue Remedy.

HOMOEOPATHY

Specific remedies for nosebleeds, to be taken every 2 minutes for up to ten doses, are: Arnica 6c for a nosebleed following injury; Ipecac 6c when blood is bright red; Phosphorus 6c for bleeding induced by violent nose-blowing; Hamamelis 6c for a nosebleed accompanied by a headache aggravated by sitting forward; or Ferrum phos. 6c for bright red blood, when the person feels faint, and especially useful if looking pale.

Specific remedies for nasal polyps, to be taken 4 times daily for up to 3 weeks, are: Calcarea 6c for loss of smell, swollen bridge of nose, dry, sore, ulcerated nostrils and offensive yellow catarrh, cold hands and feet; Phosphorus 6c for nasal polyps that bleed easily; and Psorinum 6c for chronic post-nasal drip, down the back of the throat, when the person is weak and chilly.

MEDICAL TREATMENT

Treatment for nosebleeds requiring medical attention includes the insertion of small inflatable balloons in the upper part of the nasal cavity and packing with a gauze wick. Any accompanying injuries to the head and face would be dealt with appropriately. Nasal polyps can be removed surgically under a general anaesthetic, but they have a tendency to recur.

In sports where a hard ball is used, such as baseball or cricket, a protective face mask will help avoid injury.

Foods rich in zinc may help ease a nasal polyp condition.

nose bleeds & nasal polyps

Sleep apnoea (disrupted breathing during sleep) is linked to snoring, and is caused by poor tone in the upper throat muscles and a fat-laden tongue, which collapses during sleep, blocking the windpipe. The lack of oxygen alerts the brain, the disturbed sleeper breathes, goes back to sleep and the process repeats itself.

sleep apnoea

SYMPTOMS

- Snoring
- Headache or fatigue on waking
- A bad taste in the mouth and foul breath on waking
- Daytime drowsiness

The wild olive. The oil from this plant is used with oils from sunflower, peppermint, almond and sesame to combat snoring.

THE CURES

NATUROPATHY

Measures include a wholefood diet and appropriate exercise to help shed excess fat. Special exercises might be designed to improve the tone of the mouth and throat muscles. Fresh air, or an ioniser to improve air quality, might be useful. One patent natural remedy comprises a throat spray containing a mixture of five oils – olive, sunflower, peppermint, almond and sesame, with supplementary vitamins B_6, C and E.

VITAMINS AND MINERALS

Avoid alcohol consumption last thing at night, and altogether if you need to lose weight. Avoid rich, heavy meals that either interfere with sleep or make you sleep more heavily. Eat plenty of fresh fruit and vegetables to supply vitamin C and bioflavonoids; avocados, bananas, brewer's yeast, rice and salmon to supply vitamin B_6 (pyridoxine); and wheatgerm, wholemeal flour, hazelnuts, walnuts and sunflower seeds and their oils for their vitamin E content.

Specific dietary supplements include the B-complex vitamins, vitamin C with vitamin E, calcium, bioflavonoids and magnesium.

HERBALISM

Extracts of almond, sesame and olive have been used to reduce severe sleep apnoea. Decongestant treatments can also help where allergy or infection is a problem, see hayfever (page 32) and sinusitis (page 38).

AROMATHERAPY

Remedies are as for sinusitis and hayfever.

HOMEOPATHY

The severity of sleep apnoea tends to increase as the night (or hours asleep) progresses. Remedies tackling this aspect of the disturbance include Arnica, Arsenicum, Bryonia, Opium and Pulsatilla – take a strength of 6c at half-hourly intervals for an hour and a half before retiring, for up to a fortnight. The consequences of a night's sleep continually disturbed by sleep apnoea include a dull, thudding headache, drowsiness and mild depression. These remedies should be helpful: take 1 hour before bedtime for 10 consecutive nights, and repeat the dose if you are woken by a nightmare or if you wake and cannot fall asleep again: Aurum 30c for severe depression after dreams of hunger, dying or problems at work; and Gelsemium 6c for a person whose head feels full and swollen, when the face is purple and looks congested,

An ioniser will help to purify the air and may enable the sleeper to breathe more easily.

and the facial expression is dull and heavy, when the limbs are weak and shaky, and the pupils seem to be slightly dilated.

MEDICAL TREATMENT

Surgery to the palate is sometimes resorted to in the case of patients at a severe risk of heart attack or stroke. Medical advice generally is to lose excess weight (sleep apnoea is relatively rare in people of normal or sub-normal weight), and perhaps to see an ear, nose and throat consultant with a view to identifying causes such as adenoids or chronic sinusitis.

Lying on your back makes it more likely that your windpipe will become blocked during sleep. Try to sleep on your side.

PREVENTION

Lose surplus weight (a fatty tongue is a major windpipe blocker)
Avoid sleeping on your back
Use a specially designed oral vestibular shield – a shaped plastic device which promotes breathing through the nose by effectively blocking the mouth

---

CAUTION

• *Sleep apnoea has been linked to an increased risk of stroke and heart attack*
• *Seek medical help if the condition persists*

sleep apnoea

Sinusitis is inflammation of the mucous membrane lining the facial sinuses – hollows within the bones of the forehead and on either side of the nose. Sometimes, the interconnecting channels between sinuses and the nasal cavity become blocked because of membrane swelling. Infection is almost always the cause, and symptoms commonly occur after a head cold.

sinusitis

SYMPTOMS

- Feeling of pressure in the forehead and face
- Pain and tenderness over inflamed sinuses
- A blocked nose with thick catarrh
- Headache
- Fever

THE CURES

NATUROPATHY
Naturopathic practitioners may recommend a 2–3-day fruit juice fast and hydrotherapy in the form of inhalations to treat acute cases of sinusitis.

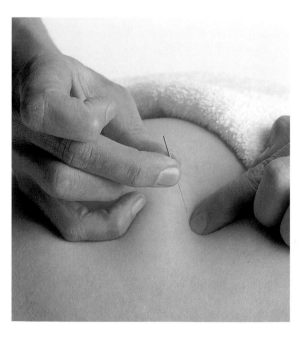

Both acupuncture and reflexology may successfully relieve recurrent sinusitis by combating stress and boosting immune defence systems.

Suspected food allergies might be investigated and treated by applied kinesiology (see page 230). Severe catarrh sometimes responds to a cutting out all dairy products from the diet. Ionisation therapy (see page 36) may also improve nasal stuffiness.

VITAMINS AND MINERALS
A wholefood diet is recommended, eliminating any items that may be responsible for an allergic reaction in the nasal and sinus linings. This diet should be supplemented with plenty of fresh fruit and vegetables and their juices taken daily to provide extra vitamin C, E and A (as beta-carotene). Specific dietary supplements of these and of pyridoxine (vitamin B_6), zinc and selenium might also be advisable if you find it difficult to stomach 6–7 helpings of fresh fruit and vegetables on a daily basis.

HERBALISM

Medical herbalists may prescribe a herbal tea containing tinctures of horehound, mullein, coltsfoot leaves and wild cherry bark. Fenugreek is also commonly used as an expectorant for catarrh (it encourages the elimination of catarrh by nose-blowing or coughing). Fenugreek tablets are available, or you can make fenugreek tea. Take a dessertspoon of the crushed seeds or a handful of the fresh plant (sold as fresh sprouts like alfalfa in supermarkets), and steep in steaming water for 10 minutes. Strain and drink 2–3 cupfuls daily. Eucalyptus leaves, crumpled in the hand and inhaled or added to boiling water for a steam inhalation, relieve congested sinuses.

To relieve nasal congestion, crumple eucalyptus leaves in the hand and inhale.

AROMATHERAPY

Try an inhalation of steam or vapour from an oil burner containing 3–4 drops of niaouli, tea tree or benzoin. For sinusitis with a blocked nose and facial pains, and thick catarrh, practitioners often prescribe inhalations of Baume de Canada (Canada balsam), which is very potent and not recommended for self-treatment.

HOMEOPATHY

Take every 2 hours for up to 2 days: Kali bichrom. 6c for rope-like nasal secretions, and feeling of pressure on either side of the nose; Pulsatilla 6c for pain mainly above the eyes and over the upper cheeks, some nasal stuffiness, yellow catarrh, symptoms that are worse indoors, a tendency to cry, and flashes of neuralgic (nerve-related) pain on the right side of the face; Silicea 6c for throbbing, stabbing pain deep inside the bones of the face, and an itchy end of nose; Hepar sulph. 6c for an attack triggered by cold dry winds, when the person is inclined to sneeze and feel chilly and irritable, and has yellow catarrh; Belladonna 30c for fever with pain mainly over the frontal sinus (forehead), nosebleed, when the face is hot and flushed, and when pain is aggravated by lying down and by slight pressure on the forehead.

MEDICAL TREATMENT

The most common medical treatment for sinusitis combines antibiotics (to treat the infection) and painkillers such as aspirin or paracetamol (for the pain, which can be quite considerable). Sometimes an NSAID (see glossary) such as ibuprofen may be prescribed to help reduce sinus inflammation.

PREVENTION

Seek medical attention for head colds that persist despite home remedies
Blow your nose gently but thoroughly when you have a head cold, instead of sniffing infected mucus upwards
See your doctor as soon as symptoms start – most sinusitis attacks require antibiotics

Fenugreek tea can help eliminate catarrh through coughing and nose-blowing.

CAUTION

• *Avoid dry atmospheres, and cold, biting winds and draughts*
• *Avoid heavy blowing of the nose*
• *Seek medical attention urgently for injuries to the face and head (small fractures of the facial bones may distort sinus passages, increasing the risk of infection)*

sinusitis

Persistent coughs arise from infections of the upper airways, inflammation and infection of the windpipe (tracheitis), bronchitis and emphysema. Tracheitis and bronchitis usually follow a viral infection. Chronic bronchitis and emphysema are long-standing and irreversible due to lung damage from smoking or other pollutants.

persistent cough

SYMPTOMS

Tracheitis:
- Dry, painful cough
- Green or yellow phlegm, may be blood-streaked
- Stabbing chest pain

Bronchitis/emphysema:
- Cough, breathlessness
- White or grey phlegm, sometimes blood-streaked

THE CURES

NATUROPATHY

Bed-rest, fluids, and small quantities of wholefood soups are required. Steam inhalations encourage phlegm production. Mustard footbaths are recommended (see Common Cold, page 28). Apply a hot poultice of linseeds or mustard seeds to the chest or back. Ionisation therapy (see page 36) may be recommended.

For chronic bronchitis and emphysema, a lifestyle plan would be worked out to help eliminate pollutants and adverse stress factors predisposing to infection.

Cat's claw helps to build up your body's infection-fighting defences.

VITAMINS AND MINERALS

Take honey and freshly squeezed fresh fruit and vegetable juices to provide antioxidant nutrients to help combat lung inflammation and encourage recovery. Lemon and pineapple juice are particularly helpful in breaking down phlegm. Fresh sprouting alfalfa or its juice – especially during convalescence – is recommended for its rich nutrient content of vitamins, minerals and chlorophyll. Specific dietary supplements include all of the above, plus a high-potency vitamin B supplement, and 3 acidophilus capsules or a portion of organic live yoghurt 3 times a day.

HERBALISM

For chest infections, herbal practitioners may prescribe an infusion of sage, thyme and nettles, and a hot concentrated concoction of fresh elecampane root to be inhaled several times a day. You can speed your recovery with regular doses of echinacea (as medicine, capsules or tablets) to boost your infection-fighting forces. The Chinese herb astragalus and traditional Peruvian herb cat's claw are also potent immune stimulators. Black cohosh acts as a (dry) cough suppressant, and a (wet) cough expectorant.

AROMATHERAPY

To ease the symptoms of acute bronchitis or tracheitis, inhale (in steam or from a burner) 4–5 drops of cajuput oil twice daily, or place on a clean tissue under your pillow. For chronic bronchitis or emphysema, inhale pepper, pine or tea tree oil in steam or a burner, or add 2–3 drops to a very warm bath and soak for 20 minutes. For emphysema, add 2 drops each of essence of hyssop, pine and garden thyme to 2 tsp (10 ml) of soya oil and rub on the chest and back after a hot poultice.

HOMEOPATHY

Take every 2 hours for up to 2 days: Phosphorus 6c for a tight, dry, tickling cough, when the person is pale and anxious, and wants frequent drinks of iced water; Bryonia 30c for a dry, stabbing, painful cough, headache, chest pain related to coughing and relieved by propping your arms on the back of a chair, and great thirst; Antimonium tartrate 6c for bronchitis in an infant or elderly, frail person, when accumulated phlegm rattles the chest, and the person is too weak to cough it up; and Causticum 6c for coughing causing the involuntary passage of urine.

For emphysema, a back rub can be used after a hot poultice.

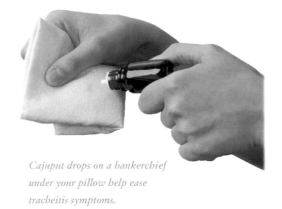

Cajuput drops on a hankerchief under your pillow help ease tracheitis symptoms.

MEDICAL TREATMENT

For a persistent cough, treatment should aim to uncover the underlying cause and treat that. Symptomatic treatment includes cough suppressants and expectorants, medications to reduce the stickiness of phlegm, and antibiotics for bacterial chest infections.

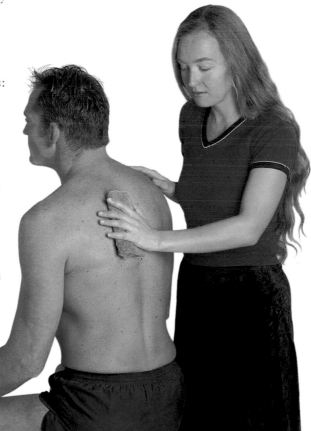

Wearing a mask whilst cycling protects you from traffic fumes.

PREVENTION

Seek medical attention for a chesty cough following a viral illness
Take the full course of antibiotics prescribed
Avoid permanent lung damage by stopping smoking and by wearing a protective mask for unavoidable fumes

CAUTION

• Take treatment advice seriously – bronchitis can progress to pneumonia
• Report streaks of blood in white or coloured phlegm during an infection
• Don't assume it's bronchitis if your cough refuses to clear – more serious causes must be ruled out by your doctor
• Stop smoking, especially if your doctor diagnoses chronic bronchitis or emphysema

persistent cough

The heart is an amazing organ, pumping blood around the body and ensuring that oxygen-rich blood reaches and nourishes every other organ. Disorders of the heart and blood vessels include palpitations, angina, high blood pressure and poor circulation. Some of these conditions can be improved with diet and exercise, while others are more serious and require medical attention.

the **heart and blood vessels**

Palpitations are an awareness that the heart is beating irregularly, or more quickly or forcefully than usual. A racing pulse following a fright, or a steep climb, is normal and does not constitute palpitations, which often come on at rest. If your heart is healthy they are nothing to worry about, and they can be triggered by nicotine, caffeine, alcohol, the menopause, anxiety or an overactive thyroid gland.

palpitations

SYMPTOMS

- A sudden awareness of your heart beat
- Pulse irregular or stronger than usual
- Pulse faster and weaker than usual
- Fluttery feeling in the chest
- Feeling faint

Artichokes are rich in antioxidants and may help reduce palpitation attacks.

THE CURES

NATUROPATHY
Advice would aim at a generally healthy lifestyle, including a wholefood diet, regular exercise and relaxation. Yoga and acupuncture reduce stress and restore balance. Hydrotherapy – holding the hands and arms in cold water for up to a minute – can slow down a racing pulse.

VITAMINS AND MINERALS
Replace cola drinks, tea and coffee with fruit juices, herbal teas and green tea, rich in nutrients that benefit the heart. Eat plenty of fresh fruit and vegetables daily, rich in the major antioxidants, and raw garlic, which is reputed to reduce palpitations.

Specific dietary supplements include vitamin E, which reduces the 'stickiness' of the blood and the risks of clotting, and octacosanol, a naturally occurring substance found in grain, known to combat stress effects on the heart.

HERBALISM
Calming herbal teas include lime, orange leaves, basil, melissa, sage and rose petals. Liquorice, and teas and drinks flavoured with this, is beneficial, as is the water in which artichoke leaves have been boiled. St John's wort, a herbal supplement available as tablets, reduces anxiety (as well as lifting mild depression). Cider vinegar on a sugar lump or mixed with a little runny honey (2–3 tbsp/30–45 ml) or added to a tumbler of water is said to stop palpitations.

AROMATHERAPY
Add 2 drops each of essences of melissa, chamomile and neroli to

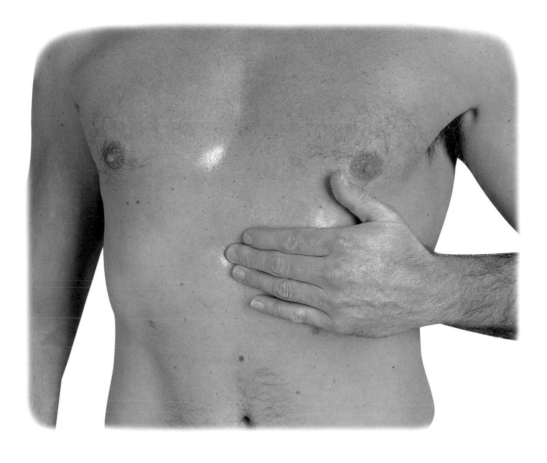

PREVENTION

Try to pinpoint and avoid personal triggers, such as spicy food or too much to eat or drink
Stop smoking
Reduce caffeine intake – found in cola drinks, chocolate, tea and coffee
Reduce stress by slow, deep breathing

CAUTION

• *Consult your doctor for recurrent attacks to rule out heart or thyroid disease*
• *Seek medical advice for palpitations that occur with chest pain, sweating or fainting*

Palpitations are quite common and usually harmless. However, frequent or prolonged palpitations may be a symptom of heart disease. Consult your doctor.

1 tsp (5 ml) of soya oil and add to your bathwater, or massage lightly into your solar plexus. Keep a tissue under your pillow moistened with a drop of rose oil for peaceful sleep.

HOMEOPATHY
Take every 5 minutes for up to 6 doses: Nux 6c for palpitations that start after too much to eat or drink, or after expending much nervous energy, when the person feels irritable and cold; Lachesis 6c for palpitations causing faintness, anxiety, a tight sensation in chest, especially if associated with the menopause; Spigelia 6c for palpitations with bad breath, when the person is thirsty for hot water which seem to relieve the attack.

MEDICAL TREATMENT
Medical treatment would include trying to find the cause of the palpitations and then perhaps recommending an electrocardiogram (ECG) or a chest X-ray.

A racing pulse can be slowed down by placing the arms and hands in a basin of cold water.

palpitations

Angina is heart pain caused by lack of oxygen, due, in turn, to partially blocked coronary arteries feeding insufficient blood to the heart. It must be distinguished from the pain of indigestion (see page 14), which similar in its effects but which is relieved by antacids. Chest pain can also arise from the chest wall itself, and from the lungs and the pleural membranes during a chest infection.

angina

SYMPTOMS

- Tight, 'clamping' sensation in central and/or left chest
- Pain down (usually left) arm and into the neck and jaw
- Triggered by exercise or emotion
- Relieved by rest and calming down
- No relief from antacids
- Person may feel sweaty, nauseous and faint

Blocked arteries restrict the blood supply to the heart muscle.

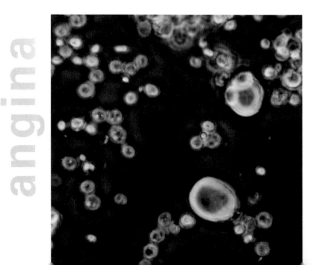

THE CURES

NATUROPATHY

Practitioners tailor their advice to suit individual patients. A wholefood diet – to lose surplus weight – would be low in sugar (sodium-based), salt and saturated animal fat, and high in fresh fruit and vegetables, which are rich in antioxidants. These nutrients help counteract the damaging effects of free radicals, unstable molecular fragments which oxidise 'dangerous' LDL cholesterol, encouraging it to clog the arteries, and increase the likelihood of clot formation. Antioxidants also give protection against 'reperfusion injury' – additional oxidative damage that ensues when the blood flow in affected body areas returns to normal (see Stroke, page 50 and Poor Circulation, pages 52–55).

VITAMINS AND MINERALS

Foods rich in the major heart-protective antioxidants beta-carotene, vitamins C, E and B_6, zinc and selenium are recommended. Co-enzyme Q10 (also called ubiquinone) is a vitamin-like substance specifically enhancing the energy metabolism of heart cells, and is found in yeast and torula yeast. Nutrients which help to prevent clot formation include vitamin B_6 (pyridoxine), gamma-linoleic acid (found in evening primrose oil), selenium and polyunsaturated fatty acids in fish oils. The chief active principle in fresh garlic, allicin, helps to reduce raised blood pressure and raised cholesterol.

The safest plan is to consult a qualified practitioner and let him or her oversee your treatment, but the following may be recommended by some naturopaths and nutritionists: vitamin C, 2000–3000 mg/day; vitamin

E, 400-800 mg/day, co-enzyme Q10, 10 mg three times a day. Magnesium, which helps to guard against arrhythmia (abnormal heart rhythm), 300-600 mg/day (either take as dolomite, which combines magnesium with its natural counterpart calcium in the correct 2:1 proportions for the body's needs; or take twice as much calcium as a separate supplement). Food sources of magnesium include nuts, sunflower seeds, fish, seafood, soya products, green leafy vegetables and wheatgerm.

HERBALISM

An old remedy consists of two foot and hand baths daily containing 2 crushed heads of garlic, and one handful each of hawthorn flowers, broom flowers and celandine leaves steeped in 3½ pt (2 litres) of warm water. Another is an infusion of a pinch each of marjoram, mint and sage to a cupful of water.

AROMATHERAPY

Inhalations, baths, foot and handbaths using 1–2 drops each of marjoram and/or melissa; also chamomile (for its sedative properties) is recommended.

BACH FLOWER REMEDIES

These can help angina sufferers whose 'short fuse', high anxiety levels and depression may be contributing to their angina attacks: Agrimony for those who hide worries behind a brave face; Aspen for apprehension for no discernible reason; Beech if critical and intolerant of others; Holly to counteract negative emotions such as hatred, envy, jealousy and suspicion.

HOMEOPATHY

Give one dose of the following every 1–2 hours: Cactus 6c when the chest feels as though it has an iron band around it, there is low blood pressure, sweating, pain down the left arm and difficulty breathing; Latrodectus 6c for violent chest pain, numbness in fingers, a weak, rapid pulse; Lilium 6c for when the chest feels as though held in a vice, pain down right arm and palpitations.

DANCE THERAPY

This offers a gentle form of exercise, directly beneficial to heart and blood vessels, and to emotions.

YOGA AND MEDITATION

Ideal therapies for someone with angina, or following a heart attack (when approved by your doctor). The balancing, emotionally calming effects ease anxiety, depression and intolerant behaviour. The gentle stretching and deep breathing also enhance muscular fitness and oxygen delivery throughout the body.

MEDICAL TREATMENT

Nitrate drugs to control angina come as skin patches, sprays and tablets to dissolve under the tongue. Transplant surgery can give some patients a new lease of life by replacing their blocked coronary arteries with new vessels fashioned from veins taken from the legs.

PREVENTION

Maintain a healthy lifestyle and lose weight if necessary
Stop smoking
Have regular cholesterol and blood pressure checks
Take regular gentle exercise (not outside in very cold weather) – stop at once if pain occurs
Consider counselling or anger management for emotional outbursts

CAUTION

• Consult your doctor about unexplained chest pains
• Seek medical advice for chest pain unrelieved by rest or antacids
• Take all medications exactly as prescribed – if some produce side effects, tell your doctor
• Resist the temptation to return to unhealthy eating and lifestyle

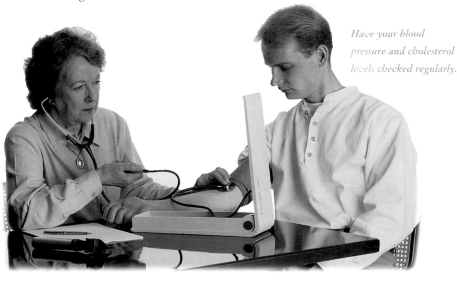

Have your blood pressure and cholesterol levels checked regularly.

angina

Raised blood pressure (BP) is the greatest risk factor for heart attacks and strokes. Millions have been spent in researching its causes, developing new drugs to control it and establishing preventive measures. Hypertension is known as the 'silent killer' because it is often symptomless. It can be hard to persuade apparently fit patients to alter their lifestyle or take medication.

high blood pressure

SYMPTOMS

- Headaches, especially on waking
- Feeling light-headed
- Dizzy spells
- 'Blackouts'

THE CURES

Regular exercise and a healthy lifestyle can help prevent high blood pressure.

NATUROPATHY

Measures include nutritional advice, a suitable exercise plan and stress reduction.

VITAMINS AND MINERALS

Follow a low-salt, low-saturated-fat wholefood diet, emphasising fresh fruit and vegetables and their juices, wholegrain products, chicken, soya products and fish (especially the oily variety such as salmon, tuna, mackerel and sardines). Nuts and seeds, grains, lentils and other pulses would also be included for their fibre, complex carbohydrates and other nutrients.

Specific dietary supplements include vitamin E* with selenium for its antioxidant benefits to the heart and blood vessels, and its anticoagulant (anti-blood clotting) effects; fish oils and evening primrose oil, which lower levels of harmful cholesterol, combat clotting and reduce mild to moderate hypertension; stress-beating antioxidants beta-carotene (natural source of vitamin A), B-complex vitamins, vitamin C with bioflavonoids, calcium, magnesium and zinc; co-enzyme Q10*, which has a major role in the metabolism of heart muscle; and the amino acids carnitine*, histidine* and taurine*, which benefit the heart, coronary arteries and blood pressure.
* *These supplements are best prescribed by a qualified practitioner for people with established heart disease or hypertension.*

HERBALISM

Preparations of motherwort are prescribed to reduce blood pressure. So, too, are infusions of broom for their diuretic properties. Decoctions of hawthorn (May) strengthen the heart which can, in turn, reduce blood pressure. Extract of kava kava relieves pain and calms emotional upset, especially useful for hypertension-related headaches.

AROMATHERAPY
Essence of ylang-ylang calms and invigorates, and is a useful adjunct to more general treatment for both hypertension and palpitations. Add 2–3 drops of the essence to bathwater or keep a small bottle of the essence on you and sniff it when upset.

BACH FLOWER REMEDIES
Holly may help a hypertension sufferer entertaining negative emotions of bitterness, jealousy and hatred. For someone deeply fatigued and drained of energy, try the Olive remedy.

Inhaling essence of ylang-ylang can calm you when vexed or upset.

Maintaining a healthy diet is important. Avoid salt or fatty foods that clog up your arteries.

HOMEOPATHY
Doses to be taken 4 times daily for up to 3 weeks: Sanguinaria 6c for a hypertension sufferer complaining of blood rushing to the head, with flushed cheeks and pulsing in the neck, right-sided head, neck and shoulder problems, and digestive problems; Nux 6c for an emotional person with a craving for alcohol, coffee and drugs which stimulate hypertension; Argentum nit. 6c for someone whose blood pressure rises due to acute anxiety and nervousness, with dizziness, headaches and a pounding pulse.

MEDICAL TREATMENT
Diuretic drugs which increase urine flow have been a first-choice medication for high blood pressure for decades. Others include beta blockers, which act on the heart muscle and constricted blood vessels; calcium antagonists, which limit the amount of calcium entering the cells; and ACE inhibitors, which inhibit the activity of an enzyme involved in blood pressure maintenance. Overall, doctors promote healthy dietary and lifestyle changes, hoping to minimise the quantities of drugs prescribed.

PREVENTION
Lose excess weight
Eat healthily
Take regular exercise
Avoid excess alcohol

CAUTION
• *Have your blood pressure checked every 2–3 years, especially if you take oral contraceptives*
• *Untreated hypertension damages the kidneys, heart muscle, eyes and other organs*
• *Take all medication as prescribed*
• *Don't just stop taking prescription medicines if troublesome side effects occur – your doctor will provide a substitute*

high blood pressure

A stroke results from damage to an area of the brain, due to obstructed blood supply. Causes include pressure following haemorrhage from a ruptured blood vessel, a clot in an obstructed brain artery, or an embolism. Symptoms lasting over 24 hours signify a full stroke. Their disappearance after a few hours indicates a 'mini-stroke' or TIA (transient ischaemic attack).

stroke

SYMPTOMS

- Sudden loss of speech or movement
- Sudden heaviness in the limbs
- Confusion
- Dizziness
- Loss of consciousness

Swimming can help stroke sufferers regain some strength and movement in their limbs.

THE CURES

NATUROPATHY

The advice is essentially the same as for angina (see page 46). For fully conscious patients able to eat and drink, a light wholefood diet would be prescribed, substituting all saturated with polyunsaturated fats. Gentle manipulative therapy would be carried out, and gentle exercise recommended. Hydrotherapy might be utilised in patients where the restoration of limb movement would be aided by carefully supervised swimming lessons.

VITAMINS AND MINERALS

The emphasis would be on antioxidant-rich fresh fruit and vegetable purées and juices. Choline, found in soya products, cabbage, cauliflower, chickpeas, green beans and eggs, is believed to have a beneficial effect upon brain function and may be recommended for recovering stroke patients. Choline and antioxidants help minimise damage caused by reperfusion – the restoration of blood flow and oxygen to an area of the heart or brain temporarily deprived of it during a stroke. Choline is also a major constituent of lecithin, found in the same foods as choline, and often recommended as a supplement for the same purposes (the human brain is 40% lecithin). Specific dietary supplements are as for angina.

HERBALISM

A course of treatment should be drawn up for the patient by a qualified medical herbalist. He/she might prescribe a preparation of yarrow, together with medications that improve the circulation in the extremities and skin, such as elderflower, rosemary, hyssop and buckwheat. Nervous restoratives to reinvigorate a debilitated central nervous system might also help, such

as damiana, oats, lady's slipper, ginseng, rosemary and lavender.

AROMATHERAPY

Scents such as lavender and rose are comforting in themselves, so adding a few drops to the bathwater of a stroke patient is doubly useful. Lavender is said to help restore movement in weak muscles; it certainly relieves headache and helps to disperse fluid retention. Rose essence also benefits the nervous system, and helps restore balance and calm.

BACH FLOWER REMEDIES

These also come into their own in patients who have undergone a severe shock, and may be depressed, confused and/or irritable. Rescue Remedy administered as soon after the stroke as the patient is fit to take it can diminish much of the anguish (consider giving some to family members or other carers, too). The components of Rescue Remedy can also be given singly with benefit – Rock Rose for fear and panic, Cherry Plum for bothersome, uncontrolled and irrational thoughts, Clematis for poor concentration and absent-mindedness, Impatiens for

impatience and irritability, and Star of Bethlehem for all the effects of serious news, or fright following an accident.

HOMEOPATHY

Consult a practitioner for the greatest benefit, but the following can be given every 15 minutes (provided the person can swallow), for up to 10

Counselling can help the patient manage anger or anxiety.

doses, while awaiting medical help: Belladonna 30c for someone with a hot, flushed face, headache, and eyes wide and staring; Nux 6c at the first sign of the attack, especially when precipitated by a heavy meal or drinking binge; and Aconite 30c for someone panicky and fearful of dying. A remedy to be taken 4 times daily for up to 2 weeks after a stroke is Aconite 6c.

MEDICAL TREATMENT

Drugs to prevent further blood clotting may be used, together with careful nursing and physiotherapy and/or speech therapy to help restore lost function.

Lady's slipper can give a boost to a flagging nervous system.

PREVENTION

Monitor blood pressure
Maintain healthy blood vessels through lifestyle
Maintain healthy cholesterol levels
Stop smoking
Counselling for anger management or anxiety

CAUTION

• *Seek urgent medical help for blurred consciousness or abnormal speech*
• *Even the briefest attacks require medical attention*
• *Sudden unexplained numbness, tingling and weakness in a limb must be investigated*
• *Alcohol overload – binge-drinking – increases the risk of a stroke*

stroke

Most circulatory problems are due to constricted arteries or weak veins. Specific remedies exist for localised disorders such as Raynaud's phenomenon and varicose veins. Raynaud's phenomenon turns hands cold and white by sending small arteries into spasm. Triggers include cold, vibration and fear. Normal hands also turn bluish-white when exposed to the cold.

poor circulation: hands

SYMPTOMS

• Hands turn pale then blue
• Hands may hurt at first
• Gradual feelings of numbness
• Frostbite kills tissues, which may need to be excised to avoid ulceration or gangrene

Sufferers are advised to avoid cold and wet conditions, and where this is not possible, to wrap up warm.

THE CURES

NATUROPATHY
Hydrotherapy will be prescribed in the form of hand baths, tepid to warm, when relieving symptoms of reduced blood flow, alternated with very warm and cold hand baths to stimulate circulation. Massage is also effective in encouraging the delivery of fresh blood to the hands and elsewhere and encourages the absorption of aromatherapy essences through the skin and into the bloodstream. Advice on helpful lifestyle changes would include diet, exercise and the avoidance of unnecessary vibration and of cold, wet conditions.

VITAMINS AND MINERALS
Avoid coffee, tea and alcohol for very troublesome symptoms, and eat a wholefood diet rich in vitamin C with bioflavonoids and vitamin E. Foods beneficial to the circulation include onions and garlic, citrus fruit, peppers, acerola cherries and rosehips, blackcurrants and rye.

HERBALISM
Bilberry extracts are used to improve the circulation and health of blood vessels throughout the body. Ginger

Strong vibrations can be a trigger for muscle spasms associated with Raynaud's phenomenon.

and its products are circulatory stimulants, promoting improved blood flow. Hawthorn berry extracts relieve the spasm in constricted blood vessels and improve blood flow. Fresh parsley, and teas made from parsley or sage, are also beneficial.

AROMATHERAPY
The addition of a few drops of essential oils of rose, lemon, neroli or cypress to a carrier oil used to massage the hands relieves the discomfort and helps sluggish circulation to return to normal.

HOMEOPATHY
For Raynaud's phenomenon, take every 30 minutes for up to 10 doses: Secale 6c for a burning sensation in fingers (or toes), aggravated by heat, and when the the rest of the body feels cold; Carbo veg. 6c for icy cold, mottled skin whose natural colour returns when the area is fanned; and Pulsatilla 6c when applying heat or

letting the limb hang down makes symptoms worse.

DANCE THERAPY
This, or any other type of exercise that appeals, entails both gentle stretching and bending, and some sort of challenge to the cardiovascular system. Brisk walking, gentle jogging, swimming in water of a suitable temperature and horse riding are good.

MEDICAL TREATMENT
Infrequent Raynaud's phenomena require no medical investigation but persistant or painful episodes should initiate a consultation to rule out any underlying disease.

Massaging the hands can improve sluggish circulation and relieve the discomfort.

poor circulation: hands

When blocked (furred up) arteries cause poor circulation in the legs and feet, walking becomes a problem. Typically, calf or thigh pain in the affected leg consistently halts the walker after, a short distance, and the person is obliged to rest until the pain-provoking lactic acid in the affected muscles has dispersed. Normally, this is removed by veins draining the area.

poor circulation: legs

SYMPTOMS

- Deep thigh or calf muscle pain brought on by exercise
- Pain relieved by rest
- The foot of the affected leg may be pale and chilly
- Extremities always seem cold, especially in bed at night

Cramping muscles in the legs after exercise are a symptom of poor circulation.

THE CURES

NATUROPATHY
For poor circulation in the legs and feet, a naturopathic practitioner would employ hydrotherapy (warm and alternating cold and warm foot baths), massage, and vibratory stimulation (electric foot bath massagers), dietary and exercise advice, and weight reduction where applicable.

VITAMINS AND MINERALS
Diet is recommended as for angina (see page 46). For foods generally beneficial to the circulation, see Hands, page 52. Specific dietary supplements include antioxidant vitamins and minerals: A (beta-carotene), vitamin B complex, vitamin C with bioflavonoids and vitamin E, plus selenium, magnesium, calcium and zinc.

HERBALISM
Valerian is best known for its mild sedative properties, but it also relaxes blood vessel spasm, and may be prescribed for mild cases of small artery disease as part of a comprehensive treatment programme. Red clover relieves smooth muscle spasm in both lower-leg arterioles (tiny arteries) and the air tubes of the lungs. It is also a powerful antioxidant, promoting tissue strength and repair, helping to protect blood vessels from further damage.

AROMATHERAPY
To promote good circulation, add a few drops of these essences to a warm (not hot) bath, or to a massage oil:

lemon, cypress, lavender. Oil of wintergreen can also be massaged onto cold feet and cramping calves, as it boosts local blood flow (avoid any areas of broken skin).

BACH FLOWER REMEDIES

Many heart attack sufferers have what is known as a type A personality, which makes them more prone to high blood pressure, and to disorders of the coronary and other arteries. Type A behaviour (TAB) traits for which Bach Flower Remedies may be especially suitable include workaholism and ambitious strivings (Vervain), impatience and irritability (Impatiens), fearfulness

To boost circulation in feet and calves, massage with oil of wintergreen.

and chronic anxiety (Aspen, Cerato or Mimulus). Depression can be another aspect of TAB – suitable remedies might include Wild Rose, Gorse and Honeysuckle.

HOMEOPATHY

To be taken twice a day for a month, in addition to general lifestyle changes as necessary: Baryta carb. 6c for an elderly sufferer, with high blood pressure and palpitations, especially if they also have an aneurysm (weakness in the arterial wall); Phosphorus 6c for someone with frequent fainting spells, with a craving for salt, who is very nervous and highly strung; Vanadium 6c for someone with fainting, dizziness, confusion, general mental deterioration, liver disorders and when the heart feels compressed within the chest; Glonoinum 6c for someone with a tight, congested headache, and a pounding sensation in the arteries.

MEDICAL TREATMENT

Surgery is usually necessary to restore poor circulation caused by clogged major arteries. A diseased artery may be replaced with a refashioned vein from the patient's body; or the atheromatous plaque blocking it may be compressed using a small blown-up balloon inside the vessel and sometimes a stent (a spring-like device) inserted to keep the cleared route open.

PREVENTION

Follow diet advised for healthy arteries (see Angina, page 46)
Take regular weight-bearing exercise
Stop smoking
Avoid being overweight

Valerian can be used to relax muscle spasm in mild cases.

CAUTION

• Report troublesome symptoms to your doctor
• Don't assume your arteries are diseased – you may just have Raynaud's phenomenon (see page 52)
• Don't try to push yourself through calf pain triggered by walking – you need medical attention

poor circulation: legs

Fainting is a temporary loss of consciousness due to a reduced blood supply to the brain. Standing still for hours causes blood to pool in the legs and feet. Standing up quickly overtaxes the adjustment of the blood vessels from a supine to a vertical position. Terror or an emotional shock may cause slowing of the heart, which then pumps less oxygenated blood to the brain.

fainting attacks

SYMPTOMS

- Sweating
- Nausea
- Objects 'swim' before the eyes
- Black dots appear in the visual field
- The person falls to the ground

Splashing cold water on the temples and forehead provides some relief.

THE CURES

NATUROPATHY

Splash cold water on the forehead and temples. Provide fresh air from a window or fan. Ammonium smelling salts held to the nostrils can help to restore consciousness. Sips of cold water provide relief.

VITAMINS AND MINERALS

A mostly wholefood diet, with emphasis on raw and lightly cooked fresh fruit and vegetables and their juices, should supply most nutrients required for health. Anaemia (where the blood carries less oxygen than usual, due to iron deficiency) increase the risks of fainting attacks. Lean red meat is rich in iron, as is enriched bread, cereals and wholegrain products, lentils and chickpeas, parsley, spinach, offal, seafood, molasses (black treacle), nuts and egg yolk. Tea, coffee and dairy products reduce the absorption of iron from food (because of their calcium content) and should be avoided, while freshly squeezed orange juice, with its high vitamin C content, promotes it.

The RDA of iron – 18mg – is the minimum needed for humans to function, and inadequate if you are over 50, breast-feeding or lose iron monthly in heavy periods. Supplements should be taken in a chelated form (see glossary) to ensure optimal absorption, in addition to a multivitamin/mineral supplement to ensure balanced nutrition.

HERBALISM

Schizandra is widely used in Chinese herbal medicine for its tonic effect on the nervous system, increasing the speed of reflexes and nerve responses and improving mental clarity. Preparations of rhodiola (native to

Russia and parts of Asia) boost heart function, improve stamina and enhance stress tolerance.

AROMATHERAPY

Citrus essences of orange, lemon and mandarin all help to combat stress and improve the function of veins and other blood vessels. Essence of petitgrain, obtained from the leaves, twigs and small, green, unripe fruit of the orange tree, is a sedative, relaxant and cardiac tonic. Lavender essence added to smelling salts improves their aroma.

HOMEOPATHY

Remedies can be taken every 5 minutes for up to 7 doses when feelings of faintness come on, or on immediately regaining full consciousness: Nux mosch. 6c for faintness linked to shortness of breath and uncustomary exercise; Aconite 30c when brought on by fright, and the person is pale, anxious, and terrified of dying; Gelsemium 6c when faintness is brought on by fright and the person feels weak and trembling; Nux 6c for fainting at the sight of blood; Ignatia 6c for faintness following emotional shock; and Opium 6c when fainting is brought on by fright and the person is numb with shock.

MEDICAL TREATMENT

This would include laying the person down – either flat, with legs raised, or in the recovery position. A hot, sweet drink may be given, and also, for example, advice about avoiding low blood sugar or the pooling of blood in the lower limbs.

Aromatherapy oils containing essences of citrus fruits improve the function of blood vessels.

If you are feeling faint, sit down with your head between your knees until you return to normal.

PREVENTION

Contract and relax calf muscles when standing still for long periods
Get up slowly after sitting or lying down
Avoid overheated, stuffy rooms and tightly fitting clothes
Sit down with your head between your legs if you feel faint

CAUTION

• *Don't sit a fainting person upright – their head needs to be lower than their body*
• *Call for medical assistance if the person does not come round within 5–6 minutes*
• *Place in recovery position in case of vomiting*
• *Do not pour brandy or any other liquid down the throat – offer a drink only when the person is fully conscious again*

fainting attacks

Leg veins channel blood upwards against the force of gravity. Veins deep in the tissues are supported by the muscles, and the flow of blood is encouraged upwards by exercise. Standing still encourages blood to pool in the deep leg veins, creating a back pressure that is transmitted to veins just below the surface. These can then become varicose – overstretched and bulging.

varicose veins

SYMPTOMS

- Blue or purple veins appear on the thigh and/or calf
- Legs ache and swell
- Skin over the bulges may tear easily, especially in older people
- Varicose eczema – an itchy rash over the affected area – may develop

Fresh rhubarb, prunes and plums are rich in antioxidant nutrients.

THE CURES

NATUROPATHY

Relevant lifestyle measures include a wholefood diet, stopping smoking, weight reduction and daily exercise, including going barefoot (or wearing open sandals that encourage the toes to grip naturally), to maximise use of calf muscles. Painful varicose veins can be relieved by splashing the area with cool then very warm water. Exercise would be recommended to improve overall health and cardiovascular fitness, and tone thigh and calf muscles in particular.

VITAMINS AND MINERALS

Wholegrain flour products, and plenty of fresh fruit and vegetables, rich in antioxidant nutrients and fibre, guard against constipation. Fresh fruit and vegetable juices rich in vitamin C and beta-carotene (vitamin A) provide naturally occurring vitamin C with bioflavonoids – especially carrot, celery and parsley juice, 3 parts of either or both of the first two, to 1 of parsley. Fresh rhubarb, plums and greengages, and prunes and their juice, can keep the most sluggish bowels regular. Avoid coffee, cola drinks and refined sugar, or reduce consumption to a minimum. Specific dietary supplements include beta-carotene (vitamin A), B-complex vitamins, vitamin C with bioflavonoids, especially rutin and hesperidin (which can also be bought separately), and vitamins D and E. The last-mentioned relieves varicose vein inflammation (phlebitis) or helps to prevent it. It is also good for varicose eczema or varicose ulcers, both of which can benefit from pure vitamin E oil or cream applied directly. Honey was recommended as a varicose ulcer application by

Elevating your legs allows blood to circulate upwards.

Hippocrates in the fourth century BCE; and modern treatment methods are utilising this – and seaweed applications – once more. Cider vinegar relieves painful, swollen varicose veins in some sufferers, besides encouraging weight loss: add 2tsp (10ml) organic cider vinegar to a tumbler of fresh cold water, and drink 3 times a day.

HERBALISM
Extracts of butcher's broom (*Ruscus aculeatus*) are prescribed to prevent and treat piles and varicose leg veins. It promotes circulation in the lower limbs and combats inflammation. Gotu kola (*Centella asiatica*) extracts have been shown to boost venous (vein) circulation in the lower legs and improve the condition of varicose veins.

AROMATHERAPY
Clove essence added to pure cold water is used to wash varicose ulcers and eczema. Practitioners sometimes make up a varicose vein ointment based upon essences of benzoin and cypress, mixed with sweet almond oil and extracts of pure beeswax.

HOMEOPATHY
Tincture of Hamamelis applied to a painful varicose vein area can bring quick relief. Remedies to take every 12 hours by mouth for up to 7 days include Hamamelis 30c for varicose veins that feel bruised and sore (often present with piles); Pulsatilla 30c for veins aggravated by warmth and letting legs hang down, especially during pregnancy, and when the person feels chilly; and Carbo veg. 30c for skin mottled and marbled around the varicose veins.

MEDICAL TREATMENT
Medical advice normally includes excess weight loss, exercise, eating and maintaining a healthy diet and the use of support stockings. Varicose veins that defy these measures often need sclerosing injections to make them shrivel up; or surgery to remove them altogether.

Butcher's broom promotes good circulation and fights against inflammation.

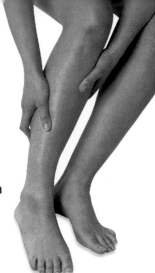

This describes when the legs itch, prickle or burn, and jerk or twitch involuntarily. Symptoms are worse after going to bed, and affect 5–10 per cent of people. The chief cause is the slow drainage of blood from the lower limbs; others include an excess of caffeine, withdrawal from alcohol or tranquilliser dependence, diabetes and deficiency of iron or vitamin B.

restless legs

SYMPTOMS

- Inability to keep legs still after retiring for the night
- Lower legs thrash about or jerk uncontrollably
- Prickling, crawling sensation just below skin of legs
- A burning sensation, although skin may be cool to the touch

Chamomile tea will help relax muscle spasms and provide relief.

THE CURES

NATUROPATHY

The same lifestyle modifications as for varicose veins (see page 58) will be recommended. Try hydrotherapy in the form of leg and foot baths and cool compresses, including aromatherapy essences (see below). Any form of healthy exercise involving foot contact with the ground, and yoga asanas (postures) to reduce tension and improve the circulation.

VITAMINS AND MINERALS

Follow a wholefood diet as for varicose veins (see page 58), but with additional emphasis upon foods rich in iron (red meat and offal, black treacle, cheddar cheese, egg yolk, wheatgerm, seaweed, nuts and lentils) and the B vitamins (brewers' yeast, wholewheat flour, beef kidney and liver, sunflower seeds and cashew nuts). Sources of vitamin C with bioflavonoids are extremely important, too (found as the brightly coloured natural nutrients in the pulp, peel (and pith) of citrus fruit, green peppers, tomatoes, broccoli, grapes, paw paw and cherries). Specific dietary supplements are the whole range of antioxidants, especially the bioflavonoids with naturally occurring vitamin C, folic acid and vitamin E.

HERBALISM

Add a few drops of tincture of witch hazel to cold water, and dab onto irritated areas. Chamomile tea is a mild sedative, and relaxes muscular

spasm. Preparations of butcher's broom taken an hour before bed can relieve restless legs.

AROMATHERAPY

A well-known remedy utilises essence of clary sage. Add 4 drops of clary sage and 3 drops each of chamomile and orange essence to 1tbsp (15ml) sweet almond or grape oil. Following a warm (but not hot) bath or shower, use to massage the legs in an upward direction from the soles of the feet to the knees, until all is absorbed. Lie down for at least 20 minutes, with your feet propped on a pillow.

DANCE THERAPY

This might be used beneficially, especially the type that involves slow, strong leg movements that utilise relevant muscles. Yoga would also be an applicable form of exercise, as would t'ai chi.

HOMEOPATHY

Specific remedies to be taken 4 times daily for up to 14 days: Tarentula 6c for legs that twitch and jerk during the day as well as at night, with an irresistible urge to move them continually, accompanied by uncontrollable yawning; Arsenicum 6c for legs that are constantly on the move, with restlessness, anxiety and feeling chilly; Belladonna 6c for legs jerking and cramping, when the person feels hot but has cold hands and feet, the slightest jarring aggravates spasms, and discomfort increases when the person tries to go to sleep; Kali carb. 6c for jerking that becomes much worse between 2–4am; Ignatia 6c for legs restless in sleep that wake the person so that they feel that he or she will never sleep again – especially after grief or a love affair that has ended.

MEDICAL TREATMENT

Exercise, weight reduction, and possibly dietary advice would be the typical treatments offered. Medication takes the form of paroven, containing rutosides, which are a form of bioflavonoid.

T'ai chi practitioners believe that this therapy is beneficial to people suffering from circulation problems.

All of these foods are rich in vitamin C with bioflavanoids, and should be eaten to help manage the condition.

restless legs

When a clot (or thrombus) forms in a deep vein, usually in the leg or pelvis, it obstructs the return of blood to the heart. Fragments of the clot may be carried to the lungs, forming a pulmonary embolism that can prove fatal. DVT has recently been linked with travelling on long-haul flights, where passengers are at risk if they do not move around the plane sufficiently during the journey.

deep vein thrombosis (DVT)

SYMPTOMS

- Pain deep in the calf (or lower abdomen)
- Swelling and tightness of the affected area
- Reddening of skin (over calf thrombus)

Drink a blend of freshly squeezed fruit and vegetable juices the day before flying.

THE CURES

NATUROPATHY

As prevention, regular exercise to lose surplus pounds would be added to nutritional advice and the need stressed for an adequate intake of fluids. Plain tap or bottled mineral water is excellent. Treatment of deep vein thrombosis (DVT) would aim at supplementing orthodox medical treatment, probably with hydrotherapy (foot and hand baths), compresses and poultices.

VITAMINS AND MINERALS

Follow a wholefood diet with fresh fruit and vegetables, seeds, nuts, grains, pulses and wholewheat (or other) products, plus low-fat dairy foods, for optimal health. During the 24 hours prior to travelling, however, and on the flight itself, it is especially helpful to avoid alcohol and rich, fatty foods, and drink freshly squeezed fruit and vegetable juices. To carrot or apple juice, add celery, which helps to remove excess fluid (and avoid swelling), lettuce for its calming properties, and a little watercress or spinach to purify the blood. A dash of Worcestershire sauce peps up the flavour of vegetable juices; a pinch of ground cloves, cinnamon or nutmeg does the same for fruit juice.

Vitamin E is prescribed in relatively large doses by alternative practitioners to treat angina or following a coronary, so normal-size doses can beneficially be added together with selenium to the other main antioxidants beta-carotene (vitamin A), B-complex vitamins, vitamin C with bioflavonoids, vitamin D, and magnesium, calcium and phosphorus.

HERBALISM
Extracts of Irish moss, used as a gelatine substitute by vegetarians, can be used to reduce the risks of thrombosis of all types. Tonka (or Tonquin) beans contain coumarin, an anticoagulant similar to one of the body's own, and can be used under professional supervision to help prevent deep vein thrombosis, and also to help prevent pieces of clot already formed from breaking off into the bloodstream. Gotu kola and butcher's broom (see Varicose Veins, page 58) can also be of use in promoting the healthy flow of blood in the veins of the legs.

AROMATHERAPY
Use the same leg massage oil as suggested for varicose veins (see page 58), or add a few drops of lavender or orange oil to your bath, or inhale in steam or from a burner.

HOMEOPATHY
These specific remedies can be taken every 2 hours for up to 6 doses while awaiting diagnosis and treatment: Bothrops 6c for when the right side of the body is most involved, the limbs are swollen and cold, and the symptoms follow severe bruising; Hamamelis 6c for deep vein thrombosis accompanied by great

Flying can really dehydrate the body and this will thicken the blood. Make sure that you keep properly hydrated by drinking extra water throughout the flight.

pain, varicose veins and exhaustion; Lachesis 6c for primarily left-sided body symptoms, with pain and swelling relieved by warmth, and purplish-blue hands and feet.

MEDICAL TREATMENT
Doctors prescribe anticoagulants (anti-clotting drugs) such as warfarin for people at risk of developing blood clots, and to dissolve clots already formed. Pain can be controlled with simple analgesics such as paracetamol. Clots can also be removed surgically.

PREVENTION

Avoid cramped, confined seating but if unavoidable (on an aircraft, for example), stretch your main muscle groups at half-hourly intervals
Get up and walk around as often as you can
Drink extra water
Avoid tight, constricting clothing and belts
Lose excess weight
Avoid oral contraceptives and hormone replacement therapy (HRT) if you or close relatives have ever suffered from blood clots

An extract derived from Irish moss has been used to reduce the risk of thrombosis developing.

CAUTION

• *Seek medical advice without delay if the symptoms of DVT appear*

deep vein thrombosis (DVT)

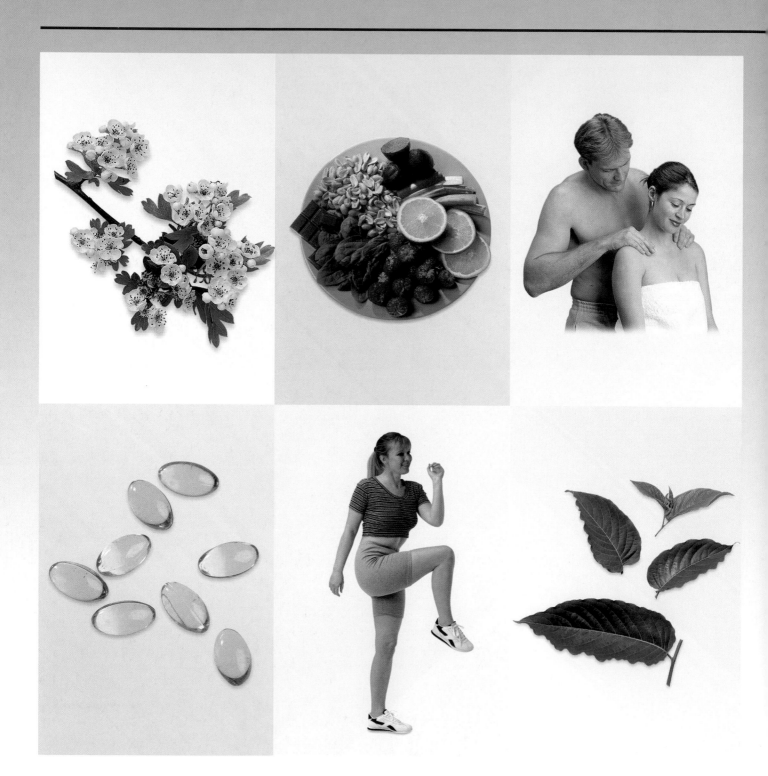

Ailments of the urinary and genital systems include cystitis, genital warts, painful periods and vaginal discharge. Many of these conditions can be particularly uncomfortable, but once diagnosed can usually be treated effectively, and some problems can be helped by drinking plenty of fluids, taking regular exercise and following basic hygiene rules.

the **urinary and genital** systems

This severe pain is caused by the blockage of a ureter – one of the two tubes that transport urine from the kidneys to the bladder – by a stone (calculus). The ureter's smooth, muscular walls contract to push the stone into the bladder from where it can be expelled. The stones, derived from calcium or from urate salts, vary from the size of a grain of sand to an inch (2.5 cm) across.

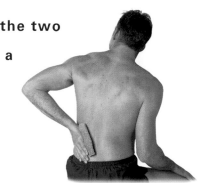

renal colic

SYMPTOMS

• Dull pain in the loins (the region of the back and side of the body between the lowest rib and the pelvis) aggravated by movement
• Pus and/or red blood cells in urine
• Very severe colicky pain passing in spasms from loin to groin
• Pain may extend into testicles, vagina or inner thighs

Medical herbalists often prescribe extract of maize tassels as a treatment for renal stones.

THE CURES

NATUROPATHY
Recommendations would include a wholefood diet, regular exercise and hydrotherapy in the form of hand, foot and body baths in water containing relevant herbs and plant essences. A compress over the kidney area (see Herbalism, below) may relieve pain.

VITAMINS AND MINERALS
Besides a wholefood diet based on grains, pulses, nuts and seeds, low-fat dairy foods, and fresh fruit and vegetables and their juices, a naturopathic doctor might suggest avoiding certain foods, depending on the type of stone that you are passing. People making oxalate stones should omit oxalate-rich foods such as rhubarb, spinach, peanuts, oranges, chocolate, beetroot, strawberries and tea from their diets. In the case of urate stones, appropriate foods to eliminate include purine-rich offal, sardines and fish roe. Gout sufferers should avoid or greatly reduce their alcohol intake. An ample daily intake of tap or bottled water would also be advised (but do check the calcium content of both of these, and choose low-calcium varieties if your stones contain calcium).

Specific dietary supplements include vitamin B_6 (pyridoxine), which helps to reduce the level of oxalate and oxalate salts in the urine by limiting the body's production of oxalic acid. A chelated magnesium supplement is also reputed to aid the elimination of oxalates from the body by making them more soluble in

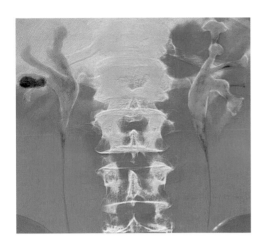

The body has two ureters, one for each kidney. The ureters carry waste from the kidneys to the bladder.

urine. Defatted rice bran – ¾ oz (20 g) taken daily – has been shown to reduce the formation of stones formed from high concentrations of calcium in the urine.

HERBALISM

Extracts of maize tassels, burdock leaves, dog's tooth root and borage flowers are all usually prescribed by medical herbalists for the treatment of renal stones. A cold compress over the kidneys using any or all of the above extracts, plus a handful of celandine leaves, should relieve pain. If none of these are available, try 1 tsp (5 ml) of the bark of a lime tree, adding a generous pinch of fresh mint, infused in a small teapot of boiling water for 6–7 minutes and drunk 3 times a day.

AROMATHERAPY

A few drops of borage oil can be added to sweet almond oil and used to massage the lower abdomen and kidney areas (just above waist level on either side of the spine) to relieve discomfort and pain. Gaiac oil from *Lignum vitae* (the tree of life) is used by qualified practitioners to treat many renal problems, and also gout. (Do not self-administer this oil.)

HOMEOPATHY

The following treatments can be given as often as necessary during an attack of renal colic while awaiting the doctor's arrival; Berberis 6c for stitch-like pain between the lower ribs and hip bone when urinating, pain aggravated by movement and which radiates from a specific point but is relieved by lying on the painful side; Mag. phos 6c for right-sided pain stabbing towards the genitals and down the right leg, with nausea and vomiting, or right-sided pain shooting into the rectum and causing an urge to open the bowels; Nux 6c for a weak urine flow which stops altogether when the person strains to pass it – and the person is cold and irritable; Tabacum 6c for pain darting down the ureter, with nausea and a cold sweat; and also Lycopodium 6c for pain on the right side which stops at the bladder and does not reach down the leg, also pain in the back relieved by urinating, clear urine with red or sediment in it, and when the symptoms worsen between 4–8 pm.

MEDICAL TREATMENT

Once renal colic has been diagnosed by a doctor, immediate treatment comprises a powerful painkiller, increased fluids and plenty of bed-rest in the hope that the stone will eventually be passed. Failing this, an ultrasound would have to be used to try and locate the stone, which could then be either fragmented by means of lasers or removed surgically.

PREVENTION

Excess uric acid in gout sufferers' urine gives rise to urate stones – have regular checks
Some diuretic drugs increase uric acid in blood and urine – have regular medical checks
Concentrated urine gives rise to stones – drink 3½ pt (2 litres) of water daily
A healthy urinary system involves frequent emptying of the bladder. Stagnant urine in the bladder can cause infection and make a urinary condition worse.

These foods are all rich in oxalates. People making oxalate stones should avoid them.

CAUTION

• *Seek medical advice for unexplained loin pain and/or blood or pus in your urine*
• *Seek urgent treatment for attacks of renal colic – the severe pain can cause collapse and shock*
• *Retain any small stone that passes out of your bladder for chemical identification later*

renal colic

Although it has several causes, cystitis (bladder inflammation) is generally used to describe a urine infection. It is much more common in women because their short urethra makes the bladder's interior more readily accessible to bacteria from the anus (the usual source of infection), and other sources.

cystitis

cystitis

SYMPTOMS

- Passing frequent, small amounts of urine
- Getting up several times in the night to empty the bladder
- Scalding pain on emptying bladder
- Cloudy, bad-smelling and/or blood-stained urine
- Low back or stomach pain with or without a temperature

Lavender tea has long been used as a cystitis treatment. It can be sweetened with honey.

THE CURES

NATUROPATHY

Lifestyle advice would include a wholefood diet, and hydrotherapy hygiene measures aimed at minimising the passage of bacteria from the anus to the vulva. Examples include passing urine immediately after sexual intercourse, and washing the perineal area (between the rectum and vulva) while still sitting on the toilet. (This can be done by pouring cold boiled water from a bottle onto the perineum and allowing it to wash over the vulva and anus). Advice would also include the use of toilet paper from front to back and washing and drying the anus after opening the bowels. Loose-fitting cotton underwear in place of tight-fitting synthetic pants reduces sweat and the risk of bacterial infection.

VITAMINS AND MINERALS

A wholefood diet that included plenty of antioxidant-rich fresh fruit and vegetables to boost immunity would be recommended. Drink at least 3½ pt (2 litres) of water, cranberry juice or barley water daily. Foods containing fresh fennel, celeriac, parsley and garlic are also beneficial.

Specific dietary supplements: propolis taken over several days is said to relieve cystitis, as is dolomite, a naturally occurring magnesium/calcium supplement, also taken over several days. Some therapists recommend a gram or so of vitamin C daily, to abort a cystitis attack. Being acidic, this would probably intensify the pain of passing urine, but ascorbic acid's antibacterial and anti-inflammatory properties could work upon the bladder wall.

HERBALISM

Lavender tea is an age-old cystitis remedy. Add 1 tsp (5 ml) dried lavender flowers to 1 pt (570 ml) boiling water, infuse for 5 minutes. Sweeten with honey if desired. Sip a cup 6 times daily during an attack.

AROMATHERAPY

Add 3–4 drops of chamomile, eucalyptus, pine or sandalwood essence to a bath. Inhale essences of cajuput, cedarwood or niaouli in steam or heated in oil in a burner. Make a hot compress with any of these oils and apply to bladder area.

HOMEOPATHY

Remedies can be taken every half hour for up to 10 doses: Cantharis 30c for burning, cutting pain in the lower abdomen which is too painful

Cranberry juice is often recommended to combat cystitis.

to ignore, a nonstop urge to urinate, with only a small trickle or blood-stained urine passed, and lower backache which is worse in the afternoons; Belladonna 30c for a burning sensation in the urethra, urine bright red with small blood clots, a bladder sensitive to jarring, and a continuous urge to empty the bladder; Dulcamara 6c for an attack that starts after getting damp and cold, or after exertion with urine frequent and blood-stained.

MEDICAL TREATMENT

Antibiotics are prescribed – after a urine specimen has been produced but before the results have been obtained from the laboratory. Fluids, bed-rest and pain relief are recommended. Further attacks may require investigation.

Add a little sandalwood essence to a hot bath to relieve the symptoms of cystitis.

cystitis

Urethritis (inflammation of the urethra, the bladder outlet tube) shares some symptoms with cystitis, but is more often due to chemical or mechanical triggers than infection. Overconcentrated urine, allergens, foreign bodies and contact with irritants such as shampoo, deodorants and condoms are all common culprits. The majority of sufferers are women.

urethritis

SYMPTOMS

- A burning sensation on passing urine
- Need to pass urine more often
- Discomfort often starts immediately after intercourse
- Symptoms are relieved by sitting in a tepid bath

Nasturtium flowers provide effective relief from urethral inflammation.

THE CURES

NATUROPATHY
A naturopath would recommend hydrotherapy in terms of drinking adequate amounts of fresh or bottled water daily (more when appreciable amounts are lost as sweat), and of using water to relieve symptoms. Sitting in a warm or tepid bath, splashing the vulval and urethral area with cold water, bathing after intercourse and applying cold compresses all relieve the stinging.

VITAMINS AND MINERALS
A wholefood diet would be recommended, avoiding common food allergens (see Prevention box). Freshly squeezed carrot juice mixed in equal proportions with either apple or celery is a recognised remedy for urethritis symptoms.

Specific dietary supplements are antioxidant vitamins and minerals similar to those suggested for mouth ulcers (such as beta-carotene, which relieves inflammation and helps to repair mucous membranes).

HERBALISM
Medicines containing extracts of cranberry, goldenseal root, nasturtium flowers and juniper berry are all recognised treatments for urethral inflammation.

AROMATHERAPY
Add a drop or two of essential oils of cypress, pine (which is particularly beneficial), parsley or niaouli to cool water and bathe the urethral opening with quick splashing movements, or soak a clean cloth, soft paper towel or cotton wool in it and apply to the sore area.

Drink plenty of water to dilute the urine and ease the pain of urination.

HOMEOPATHY

Give one dose every 1–2 hours: Staphisagria 6c for increased frequency of urination and a burning sensation as urine is passed, starting after intercourse or after catheterisation for a surgical operation, when the burning sensation is constant, and the urethra feels as though a drop of urine is passing down it all the time, even when you are not opening the bladder; and Sarsaparilla 6c for burning inside the urethra triggered by urinating, with urgency and pressure to pass urine which looks thick and slightly opaque, and when the person feels thirsty.

MEDICAL TREATMENT

Urethritis is often misdiagnosed as a urinary tract infection; this is because a scalding sensation when urinating is such a common feature of cystitis. As it is customary (and wise) in the case of cystitis to start an antibiotic course before the laboratory results of the urine sample are known, many patients with urethritis find themselves taking antibiotics unnecessarily. Doctors treat urethritis, when it can be identified, with advice to avoid likely irritants (see Prevention box), and with alkalising agents to reduce the urine's acidity (and hence the pain of passing it). A teaspoon of bicarbonate of soda with a little warm water and a squeeze of orange juice for flavour has the same effect.

urethritis

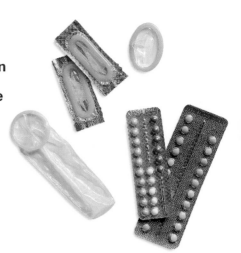

Genital warts develop as soft, pink, finger-shaped growths in and around the genital region and around the anus. They are caused by a virus, some strains of which are known to increase the risk of cervical cancer. Men can carry the virus without developing warts. An annual smear is a wise precaution for all partners of known carriers.

genital warts

SYMPTOMS

- Pink, soft, growths in genital area varying in length from matchhead-size to ⅓ in (1 cm)
- May itch, and bleed if scratched
- May smart and sting after intercourse and when in contact with urine

Astraglus can be bought in Chinese herb stores as Huang Qi.

THE CURES

NATUROPATHY

A wholefood diet with plenty of antioxidant-rich fruit and vegetables and their juices to boost the immune defence system is recommended. Fresh air and exercise boost immunity by maximising the oxygen-carrying capacity of the blood and releasing endorphins (mood-lifting hormones). Warts are especially susceptible to charming, so relaxation exercises and meditation are recommended for genital warts.

VITAMINS AND MINERALS

The usual recommendation of antioxidant-rich fruit and vegetables will be given, to provide beta-carotene (vitamin A), B-complex vitamins, vitamin C with bioflavonoids, vitamins D and E, and the minerals selenium, zinc, calcium and magnesium. Vitamin E oil painted regularly onto the warts may hasten their disappearance. Supplements include additional forms of all of the above.

HERBALISM

Extracts of the Chinese herb astragalus increase white blood cell and interferon activity, and are available over the counter and on a practitioner's prescription as potent immune stimulators. Extracts of echinacea act similarly, and boost antibody formation against viral and bacterial activity. Fresh garlic also potentiates immune defences, and can

Fresh air and exercise help boost the immune system and combat stress.

be eaten daily, and/or the juice from freshly crushed garlic cloves applied at least twice daily to the warts.

AROMATHERAPY
The essential oils of both laurel (*Laurus nobilis*) and gaiac (from the *Lignum vitae*, or tree of life) are recognised for their specific antiviral properties. Both are best used under the guidance of a qualified practitioner (especially gaiac), but a few drops of laurel essence can be safely added to an oil burner and inhaled; or to a small quantity of warm water, and used to bathe the affected area. You can also dab the warts with essential oil of lemon.

HOMEOPATHY
For vulval warts, take 4 times daily for up to 3 weeks: Thuja 6c for fleshy warts; Sabina 6c for warts of the vulva that smart and itch; and Medorrhinum 6c for itchy warts in a woman prone to catarrh and shakiness. For penile warts, take 4 times daily for up to 14 days: Thuja 6c is the remedy of first resort, but if there is no improvement, and the foreskin is swollen and the warts bleed, try Cinnabar 6c. For warts accompanied by erectile difficulties or increased desire plus premature ejaculation, try Lycopodium 6c.

MEDICAL TREATMENT
Specific proprietary topical applications may be prescribed and can be used safely. Remember, however, not to place the compound on the surrounding healthy skin. Surgical intervention may be required if warts are disfiguring or spreading. Diathermy (burning), liquid-nitrogen application (freezing) and, very rarely, surgical excision may be required. The doctor will also give advice on having regular smears and check-ups if you find that you or your partner are carrying the wart virus.

Laurel essential oil can be used in a burner for its antiviral properties.

genital warts

Painful lovemaking in women (vaginismus) is often due to muscle spasm, pelvic inflammation, infection (see Vaginal Discharge, page 76) and thinning vaginal membranes (see Menopause, page 84). Men are examined under potency problems (see page 90). Muscle spasm is often caused by fear of penetration. Pelvic inflammation causes additional symptoms.

painful intercourse

painful intercourse

SYMPTOMS

- Penetration, even partial, may be difficult
- Muscles of pelvis and thighs clamp down when penetration is anticipated
- Full relaxation impossible even with prolonged foreplay
- Other symptoms, such as heavy or irregular periods, lower abdominal pain, fever and vaginal discharge

Inhaling calming oils or using them in a massage will help relaxation.

THE CURES

NATUROPATHY
A standard healthy wholefood diet and exercise plan would be advised. Hydrotherapy, for example warm baths containing aromatherapy essences, would be recommended to aid relaxation. Massage oils containing appropriate essences also help.

VITAMINS AND MINERALS
Comforting, relaxing foods rich in stress-beating B-complex vitamins such as eggs, fish, milk products, seafood, wholegrains and nuts, and in nerve-calming calcium (milk and its products, prawns, salmon, nuts) and magnesium (green leafy vegetables, fish, nuts) are all beneficial. Calming, invigorating juices include celery, lettuce and small quantities of spinach mixed with carrot or apple.

Specific dietary supplements include all of the above, plus brewer's yeast (tablets or powder) to provide extra B-complex vitamins.

HERBALISM
Try calming herbal teas such as chamomile, taken half an hour before bed. Valerian tablets will improve unsatisfactory sleep. Preparations of agnus castus are often prescribed for anxiety linked to stress. Aloe vera gel is an excellent, safe lubricant (check the label – some aloe vera products are meant to be taken by mouth).

AROMATHERAPY
Add a few drops of essence of rose or ylang-ylang to bathwater, or to 1 tbsp (15 ml) sweet almond oil and use as a pelvic and genital massage. Heat these essences, or oils of lavender, clove or cedarwood, in an oil burner in the bedroom, and inhale to improve relaxation.

Art therapy will enable you to relax mentally and physically, and feel comfortable in yourself.

HOMEOPATHY

To be taken every 12 hours for up to five days: Ignatia 30c for spasm resulting from a hysterical reaction to grief or a broken love affair; Plumbum 30c for extreme sensitivity of the vulva and vagina, coupled with constipation.

YOGA

With its slow, calm stretching postures (*asanas*) and deep breathing, yoga is one of the most effective methods for learning to relax. It also improves the suppleness and flexibility in the muscles of the pelvis and around the vagina as much as anywhere. Helpful *asanas* might include: the Plough, Shoulder Stand, Twist, Complete Breath and Uddiyana.

RELAXATION AND MEDITATION

These can be learned together with, or separately from, yoga. Sources include videos, DVDs, cassette tapes, evening and weekend courses, and one-to-one instruction (see also Hypnotherapy, page 244).

T'ai chi and dance therapy, art and colour therapy, music therapy, spiritual healing and laughter therapy will all help you relax.

MEDICAL TREATMENT

Vaginismus has to be distinguished from inflammatory disorders of the pelvis and other conditions by the patient's account of her problem, the presence or absence of other symptoms, and possibly tests.

Vaginal dilators in graduated sizes are available to help expand a tight vagina. Psychosexual counselling involving both partners and available on the NHS can prove very helpful.

Ylang-ylang essence can be added to bathwater to promote relaxation.

A clear, non-smelling discharge mid-cycle or before your period is normal, as is a slight show of blood mid-cycle. Vaginal discharge is often caused by infections such as thrush (Candida) or Chlamydia. The appearance, odour of the discharge, soreness and irritation generally indicate the diagnosis and can be confirmed by a vaginal swab. Forgotten tampons also give rise to vaginal discharge.

vaginal discharge

vaginal discharge

SYMPTOMS

- White discharge with yeasty odour, soreness and itchiness: thrush
- Copious, bubbly, greenish discharge with fishy odour, soreness: Trichomonas
- Blood-stained discharge, pain on opening bowels and intercourse, fever: Chlamydia
- Watery discharge with fishy odour, worse after sex and mid-cycle: gardnerella
- Yellow discharge, pain and frequency of urination within 7 days after sex: gonorrhoea

THE CURES

NATUROPATHY

Fresh air, exercise and a wholefood diet will be recommended to boost immunity, with yoga or a similar therapy to combat stress. Blot the urethral area and vulva carefully after urinating and use toilet paper in a front-to-back direction. Wear loose cotton clothes and avoid tight jeans and synthetic underwear. Douche twice daily with cool or tepid water, utilising aromatherapy essences. Thrush thrives in an alkaline environment: add 1 part vinegar to 3 parts water for a douche.

VITAMINS AND MINERALS

To prevent and overcome vaginal infections, eat as many portions daily as you can of fresh fruit and vegetables and their juices, rich in immune-boosting antioxidants. Alcohol, tea, coffee and cola drinks are best avoided until the symptoms are overcome.

For thrush, eat fresh live culture yoghurt to help replace useful bowel bacteria possibly decimated by stress or antibiotics. Plain live yoghurt can also be inserted into the vagina to combat the infection and soothe inflamed membranes directly. Some practitioners advise a low-sugar diet (which includes a temporary ban on fruit) to treat thrush, since Candida yeast thrives in a sugary environment.

Specific dietary supplements include beta-carotene (vitamin A), B-complex vitamins, vitamin C with bioflavonoids, vitamins D and E with selenium, calcium and magnesium. Zinc could be beneficially added for its mood-lifting and infection-fighting abilities.

Aloe vera gel can be used to cool and soothe a sore vulval area.

HERBALISM

Aloe vera gel has been found useful for thrush infections; use to coat a sore vulval area and the entrance to the vagina. Medical herbalists prescribe douches and compresses using extracts of goldenseal, comfrey, elecampane leaves, crab apples, bay, myrrh, bramble leaves and rose petals.

AROMATHERAPY

Add 2 drops of essence of juniper, lavender or niaouli to your bathwater, or 1 drop of any of these to a bidet.

HOMEOPATHY

Take 6 times a day for up to 5 days: Alumina 6c for a copious, straw-coloured discharge that stiffens underwear, with smarting and irritation relieved by washing in cold water; Calcarea 6c for a milky discharge causing vulval itch, which is worse after urinating and before periods; Kreosotum 6c for a milky,

Regular exercise, such as jogging, will help boost your immune system.

Rose petal extract used in a compress relieves symptoms of thrush.

itchy discharge that smells like rye bread and which is preceded by low backache and great weakness; Bovista 6c for a green discharge that smarts and stings (where Trichomonas is suspected); and Carbo veg. 6c for a corrosive greenish discharge, especially before periods (where Trichomonas is suspected).

MEDICAL TREATMENT

Doctors treat vaginal infections with the appropriate antibiotic, having established the type of organism responsible. These are either taken by mouth, or inserted into the vagina, in the form of pessaries or creams (for example, nystatin, in the case of thrush).

PREVENTION

Live yoghurt or an acidophilus supplement restores 'helpful' vaginal bacteria after a course of antibiotics
Practise safe sex, using condoms
Beware with whom you share – though usually transmitted sexually, it is not unknown to catch Trichomonas from a toilet seat, towel, flannel or swimming costume used by someone else
Boost your immunity: thrush and Trichomonas are commonly found in and around the vagina, anus, cervix and bladder, and only cause harm when you are run down
Combat stress – thrush is linked to stress

CAUTION

• *Untreated Trichomonas can cause PID (pelvic inflammatory disease)*
• *Untreated Chlamydia leads to PID, and can harm an unborn baby*
• *Get your partner checked: men can carry sexually transmitted diseases without developing symptoms*
• *Gonorrhoea can be symptomless in women – untreated, it can cause PID and infertility*
• *Gonorrhoea is often present with Chlamydia – if you have one, get tested for the other*

vaginal discharge

Menorrhagia (heavy menstrual bleeding) is somewhat subjective. However, 'flooding' (whereby blood soaks tampons, towels and underclothes) and anaemia suggest abnormal loss. Causes include hormonal imbalance, fibroids, endometriosis, pelvic inflammatory disease (PID), and an IUCD (intrauterine contraceptive device).

heavy bleeding

SYMPTOMS

- Painless, heavy blood loss suggests fibroids or a polyp – non-cancerous growths in the uterus lining
- Heavy bleeding, with severe period cramps and painful intercourse, suggests endometriosis (deposits of uterus lining cells in other areas such as the wall of the uterus, bladder, colon or rectum)
- Heavy or irregular bleeding, with painful intercourse, low abdominal pain, bad cramps, unpleasant-smelling discharge, cystitis-like symptoms, fever, nausea and vomiting, suggests pelvic inflammatory disease (PID)

Heavy bleeding means the body loses valuable iron. Carrot juice helps the body absorb iron from food.

THE CURES

NATUROPATHY

The overall policy is to boost stamina, treat individual complaints as they are identified, and combat the iron-deficiency anaemia that generally results from chronic heavy blood loss.

A wholefood diet is, as usual, recommended, with appropriate exercise and anti-stress measures. Douches and both warm and cool baths would be recommended, in addition to compresses, poultices and the inhalation of essential oils.

VITAMINS AND MINERALS

Eat whole foods, with fruit and vegetables rich in antioxidants and iron from wholemeal enriched breads, cheddar cheese, egg yolk, chickpeas, molasses, lentils and walnuts. Suitable sources of protein include fat-free organic red meat and offal, pulses, grains, nuts and seeds. A naturopathic diet often recommended for heavy periods due to fibroids and endometriosis includes 1 g of protein per kilogram of body weight per day, with a view to counteracting the injurious effects of oestrogen in the body and to speed the liver's conversion of naturally produced oestrogens into the less harmful form, oestriol. Carrot juice is most appropriate, because beta-carotene helps to maximise the food's iron content. Vitamin C also helps the body to absorb iron: try drinking freshly squeezed orange or blackcurrant juices.

Specific dietary supplements are the B-complex vitamins (especially B_6), lecithin granules, brewer's yeast, vitamin E and selenium.

HERBALISM
Herbal medicines, baths, douches, compresses and poultices made from extracts of celandine, hawthorn flowers, mallow, bramble and sage are all prescribed by medical herbalists for the treatment of heavy blood loss.

AROMATHERAPY
Cypress essence in bathwater, massage oil or an inhalation eases period cramps. To revitalise the body when you have been experiencing heavy menstrual bleeding, mix together 2 fl oz (50 ml) soya oil, 2 drops of wheatgerm oil and 3 drops each of essential oils of melissa and lavender. Massage into the lower abdomen every day, and for the same or improved effect, massage 2 drops of neat melissa or lavender oil daily into the wrists or the soles of the feet.

HOMEOPATHY
To be taken every 8 hours for up to 10 doses, starting just before period is due to commence: China 30c for intermittent bleeding, dark blood clots, cramps, headache, giddiness, faintness, and if your face is very pale; Ipecac. 30c for profuse bleeding, bright red blood, and nausea; Ferrum 30c for flooding, when blood is dark and watery, occasional flushes,

face pale, and when walking seems to improve things; and Crocus 30c when there are clots of blackish blood, sensation of movement inside uterus, and the person feels weak and sick.

MEDICAL TREATMENT
This aims at treating the underlying problem. Hormones are prescribed in the form of the contraceptive pill and hormone replacement therapy (HRT) as tablets, skin patches or gels.

Fibroids can be removed surgically, and endometriosis can be treated surgically and with hormone medications.

Massaging melissa or lavender oil into the soles of the feet each day gives the body an energising boost.

PREVENTION
The only avoidable varieties of menorrhagia are those due to the coil, the progesterone contraceptive injection and, to an extent, PID, since this can be prevented from developing from a sexually transmitted disease (see Vaginal Discharge, page 76) by prompt diagnosis and antibiotic treatment

Medical herbalists may prescribe compresses made from extract of hawthorn flowers for heavy bleeding.

CAUTION
- *Seek medical advice for persistently heavy bleeding*
- *Keep a diary of blood loss days, number of tampons or towels used, clots passed, and any other symptoms*
- *If your doctor prescribes a medication that fails to help, return so that he/she can offer an alternative*

heavy bleeding

Early painful periods – primary dysmenorrhoea – typically affect young women, disappearing after the birth of the first child. The first few periods occur without ovulation, becoming painful when ovulation is established after a year or so. Secondary dysmenorrhoea affects older women, and is usually due to fibroids, endometriosis and PID (see page 78).

painful periods

SYMPTOMS

• Pain in the lower stomach and back that starts before or on the day a period arrives
• Heavy, stricture-like discomfort felt, like flesh being clamped in a vice

Fresh mint added to water can make a soothing vaginal douche.

THE CURES

NATUROPATHY
A naturopathic practitioner would advise a wholefood diet, and periodic fruit or fruit-juice fasts as a means of cleansing the body of accumulated waste. A gentle exercise plan would be prescribed, building up tolerance to aerobic exercise. Relaxation is advised. Dysmenorrhoea (period pain) associated with headaches, nausea and vomiting, exhaustion or depression is seen by practitioners as a manifestation of an underlying disharmony within the body rather than as a chemically mediated effect, and treatment is directed towards expelling toxins and rein-stating the body's equilibrium.

VITAMINS AND MINERALS
Fresh fruit and vegetables and their juices play a major part in this treatment regimen. Juices rich in antioxidant nutrients are recommended to cleanse the body and minimise the toxic waste excreted by the uterus.

Specific nutritional supplements include B-complex vitamins to minimise stress and harmonise all bodily functions. The other antioxidant vitamins – A (beta-carotene), vitamin C with bioflavonoids and vitamins D and E with selenium – are also recommended. Others include ferrous gluconate (iron), folic acid, and pollen, taken together with royal jelly (which has been clinically shown to relieve primary dysmenorrhoea in many cases).

HERBALISM
For painful periods, vaginal douches are recommended, using a handful of each of the following added to 1¾ pt

(1 litre) of water: yarrow, mint leaves, sage and parsley. Other remedies include foot and hand baths made from 2 handfuls of fresh nettle leaves to 1¾ pt (1 litre) of water. To reduce heavy periods, make an infusion of 2 handfuls of fresh nettles in a small cup of water and drink 3 cupfuls daily.

HOMEOPATHY

To be taken hourly for up to 10 doses the moment period pains occur: Belladonna 30c for pain worse immediately before the period, with a dragging sensation aggravated by lying down, when the skin is hot and flushed, and there is bright red blood; Chamomilla 30c for severe cramping pain, especially if it is associated with great anger, and extreme restlessness; Viburnum 30c for late and scanty periods, where pain extends into the thighs; Pulsatilla 30c for scanty periods, nausea, vomiting and weepinesss; and Cimicifuga 30c for strong contractions of the uterus rather like labour pains, with headaches on the days leading up to the period.

MEDICAL TREATMENT

This aims to rule out any rare, underlying conditions that may cause painful periods by having ultrasound, blood tests and a cervical smear and internal examination. The use of the oral contraceptive pill can be considered and is helpful to some.

Royal jelly has been proven to relieve the symptoms of period pain.

Relieve stress and anxiety by following a regular exercise regime.

painful periods

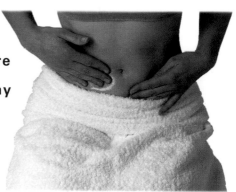

Premenstrual syndrome (PMS) is a collection of physical and emotional symptoms, which can start from a day before a period is due to 14 days beforehand, after ovulation. Many causes have been suggested, the most likely being an altered hormonal state in which the woman experiences minor hormonal changes in an exaggerated way.

premenstrual syndrome

SYMPTOMS

- Fluid retention and bloating
- Temporary weight gain
- Tender breasts
- Headaches and fatigue
- Irritability and emotional outbursts
- Weepiness and depression

Evening primrose oil has long been shown to alleviate symptoms of PMS.

THE CURES

NATUROPATHY

The benefits of a wholefood diet to PMS include the supply of many relevant nutrients and of fibre to keep the bowels regular. It is particularly important to avoid constipation, because it increases the fatigue, lethargy and bloated sensation typical of PMS. Regular appropriate exercise is also recommended, to counteract fatigue, tension and depression.

Hydrotherapy would include comforting and invigorating showers, and baths containing some of the recommended herbs and aromatherapy essences.

VITAMINS AND MINERALS

Light, low-fat sources of protein such as bean and pulse combinations, skinless chicken and turkey, pork and veal, eggs and dairy products are recommended. 'Grazing' – eating small meals within an hour of waking and sleeping, and every 2–3 hours during the day – combats the hypoglycaemia (low blood sugar) that can play a major role in PMS. Fresh fruit and vegetable sources of the antioxidants, concentrating especially upon magnesium (soya products, green leafy vegetables, wheatgerm, nuts, fish and seafood); zinc (mustard powder, oysters, wheatgerm, soya products, pork, beef and wholegrain products); vitamin C (most fresh fruit and vegetables, especially potatoes, peppers, broccoli, tomatoes, oranges and other citrus fruit, orange juice); and vitamin B_6 (pyridoxine: found in wheatgerm, fish and seafood, wholemeal flour and hazelnuts, sunflower seeds and rice).

Specific dietary supplements include vitamins C and B_6, magnesium and zinc, which promote the manufacture of helpful hormone-like chemicals called prostaglandins

Combat stress by spending extra time resting in the days leading up to a period.

from linoleic acid, present in evening primrose oil. Prostaglandins E-1 are in short supply in many PMS sufferers – reasons for this deficiency include the ageing process, viral infections, trans-fatty acids found in heat-processed oils and margarine, radiation, and a depleted immune system.

HERBALISM

Evening primrose oil: worldwide research has shown that women with severe PMS need to take this herbal medicine in higher quantities than were once recommended (2 x 500 mg capsules twice daily minimum, up to 4–6 x 500 mg capsules twice daily). This oil is not recommended for women subject to fits or seizures. Agnus castus preparations relieve a range of PMS symptoms. Reliable, safe herbal diuretics include celery, parsley, parsley piert and asparagus.

AROMATHERAPY

Useful essences include chamomile, to counteract nervous tension and irritability, and both rose and sandalwood, which lighten the mood and can enhance sexual desire (which tends to plummet in the premenstrual phase of the cycle in PMS sufferers). Geranium and rosemary essential oils have diuretic properties – add to bath or mix 2–3 drops into 2 tsp (10 ml) of sweet almond oil and smoothe into the lower abdomen. Chamomile, marjoram or lavender can be used similarly to relieve low backache and cramping stomach pain.

HOMEOPATHY

Take every 12 hours for up to 3 days, starting 24 hours before PMS symptoms are due: Lachesis 30c for symptoms that are worse first thing in the morning, and tender breasts; Lycopodium 30c for feeling bad-tempered and depressed, and craving sweet things; Kali carb. 30c for feeling taut, tense and exhausted, especially if overweight, and if symptoms are worse around 3am; Natrum mur. 30c for fluid retention, swollen breasts and if feeling sad and irritable.

MEDICAL TREATMENT

The oral contraceptive pill is prescribed in many cases, and antidepressants in rarer instances.

Sandalwood essence is a good aromatherapy oil to help lighten a heavy mood.

premenstrual

Menopausal symptoms are triggered by the fall in oestrogen that occurs at the end of a woman's reproductive years. Many who experience problems turn for relief to either hormone replacement therapy (HRT) or natural remedies. Treatment benefits include protection against bone thinning (osteoporosis), heart disease, eyesight degeneration and dementia, as well as against common menopausal symptoms.

menopause

m e n o p a u s e

SYMPTOMS

- Hot flushes
- Night-time sweats
- Mood swings, irritability, depression
- Bone fractures following minor accidents
- Poor concentration, reduced self-confidence
- Reduced sex urge (libido), painful intercourse

During the menopause eat plenty of pulses, nuts and foods with a low fat content.

THE CURES

NATUROPATHY

Recommendations include a wholefood diet for the benefit of antioxidant nutrients (which combat the ageing process) and exercise to maintain physical fitness (including cardiovascular health), and remain lithe and supple. With children possibly leaving home, and thus a lighter workload, now is the moment to organise time for yourself. Consider t'ai chi, yoga, meditation, dance therapy, art or music therapy, or shiatsu. Massage, aromatherapy and herbal medicines, cold and warm water compresses and douches all offer creative relief from menopausal symptoms.

VITAMINS AND MINERALS

Wholefoods with low-fat meat/fish and vegetarian protein sources, low-fat dairy products, pulses, grains, seeds and nuts, and as many daily helpings as possible of fresh fruit and vegetables and their freshly squeezed juices are recommended.

In addition to the standard multivitamin/mineral supplement (recommended in Naturopathy, page 184), useful dietary supplements include B-complex vitamins for their balancing effect upon both carbohydrate metabolism and highly strung emotions. Other supplements include extra vitamin C with bioflavonoids, beta-carotene (vitamin A), and vitamins D and E with the trace elements selenium, calcium, magnesium and zinc; all of these supplements help to slow down the ageing process and keep the metabolism ticking over at an optimal rate.

HERBALISM

Chamomile and black haw both combat stress and tension, tearfulness and irritability. Damiana, liquorice, saw palmetto, agnus castus and sarsaparilla all help to boost a flagging libido. General menopausal herbal remedies include helonias root, St John's wort and life root. Recommended natural menopausal supplements often contain extracts of red clover, with its high content of plant oestrogens.

AROMATHERAPY

The following essential oils are all suitable for adding to bathwater, a candle-heated oil burner, massage oil and/or warm or cool compresses for the middle or lower abdomen: rose (increases feminine self-confidence and dispels doubts about sexual attractiveness); rose and geranium to ease general menopausal symptoms; chamomile for irritability; and sandalwood, ylang-ylang, bergamot, clary sage and lavender for their antidepressant effects.

HOMEOPATHY

Specific remedies to be taken every 12 hours for up to 7 days include: Lachesis 30c for hot flushes, sweating, tight-feeling stomach, dizziness, a headache on waking, flooding during periods and being very talkative; Sepia 30c for flooding during

Keeping busy and active will help reduce menopausal symptoms.

For a flagging libido try some palmetto fruit.

periods, sweating, backache, a sinking sensation in the pit of the stomach, when the person is chilly, irritable and tearful; Bryonia 30c for dryness and thinning of vaginal membranes, constipation, and when the stools look black and burned.

MEDICAL TREATMENT

Doctors prevent and treat menopausal symptoms with HRT – hormone replacement therapy. Women who have had a hysterectomy can take oestrogens alone, but because these are linked with an increased risk of uterine cancer, progesterone is also prescribed for its protective effect on the uterus lining for women who have not had a hysterectomy.

menopause

Bartholin's glands in the vulva (female external genitalia) close to the vaginal entrance secrete lubricating moisture during sexual arousal. Blockage of a gland's opening, by dirt or a plug of mucus, traps the internal fluid and the affected gland swells, forming a cyst. Harmful bacteria can then multiply and thrive within the gland, creating pus and a painful abscess.

Bartholin's abscess

SYMPTOMS

- Throbbing, burning pain on one side of the vulva
- May feel hot, achy and unwell
- Swelling felt near vagina
- Painful to sit down, defecate, etc.

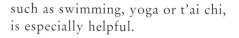

THE CURES

NATUROPATHY

Recommendations include a wholefood diet, regular exercise, hydrotherapy in the form of cool or warm herbal or aromatherapy douches and baths. Exercise that increases physical fitness and contributes to healthy vulval glands, such as swimming, yoga or t'ai chi, is especially helpful.

VITAMINS AND MINERALS

A standard wholefood diet with plenty of fluid to avoid dehydration will be recommended. Fresh fruit and vegetables contain many of the antioxidants required to boost the immune system against infection. Specific dietary supplements include beta-carotene (vitamin A), B-complex vitamins, vitamin C with bioflavonoids and E with selenium; also zinc.

HERBALISM

Burdock root has powerful anti-inflammatory, antibacterial and immune-boosting properties, and preparations in tablet form are often prescribed where infection threatens, as a blood cleanser and general detoxifier. In Europe, compresses are made using freshly crushed chervil

Burdock root can be used to calm down inflammation and give the immune system a boost.

and/or parsley, and applied to many different types of abscess.

AROMATHERAPY
Add a few drops of any of these oils to your bathwater, or apply a little to the abscess, using a clean cotton bud: tea tree, chamomile, clary sage, rosemary, Baume de Perou (balsam of Peru), or patchouli. To draw a Bartholin's (or other) abscess to a head, make a warm oatmeal poultice (see Aromatherapy, page 202) with a few drops of lavender, patchouli, tea tree or thuja essence and apply to painful swelling for 20 minutes or so, twice daily if necessary.

HOMEOPATHY
Baryta carb. 6c can be taken 4 times a day for up to 3 weeks. However, it is very unlikely that anyone would put up with a painful swelling in the vulva for more than a few days; and the longer a cyst remains in place, the greater the risks of infection and abscess formation. It is therefore recommended that this remedy be

A warm oatmeal poultice used twice a day will bring the abscess to a head.

taken 4 times a day for a maximum of 5 days, before seeking conventional medical treatment. For abscess, the following specific remedies should be taken every 2 hours for up to 10 doses: Belladonna 30c for early stage of infection, when the vaginal entrance is red, hot and swollen; Hepar sulph. 6c for discharge of pus and extreme tenderness; Mercurius 6c when symptoms include fever and chill, with the person feeling very hot and freezing cold alternately.

MEDICAL TREATMENT
Antibiotics are prescribed to prevent or treat a Bartholin's abscess. Sometimes, an enlarged, very painful abscess needs to be opened and drained under local anaesthetic.

PREVENTION
Wash vulva thoroughly twice daily
Avoid tight-fitting underwear and jeans, which encourage bacterial infection
Wear loose, cool cotton pants and skirts, especially after sexual contact

CAUTION
• *Seek medical help – an untreated abscess can lead to blood poisoning (septicaemia)*
• *Throbbing, hot pain in the genital region always requires medical investigation*
• *Flu-like symptoms (temperature, lethargy, feeling unwell) commonly accompany this condition*

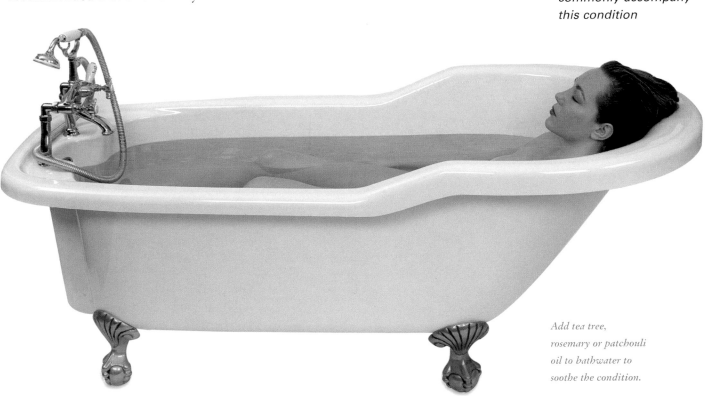

Add tea tree, rosemary or patchouli oil to bathwater to soothe the condition.

Bartholin's abscess

The male prostate gland surrounds the neck of the bladder and upper part of its outlet tube (the urethra). The fluid it produces forms part of the semen released during ejaculation (male climax). The prostate gland tends to enlarge from middle age onwards, pressing on the urethra passing through it. This interferes with emptying the bladder, and can lead to annoying symptoms.

prostate gland enlargement

SYMPTOMS

- Need to empty the bladder more often
- Getting up at night to pass urine
- Having to strain to empty the bladder completely
- Feeble urine flow – poor control over starting and stopping stream

Yoga can provide relief from the problems of prostate gland enlargement.

THE CURES

NATUROPATHY

A wholefood diet and supplements (see below), regular appropriate exercise, warm and cool baths using herbal and aromatherapeutic remedies are recommended, as are compresses for deep pelvic pain, applied over the bladder and, if necessary, to the perineum (the space between the genitals and the anus). Some yoga positions may prove helpful in the relief of this and other male pelvic problems, for example.

VITAMINS AND MINERALS

Ample supplies of water and fruit juices, especially a mixture of freshly squeezed carrot, cucumber and beetroot in roughly equal volumes, are recommended. Caffeine-containing drinks such as tea, coffee and cola should be avoided because they can aggravate benign enlargement of the prostate gland. The high intake of fresh fruit and vegetables could in itself be beneficial because of the hormone-like nutrients many plants possess. The prostate gland also contains more zinc per gram of tissue than any other organ – zinc-rich foods are therefore said to help this condition, and these include lean lamb chops, eggs, wheatgerm, pumpkin seeds, wheatgerm, fat-free milk powder and powdered mustard.

Specific dietary supplements include zinc gluconate; pollen has been confirmed in many clinical trials to reduce benign prostate gland enlargement and the symptoms to which it gives rise.

HERBALISM

Best prescribed by a qualified medical herbalist, remedies for prostate gland swelling include saw palmetto (extracts of the berries have been used for centuries as a general tonic

Zinc gluconate is taken regularly as a dietary supplement for this particular condition.

for the male reproductive system); damiana; couch grass; and horsetail. Cranberry extracts and juice ease a sore, inflamed bladder and combat urinary infection.

AROMATHERAPY
Lavender or gaiac essential oil, used to make a warm or cool compress, or added to massage oil and smoothed into the perineal area and over the lower abdomen, and lavender tea to reduce bladder inflammation (see Cystitis, page 68) are recommended.

HOMEOPATHY
To be taken 4 times daily for up to 21 days: Sabal 6c for difficult or painful bladder emptying, including spasms of the bladder or urethra; Ferrum pic. 6c for a senile person who urinates a lot at night, and complains of pressure on the rectum and a smarting sensation at the neck of the bladder; Baryta 6c for a frequent urge

to urinate, a slow stream, and when the person is thin, underweight and impotent; Thuja 6c for a frequent and urgent desire to pass urine; Iodum 6c for loss of potency, shrunken testicles, and when the prostate gland feels hard (which may be a sign of cancer).

MEDICAL TREATMENT
Drugs can now be given to shrink a benignly swollen prostate gland; in suitable cases, surgery is often preferable as a large chunk of the gland can be removed, freeing the urinary obstruction.

Zinc-rich foods such as these help ease an enlarged prostate gland.

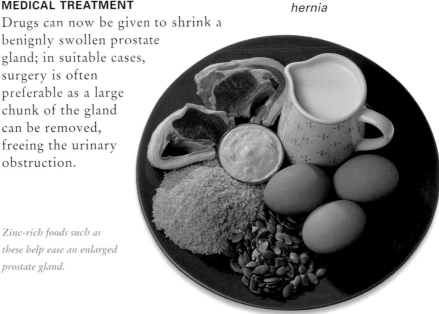

prostate gland enlargement

Potency problems range from difficulty in obtaining, or maintaining, an erection, to an inability to ejaculate during a climax. The causes range from discomfort in the penis or testicles, to reduced blood supply (common in middle-aged or older diabetic men and those with clogged arteries), anxiety, tension or other emotional disorders.

potency problems

SYMPTOMS

- Partial erection only – the penis may be too floppy and limp for penetration
- Erection satisfactory until penetration attempted, when it disappears
- Pain experienced in penis or testicles when intercourse attempted
- Prevailing anxiety or depression reduces libido (sexual urge) and/or causes erectile failure

Freshly squeezed red cabbage, celery and lettuce juices are recommended as part of a wholefood diet.

THE CURES

NATUROPATHY

This is a particularly valuable therapy for complaints such as potency problems which tend to have multiple causes. A wholefood diet would lie at the centre of any treatment, together with regular exercise and effective relaxation. Hydrotherapy might be employed to administer herbal and/or aromatherapy remedies in baths and sweet-smelling compresses.

VITAMINS AND MINERALS

A wholefood diet with a high percentage of raw fresh fruit and vegetables would also include freshly squeezed juices. A particular combination recommended to improve potency comprises 5 fl oz (140 ml) red cabbage juice, 3 fl oz (85 ml) celery juice and 2 fl oz (55 ml) lettuce juice. Drink twice daily (if the taste is not to your liking, add some ground spice such as clove, nutmeg, and/or a dash of Worcestershire sauce or a little orange juice). Oily fish and fish roe contain fatty acids that help make healthy sperm.

Specific dietary supplements include zinc gluconate, pollen (see Prostate Gland Enlargement, page 88), and a high-potency vitamin B-complex to counteract tension and stress. Calcium and magnesium, among the antioxidant nutrients, are especially beneficial in cases of anxiety and 'feeling wound up'.

HERBALISM

Most of the herbal remedies prescribed for prostate gland are also recommended to help improve potency. Siberian ginseng is also used, as are elixirs of basil, celery and savory mixed with fortified wine. Sip very strong mint tea or some ginseng tea half an hour before lovemaking.

AROMATHERAPY

Essence of cedarwood is reputed to stimulate the sexual senses. Add to a massage oil, or to bathwater, place a few drops on the bed linen, or heat in a candle burner, dissolved in sweet almond oil. Other erotic essences include rose, ylang-ylang, lavender, clove or ginger.

HOMEOPATHY

Take every 12 hours for up to 5 days: Lycopodium 30c for a surge of desire with the anticipation of failure, and when the penis is cold and small; Agnus 30c when the erection is not firm enough for penetration, general weakness, when the penis is small and cold, especially if intercourse has been very frequent or if erectile problems have recently come on; Selenium 30c for erectile problems associated with dribbles of semen while asleep, increased desire for sex and erotic fantasies; and Arnica 30c following a bruising injury to the penis.

ALTERNATIVE THERAPIES

Acupuncture, yoga and relaxation or meditation, dance and music therapy, art therapy, laughter therapy, and t'ai chi could all play useful roles (depending upon personal tastes).

MEDICAL TREATMENT

Any of the above therapies may be suggested by a doctor after diagnosis. Viagra is used to

Acupuncture boosts circulation, nerve impulses and sexual energy.

boost the circulation to the penis and promote erections but it is not suitable for people suffering from angina or other heart problems. Medicines known to affect potency include alcohol, diuretics, several prescribed for high blood pressure, barbiturate anticonvulsants, appetite suppressors, some peptic ulcer drugs and some antidepressants.

Alternative therapies such as laughter therapy may help you to relax.

potency problems

Ailments of the nerves and spinal cord include sciatica and trapped or compressed nerves, causing shooting pain. Illnesses to do with the brain can be particularly distressing, with symptoms ranging from headaches and migraines to memory loss, dizzy spells or depression, to name but a few. Many of these conditions can be treated or at least managed once diagnosed.

the **brain, spinal cord and nerves**

Headaches affect all of us at some time. Migraines often confine sufferers to bed in a darkened room, and cause additional problems such as nausea, vomiting and abdominal pain. Tension headaches produce head pain only, but can last much longer. Like migraines, they are triggered by fatigue, stress and tension. Both types of headache can respond readily to alternative treatments.

migraines & tension headaches

SYMPTOMS

Classical migraine
- Intense throbbing on one side of the head
- Warning symptoms: zig-zag lines, flashing lights, facial tingling
- Nausea and vomiting

Tension headache
- Tight band around skull
- Head pain pulsing in time with the heartbeat

Stress can often bring on a migraine. Take time to relax each day.

THE CURES

NATUROPATHY

A wholefood diet, stress reduction and therapies to relieve the effects of stress would be recommended. Hydrotherapy may be prescribed in the form of swimming as an easily accessible and stress-relieving exercise, and as a cold compress in the treatment of tension headaches or migraines. A tendency to either hypoglycaemia or sinusitis, both headache triggers, would be noted, as well as current prescription medicines such as oestrogen in the contraceptive pill. Applied Kinesiology (see page 230) might be used to help identify food allergens. Also, because some severe headaches are caused by constriction of the arteries supplying the scalp and brain, the application of hot air via a bonnet hairdryer can sometimes terminate attacks.

VITAMINS AND MINERALS

Small, regular wholefood meals and snacks to eliminate hypoglycaemia as a migraine trigger are recommended. Eliminate processed foods containing MSG (monosodium glutamate), used widely in Chinese cooking, and nitrate and nitrite preservatives found in hot dogs, ham, bacon and salami.

Common migraine food triggers include chocolate, cola, pork, onion, garlic, corn, eggs, citrus fruit, wheat, coffee, alcohol, cheese, chicken livers, pickled herrings (rollmops), broad bean pods and tinned figs. For migraines or tension headaches linked with a hangover, gastric upset, fatigue and/or nervous tension, make up a fresh juice mixture comprising 2 parts of tomato to 1 of celery, plus 2 tsp (10 ml) onion juice if onions are not a trigger. Take one wineglassful every 2 hours until symptoms disappear.

Specific dietary supplements include vitamin B_3 (niacinamide), which can help prevent or ease severe migraine. Others to relieve severe headache in general include calcium pantothenate and pyridoxine (vitamin B_6) – especially good for headaches linked to PMS (see page 82). Both of these should be taken as part of a B-vitamin supplement added to the recommended multivitamin/mineral supplement. Pollen is also reported to relieve severe attacks effectively.

HERBALISM

Feverfew is a renowned migraine remedy, which helps constricted blood vessels in the brain to relax, and counteracts any inflammation. Valerian preparations combat irritability and nervous tension, and improve sleep. A cold compress on the forehead using extracts of chamomile, lavender, thyme or basil can help soothe away most headaches.

AROMATHERAPY

Bathe the forehead with cool water after adding 2–3 drops of lavender, clary sage or rosemary. Massage using 1 tsp (5 ml) grapeseed oil mixed with 1 drop of lavender, melissa, basil or juniper oil (or chamomile oil for severe nervous tension), or inhale cajuput, geranium, lemon grass or oregano in steam or from a burner.

HOMEOPATHY

For tension headaches, take remedies every 10–15 minutes for up to 10 doses: Glonoinum 30c for a headache pounding in time to heartbeat, worsened by bending over; Ignatia 6c for a headache causing a tight band across the forehead or skull; and Ruta 6c for a pressing, bruising headache linked to fatigue, aggravated by reading and relieved by rest. For migraine attacks, take every 15 minutes for up to 10 doses, preferably at the earliest warning sign: Iris 6c for blurred vision, a tight-feeling scalp, a right-sided headache, and when vomit is mostly bile; Spigelia 6c for a sharp, severe pain over the left eye, pain pulsating with heartbeat, worsened by sudden movements; and Pulsatilla 6c for a headache worse in the evening or during a period.

MEDICAL TREATMENT

Painkillers such as paracetamol or NSAIDs, and specific migraine medication, which acts directly upon the blood vessels in the brain, will be recommended.

Massage temples, shoulders and the back of the neck just within the hairline.

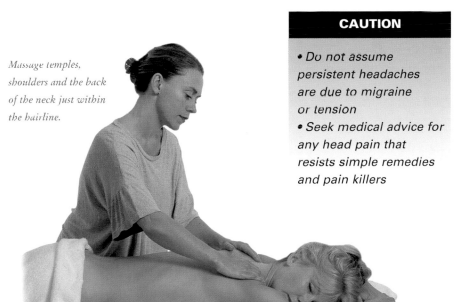

Rich, spicy or fatty foods can trigger migraine attacks and are best avoided.

migraines & tension headaches

Causes of a failing memory include psychological or emotional trauma, nervous tension, fatigue and a depleted blood supply to the brain. Dementia (including Alzheimer's disease) causes progressive changes in the brain such as plaque formation or clogged arteries, which destroy normal cognitive (thought-linked) functioning.

memory problems

SYMPTOMS

- Difficulty remembering recent events
- Reduced powers of expression, due to forgetting words and/or substituting inappropriate ones
- A tendency to repeat things or ask the same questions many times over
- Vivid long-term memory, such as childhood events but recent events easily and frequently forgotten
- Personality changes and mood swings as the disease progresses.

Keep up your protein levels. Boiled eggs, steamed fish and fresh chicken are all rich in protein.

THE CURES

NATUROPATHY
A wholefood diet, stress reduction and therapies to relieve the effects of stress would be recommended. Hydrotherapy may be prescribed in the form of swimming as an easily accessible and stress-relieving exercise for people of any age.

Current prescription medicines would be noted, as those that lower the mood can also interfere with memory and mental well-being. The person's lifestyle would be assessed from the holistic viewpoint (see page 184) and suggestions made where appropriate to improve general health and reduce stress levels.

VITAMINS AND MINERALS
Small, regular wholefood meals and snacks tailored to suit the person's tastes, lifestyle and capacity would be recommended – for example, puréed and liquidised fruit and vegetables and their juices would be more appropriate for someone with dentures than masses of wholefood breads, pastas and grains. The need for antioxidants is vital, to help prevent or relieve ageing signs in the brain. Protein should be taken daily in some form; for example, a boiled egg, poached or steamed fish, a little fresh chicken, liver or kidneys.

Specific dietary supplements include a multivitamin/mineral supplement, with extra vitamin C with bioflavonoids, fish oil (which many older people already take, and which contains essential fatty acids vital for brain function). Extra B vitamins where stress is a problem, plus vitamin E with selenium for its beneficial effect upon blood vessels, and zinc to improve immunity to colds and flu and lift a low mood, are also recommended.

HERBALISM

Ginkgo biloba extracts have been shown to improve memory, alertness and general mental function, primarily through their beneficial effects upon blood circulation and energy metabolism in the brain. Ginkgo extracts improve blood flow to the extremities as well (see poor circulation in the hands and legs, pages 52–5), and also act as antioxidants, further slowing down the brain's decline with age.

AROMATHERAPY

The herb rosemary was used by the ancient Greeks to boost memory and brain power, and the addition of a few drops of the essential oil to bathwater, as an inhalation or simply on a tissue beneath the pillow, may play a useful part in an overall prevention or relief plan.

BACH FLOWER REMEDIES

Clematis is useful for someone who is overly absent-minded, dreamy and suffers from poor concentration. Vine helps balance people who are autocratic, domineering, inflexible, tyrannical and arrogant. Walnut assists in the adjustment needed for transition or change (for example, when a partner dies or goes into hospital, the children leave home or move away, or a house move becomes inevitable).

HOMEOPATHY

Take 4 times daily for up to 14 days: Calcarea 6c for an elderly person with wandering attention, childish behaviour, who finds words hardest to remember; Plumbus 6c for words causing most difficulty, when the

Keep active, both physically and mentally. Sharing an activity with friends is good for the mind and body.

person is anaemic, colicky or suffering from a nervous condition; Sulphur 6c for difficulty recollecting words and names; Anacardium 6c for a person who is absent-minded because of inner conflict or worry, with the memory for names chiefly affected.

MEDICAL TREATMENT

Although it is still said that senile dementia and Alzheimer's disease cannot be medically treated, drugs do appear from time to time which seem to arrest the decline associated with these two complaints. In Europe, ginkgo biloba preparations are extensively prescribed for their beneficial effects in patients suffering from these conditions.

PREVENTION

Live as healthy a lifestyle as possible
Exercise mentally as well as physically, for example by doing word puzzles, crosswords or quizzes
Keep active (especially important after bereavement) – play cards, dance, meet friends, read and watch the news

CAUTION

• *See your doctor about any of the described changes as soon as they become apparent*
• *Seek medical advice about insomnia, anxiety and depression – all of which affect memory and mental function*

Ginkgo biloba improves memory, alertness, circulation and energy levels.

memory problems

We all feel anxious at times, but it becomes a medical problem when it persistently interferes with a person's happiness, work or relationships. Free-floating anxiety was first described by Sigmund Freud, who believed this sensation of dread for no known cause had a sexual origin. Other forms include phobias, panic attacks and obsessive–compulsive disorder.

anxiety disorders

SYMPTOMS

- Stomach pain, palpitations, dry mouth, and a frequent need to open bowels or empty bladder
- Difficulty in concentrating – the mind always seems to be buzzing with confusion
- Feeling of dread during the day and on waking
- Reduced ability to make decisions or complete tasks at home or at work
- For panic attacks, a sudden onset of acute fear, often triggered by a challenging situation such as shopping or crowds

THE CURES

NATUROPATHY

A wholefood diet, stress reduction and therapies to relieve the effects of stress would be recommended. Hydrotherapy may be prescribed in the form of swimming or the use of a flotation tank to induce tranquillity

Clary sage is sometimes prescribed by herbalists to allay feelings of anxiety.

and balance. Lifestyle assessment would be made from the holistic viewpoint (see page 184) and suggestions made where appropriate to improve physical, mental, emotional and spiritual health generally.

VITAMINS AND MINERALS

Small, regular wholefood meals and snacks are recommended, employing the grazing approach (meals little and often) to avoid low blood sugar, which can help induce panic symptoms. Fresh fruit and vegetable juices are especially important, to top up the defence system (which is badly affected by anxiety and stress) with antioxidants and other nutrients. Celery, carrot and/or apple juice in equal proportions, with a few tablespoons (45 ml) of fresh lettuce juice, calms frayed nerves. Sunflower seeds contain a substance that helps to quell nicotine cravings in

ex-smokers. Protein should be taken daily – for example, a boiled egg, poached or steamed fish, a little fresh chicken, liver or kidneys – but it often suits anxious people better if eaten in the middle of the day or at night rather than for breakfast.

Specific dietary supplements include a multivitamin/mineral supplement, with extra vitamin C with bioflavonoids, and B vitamins for their stress-relieving properties.

HERBALISM
Valerian is probably the best-known herb for allaying anxiety and improving poor quality sleep. Others prescribed for anxiety conditions include chamomile, clary sage, hawthorn and both melissa and mint. These can be taken as tablets, tinctures or herbal teas, while ginger, fresh or as preserved root, or in powder-containing capsules, relieves nausea due to anxiety and other causes.

AROMATHERAPY
A good head-to-toe massage by a professional therapist using plain massage oil and clary sage reduces and relieves anxiety and can produce euphoria, followed by calm sleep. Useful additions to bathwater, or to inhalations and oil burners, include ylang-ylang, lavender, mandarin and marjoram.

BACH FLOWER REMEDIES
White Chestnut helps to get rid of recurrent unwanted thoughts, as well as preoccupation with worry or conflict. Larch boosts low self-confidence and combats failure fears.

HOMEOPATHY
In cases of panic, take every few minutes for up to 10 doses: Arnica 30c as a first resort; Opium 6c for paralysing fear; Gelsemium 6c for

weakness and shakiness after panic has subsided. For overwhelming obsessive thoughts (of death and dying, or feelings of worthlessness), take Aurum 30c every 2 hours for up to 10 doses; and Thuja 30c to combat thoughts of live animals wriggling in the stomach, or that the limbs are made of glass and so brittle they may break (especially if the sufferer also has warts).

Psychotherapy, hypnotherapy and counselling would all be helpful. Stress relievers such as relaxation, meditation and yoga are especially beneficial. People with a history of emotional trauma may benefit from art, music and colour therapy, and also from spiritual guidance.

MEDICAL TREATMENT
A doctor may prescribe a course of tranquillisers such as diazepam, but they may cause addiction, and doctors are increasingly recommending natural therapies to improve sleep and anxiety problems.

Swimming works well as part of a hydrotherapy treatment, promoting a feeling of calm and well-being.

PREVENTION
Follow a healthy lifestyle including a nutritious diet and exercise to dispel stress
Talk over problems when they arise instead of bottling them up
Seek help sooner rather than later – the longer an anxiety illness remains hidden, the more deeply it can take root

CAUTION
• Seek help urgently for emotional or anxiety problems linked to thoughts of self-harm
• Do not feel stupid – anxiety can be treated
• Avoid situations linked to an established phobia, such as heights or tense social situations, until the person feels ready to cope

anxiety disorders

We all feel sad sometimes, and most of us experience catastrophes such as bereavement, redundancy or the ending of a close relationship. Grief in these situations is normal, and should be allowed to resolve itself naturally. Depression becomes an illness when mental anguish is excessively intense or prolonged, and interferes with normal functioning. It can also arise for no reason.

depression

SYMPTOMS

- Feeling sad, pessimistic, and preoccupied with loss
- Feelings of worthlessness, and of personal wickedness
- Tearfulness and general apathy
- Loss of appetite and normal sleep pattern
- Thoughts of suicide or other self-harm

St. John's wort, taken in tablet form, can help with mild symptoms.

THE CURES

NATUROPATHY

A wholefood diet, stress reduction and therapies to relieve the effects of stress would be recommended. Hydrotherapy may be prescribed in the form of swimming. An old but effective naturopathic treatment for depression used hydrotherapy in the form of a cold bath or shower once or twice daily, combined with vigorous outdoor exercise.

VITAMINS AND MINERALS

Small, regular wholefood meals and snacks, with plenty of fresh fruit and vegetables and their juices, are recommended. Foods rich in the amino acid tryptophan have been shown to increase the serotonin in the brain (a low level of which mood transmitter is found in many depressed people). Examples include turkey, fish, dried dates, bananas and cottage cheese.

Specific dietary supplements include a multivitamin/mineral supplement, with extra vitamin C with bioflavonoids, and B vitamins for their stress-relieving properties (stress is a major trigger for depressive illness). Zinc gluconate has been shown to relieve clinical depression in some people.

Nutritional supplements of tryptophan are sometimes prescribed by qualified practitioners. They (and foods rich in tryptophan) should be taken with a carbohydrate snack to facilitate the passage of tryptophan into the brain. Nuts contain bromine so help to allay anxiety, and wheatgerm is rich in vitamin E, a great energiser.

HERBALISM

Herbal teas made from basil, thyme or mint are often recommended. St John's wort has been shown in a number of clinical trials to relieve mild to moderately severe depression, and can be bought in tablet form. Ginseng also balances the body's systems and rids the body of fatigue – often a strong indication of depressive illness.

AROMATHERAPY

Try a warm, relaxing bath or massage seasoned with 3–4 drops of ylang-ylang, rose, verbena, neroli, clary sage or marjoram essences. Alternatively, inhale these from an oil burner and carry some of the oil with you to sniff during the day when times are difficult.

HOMEOPATHY

Take 3 times daily for up to 14 days for mild to moderate depression, or while awaiting medical treatment: Cadmium phos. 6c for depression with a lack of energy and stamina after a viral illness such as glandular fever or flu; Aurum 6c for feeling totally worthless, disgusted with oneself and suicidal; Nux 6c for depression coupled with great irritability, and finding fault with everyone around you.

Many other therapies – from acupuncture to Zen-mediated meditation – can prove beneficial in relieving depression.

MEDICAL TREATMENT

Depressive illness is an instance in which pharmaceutical drugs and psychotherapy have enormously important parts to play, although alternative remedies continue to be

Vigorous outdoor exercise, such as jogging, allows the body to produce endorphins, which lift the spirits.

beneficial – either combined with orthodox treatment, or used alone to help relieve mild to moderate depression. Current medications include the long-established tricyclics such as amitryptiline, and SSRIs (selective serotonin re uptake inhibitors) such as venlafaxine or fluoxetine.

All these foods are rich in tryptophan, which helps increase levels of seratonin in the brain.

PREVENTION

Seek counselling or therapy for unresolved trauma such as abuse during childhood
Talk (to your partner, family, colleagues or boss) instead of bottling up negative feelings
Watch out for depression's early warning signs: poor appetite, weight loss, early morning waking

CAUTION

• *Never tell a depression sufferer to 'snap out of it' – they cannot*
• *Never belittle a depressed person's symptoms*
• *Never ignore indications of self-harm – some depressed people threaten and commit suicide*

depression

Dizzy spells can be caused by low blood pressure (for example, when getting up too quickly after lying or sitting down, especially if you are taking medication for high blood pressure). Other causes include a substantial loss of blood, anxiety and panic attacks, low blood sugar and inner-ear disturbance (see page 156). Anaemia can also be responsible.

dizzy spells

SYMPTOMS

- The room seems to swim, especially after mild exertion – for example, going upstairs
- Loss of appetite
- Lacklustre hair and brittle nails
- Pallor
- Exhaustion
- Breathlessness

To stimulate digestion, grate horseradish root into some cider vinegar with some runny honey.

THE CURES

NATUROPATHY

Recommendations include a strictly wholefood diet (see below), with stress reduction to prevent this from worsening dizzy spells caused by anaemia. Exercise would be very gentle at first, while the body was assimilating iron and manufacturing healthier blood (anaemia prevents blood from transporting as much oxygen as your brain and body need, which is why dizziness commonly follows mild exercise).

VITAMINS AND MINERALS

Small, regular wholefood meals and snacks, with plenty of fresh fruit and vegetables and their juices, are recommended. Foods rich in iron include mussels, offal and red meat, which can safely be eaten in moderation if all fat is removed and no fat added while cooking. Vegetarian sources of iron include enriched bread and cereals, pulses, beans, egg yolk, cashew and pistachio nuts, seaweed, dark green leafy vegetables, cheddar cheese, pumpkin seeds, wheatgerm and wholewheat products. Add a couple of handfuls of spinach, parsley, dark green cabbage, kale or watercress to carrots when juicing; the beta-carotene in the latter helps to stabilise iron in the food. Thyme has the same effect – add to cooking water. Fresh orange or blackcurrant juice supplies vitamin C.

Specific dietary supplements for dizzy spells include chelated iron to maximise absorption, and vitamin C, which is needed for iron absorption and assimilation, and in the manufacture of healthy red blood cells. Take a multivitamin/mineral supplement but do not take additional supplementary vitamin E or zinc, since both interfere with iron metabolism. B-complex vitamins and folic acid all aid blood cell manufacture and metabolism.

HERBALISM

Thyme tea is recommended. A glass of parsley wine daily is an old country remedy for combating post-natal fatigue and depression, and boosting the appetite. Horseradish stimulates the appetite and digestion – try a spoonful of the sauce or cream, or grate a few teaspoonfuls (15 ml) of the raw root into a tablespoonful (15 ml) of organic cider vinegar, with runny honey. Ginseng remedies rebalance a disordered metabolism and counteract fatigue.

AROMATHERAPY

Boost the appetite and the spirits, and stimulate weary senses with essences of melissa (also called lemon balm and bee balm), rosemary, lavender and orange. They are all wonderful just to inhale when feeling fatigued – carry some with you to sniff as required, add to washing and bathing water and heat in an oil burner.

HOMEOPATHY

Take every 12 hours for up to 2 weeks: China 30c for anaemia due to blood loss, where the person is chilly, hypersensitive and tired; Ferrum 30c for anaemia where the face is pale but flushes easily; Calcarea phos. 30c for anaemia that arises during a growth spurt (during the first 2 years of life and during adolescence) or the person is irritable, with poor digestion; Picric ac. 30c for anaemia coupled with mental overload; and Natrum. mur. 30c for anaemia in a person with constipation, a muddy complexion, headache, dry mouth and lips, and a tendency to suffer from cold sores.

MEDICAL TREATMENT

For dizzy spells due to anaemia, a doctor would treat the cause, such as heavy periods or poor nutrition. The anaemia would be treated with iron and folic acid supplements or iron injections.

Iron supplements can be bought easily from most good health food stores.

Milk, tea and coffee hamper iron absorption, so do not drink these with your meals.

dizzy spells

MS is a chronic disease of the nervous system in which the myelin sheaths, which protect and insulate the nerves of the brain and the spinal cord, become damaged, resulting in loss of nerve function in body areas served by the affected nerve. Symptoms tend to fade and recur, especially at first, but progressive physical disability is the most common outcome. The causes of MS are unknown.

multiple sclerosis (MS)

SYMPTOMS

- Blurred vision in one or both eyes
- Muscular spasms and weakness
- Patches of numbness anywhere on the body
- Loss of control over bladder and bowels
- Mobility problems as disease progresses

THE CURES

NATUROPATHY

A strictly wholefood, low-fat diet (see below), with stress reduction to prevent unnecessary fatigue and strain, would be recommended. Gentle strengthening and remedial exercise would be advised according to the person's capabilities. Relaxation and meditation with, perhaps, visualisation may also be advised. Since diet has such a prominent role in the alternative approach to MS, applied kinesiology or dowsing may be employed to identify personal food allergens.

VITAMINS AND MINERALS

Recommendations include small, regular wholefood meals and snacks, based on the macrobiotic philosophy, which advocates eating plenty of cereals and grains, and fresh, organic, preferably locally produced fruit and vegetables and their juices. Animal fats will be banned, consumption of dairy products limited, and low-fat items always used. Fresh polyunsaturated fats and oils will be used where required.

In addition to a daily multivitamin/mineral supplement, specific dietary supplements including additional stress-beating vitamin B-complex, vitamin C with bioflavonoids, vitamin E, selenium and zinc are usually recommended. Some MS sufferers have been found

Evening primrose oil has been of benefit to some MS sufferers.

to benefit from high doses of evening primrose oil and, while research progresses, it is thought that a fault in the body's ability to convert the essential fatty acid cis-linoleic acid, found in most people's diets, into beneficial group E1 prostaglandins may help to explain this disease, similar to the mechanism underlying the problems many PMS sufferers experience (see page 82). The benefits from diet and supplementation seem chiefly to consist of stabilising MS and preventing further deterioration from the disease, and should be implemented as soon as possible after a diagnosis is made. They do not appear to benefit people with advanced forms of the disease.

HERBALISM

Ginseng helps to correct metabolic imbalances and combats stress and fatigue. The Chinese herb astragalus also increases stamina and boosts the immune system (some research suggests a viral cause of MS).

Massaging tired and painful muscles may help to stimulate them.

AROMATHERAPY

Juniper essence – 2–3 drops in 4 tsp (20 ml) plain carrier oil – makes a stimulating massage oil for fatigued, painful muscles. The oil may also help to maximise the function and movement of any muscles that are partially paralysed.

OTHER THERAPIES

MS is an illness that affects the emotions as well as the body, with mood swings, depression and personality changes. Art and colour therapies, music therapy, psychotherapy, relaxation and meditation (with visualisation) all have much to offer.

MEDICAL TREATMENT

Oxygen therapy, steroids and other approaches attempt to delay or reverse the disease's progress. Otherwise, the treatment is largely supportive, including physiotherapy, a bladder catheter to deal with urinary incontinence, psychotherapy and counselling.

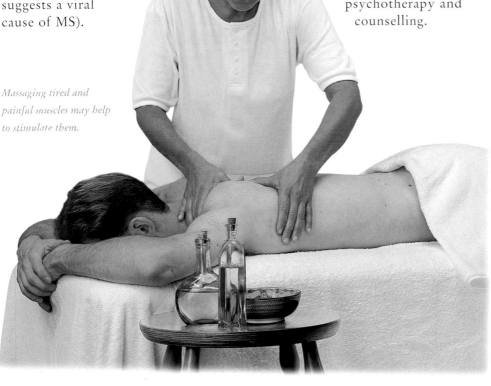

PREVENTION

Because the causes of MS are unknown, it is impossible to prevent it

Juniper essence can be used to make a stimulating massage oil.

CAUTION

• *Seek medical advice as soon as possible for any of the symptoms described opposite*
• *The symptoms all have numerous causes besides MS – for example, calf muscle spasm may be due to poor circulation*
• *The earlier MS is diagnosed, the better the chance of relief through treatment*

multiple sclerosis (MS)

Lapses in consciousness have many causes including hypoglycaemia, dizzy spells, high blood pressure, fainting and strokes. For giddy spells due to inner-ear disturbances, see pages 157–158. Epilepsy is an indication of abnormal brain function, often characterised by seizures or loss of consciousness. The most common forms are petit mal and grand mal.

loss of consciousness & epilepsy

SYMPTOMS

Petit mal
- Brief loss of conscious awareness that may go unnoticed by others
- Person feels he/she has lost a few moments, or may appear vacant for seconds at a time

Grand mal
- Headache, yawning, dizziness and feelings of unreality are all warning signs
- Loss of consciousness
- Muscles, especially of the jaw, contract strongly then convulse (have a fit or seizure)
- Person may vomit or pass urine

Regular wholefood meals including organic vegetables are recommended.

THE CURES

NATUROPATHY
A wholefood diet would be recommended, high in raw foods, with a special caution to avoid artificial additives (which are suspected of triggering convulsions in some patients). Other aspects of lifestyle, especially exercise habits, stress factors and sleep patterns would also be scrutinised with a view to overall improvement. Because so many factors affect, and are affected by, grand mal epilepsy in particular, even small positive changes (avoiding low blood sugar with small, frequent meals, reducing stress with regular relaxation) can significantly improve well-being and reduce the frequency of attacks.

VITAMINS AND MINERALS
Small, regular wholefood meals and snacks, with plenty of cereals and grains, and fresh, organic fruit and vegetables and their juices would be recommended. Calming foods, such as wholegrains and pulses, seeds and nuts, calcium-rich low-fat dairy products, and magnesium-rich green leafy vegetables are all good choices.

Specific dietary supplements include the stress-beating vitamin B-complex, vitamin C with bioflavonoids, vitamin E, selenium and zinc. Supplementary taurine, an amino acid present in eggs, fish, meat and milk, is prescribed by some naturopathic/nutritional practitioners in the treatment of epilepsy. Calcium and magnesium very occasionally help reduce frequency of attacks; try naturally occurring dolomite containing 2 parts of calcium to 1 of magnesium – the form most tolerated by the body.

HERBALISM
Preparations of skullcap are sometimes prescribed alongside orthodox medicines to control attacks. Calming herbs may also help, such as chamomile, melissa, orange blossom or mint tea, lettuce and its extracts, valerian tablets and tinctures, all of which should be used only with the collaboration of an orthodox and an alternative health professional.

AROMATHERAPY
Soothing baths, compresses for the forehead, inhalations in steam or oil burners, and tension-relieving therapeutic massage using any of these aromatherapy essences – ylang-ylang, lavender, mandarin and petitgrain – are recommended.

HOMEOPATHY
To be taken every 60 seconds for up to 10 doses immediately after a person stops jerking and twitching: Aconite 30c for a fit brought on by fright or fever; Cuprum 6c for a violent seizure, when the face and lips turn blue, and the thumbs are clenched inside the fists; Ignatia 6c for a fit brought on by emotional trauma, when the face is pale, and when twitching starts in the face; and Belladonna 30c when a person is feverish, flushed, with eyes wide and staring and when symptoms are aggravated by jarring or jolting.

MANIPULATION THERAPIES
Osteopathy, including cranial osteopathy, may be used to correct structural imbalances, as may the Alexander technique. Remedial massage would undoubtedly be beneficial, especially of high tension areas including the scalp, neck and shoulders, and would incorporate appropriate aromatherapy essences.

EXERCISE AND RELAXATION
Yoga and simple relaxation are helpful, although meditation is sometimes not recommended for people in whom a trance-like state may induce further seizures. T'ai chi and dance therapy may be beneficial, as might art, colour and music therapy.

MEDICAL TREATMENT
Anticonvulsant drugs are the mainstay of epilepsy treatment, together with lifestyle modifications similar to those that promote relaxation. Diazepam (Valium) may also be prescribed where necessary to combat harmful tension and reduce the risks of seizures.

Orange blossom is often used by herbalists for its calming effect.

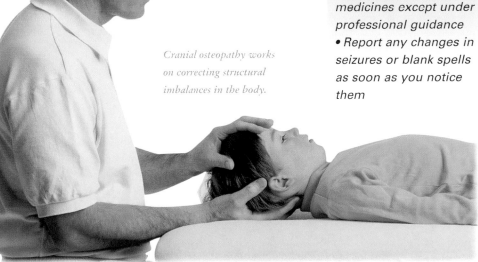

Cranial osteopathy works on correcting structural imbalances in the body.

PREVENTION

Avoid grand mal triggers such as flashing lights, loud music, fatigue, stress and hot, smoky rooms

CAUTION

• Petit mal attacks are easy to miss – consult a doctor about any blank moments in yourself or others
• Do not stop or reduce anticonvulsant medicines except under professional guidance
• Report any changes in seizures or blank spells as soon as you notice them

loss of consciousness & epilepsy

Probably the same illness as post-viral syndrome, ME may result from damage to the immune system by a viral infection which greatly increases its sensitivity to toxins, viruses and bacteria, stress and other irritants. Once thought to be 'all in the mind', acceptance of ME as a physical disorder has spread worldwide over the past 25 years, although much remains to be discovered.

ME: myalgic encephalomyelitis

SYMPTOMS

- Overwhelming physical and mental fatigue
- Muscle and joint pains
- Headaches
- Abdominal pains
- Poor memory and concentration
- Panic attacks, mood swings and depression

Including oily fish in your diet helps to boost your brain function.

THE CURES

NATUROPATHY

A wholefood diet would be recommended, high in raw foods, with a veto upon artificial additives (suspected of triggering symptoms in some ME patients). Exercise, stress factors and emotional well-being would also be assessed, with a view to maximising energy levels and boosting immunity. Hydrotherapy would be recommended, using appropriate oils (see below). Many factors affect, and are affected by, ME, and small, positive changes, such as identifying and avoiding food allergens, stress reduction, counselling and a positive attitude can produce remarkable improvement.

VITAMINS AND MINERALS

Recommendations include small, regular wholefood meals and snacks, with daily protein to boost stamina, oily fish (sardines, tuna and salmon, for example) to boost brain function, and plenty of fresh, organic fruit and vegetables and their juices for their antioxidant content. Foods rich in the amino acid tryptophan (e.g. turkey breast, dried dates, fish, bananas and peanuts), with a carbohydrate snack, boost levels of the mood-lifting chemical serotonin in the brain, improving sleep and allaying anxiety and panic. Alfalfa, added to salads or soups, is one of the richest known sources of antioxidants, iron and other minerals (and is prescribed by herbal practitioners to aid convalescence – see below). You can grow alfalfa at home by sprouting the seeds in a jam jar.

Specific dietary supplements include stress-beating vitamin B-complex, vitamin C with bioflavonoids, vitamin E, selenium and zinc, and the rest of the main antioxidants – beta-carotene, vitamin

D, calcium and magnesium (the last two of which are especially beneficial for frayed nerves and depression). B vitamins are extremely important in the treatment of ME, as they release the energy from food and pep up the metabolism. Iron and iodine (as kelp) would also be recommended. The chlorophyll-rich algae chlorella, taken as a health food and to aid detoxification, provides a wide range of antioxidant nutrients and enzymes.

HERBALISM
Astragalus is a potent immune stimulator, and also boosts endurance to exercise and general stress. Cat's claw, another powerful immune booster, also has antioxidant and anti-inflammatory properties. Korean ginseng aids recovery from illness, improves tolerance to stress, combats fatigue and boosts alertness. St John's wort counteracts mild to moderate depression and aids sleep.

AROMATHERAPY
Essence of bay or laurel can be inhaled or massaged into the chest or back in a little sweet almond oil to help overcome any viral infection present during or after the appearance of ME symptoms. Fatigue should be combated as part of a regimen planned by a naturopath or other practitioner – appropriate essences include ylang-ylang, petitgrain, neroli, lavender, melissa, clary sage, orange and mandarin.

BACH FLOWER REMEDIES
Take Rescue Remedy for the shock and dismay experienced at the start of an attack. Aspen deals with apprehension and other anxiety symptoms arising for no known reason. Gentian relieves despondency. Sweet Chestnut helps to lift total dejection.

HOMEOPATHY
The only remedy recommended for ME is China 30c, to be taken every 12 hours for up to three days while waiting for treatment from a homeopathic practitioner.

OTHER THERAPIES
ME affects the emotions and body, with mood swings, depression and personality changes. Art and music therapies, relaxation, meditation and psychotherapy have much to offer.

MEDICAL TREATMENT
Antidepressants help, lifting the mood, reducing anxiety, improving the quality of sleep and raising the pain threshold. Cognitive behavioural therapy (CBT) is also prescribed.

Gentian helps treat despondency and mild depression.

Regular, gentle exercise that does not tax the body too much is often recommended.

ME: myalgic encephalomyelitis

The symptoms of carpal tunnel syndrome are due to compression of the nerve which supplies motor activity and sensation to the thumb and first three fingers. This nerve is liable to nipping as it enters the hand at the wrist joint, passing through the carpal tunnel. Hormonal changes, inflammation or injury may be responsible.

carpal tunnel syndrome

SYMPTOMS

- Pins and needles, numbness in the thumb and first three digits
- Pains shooting up the arm from the wrist
- Symptoms worse at night
- Relieved by hanging the arm over the side of the bed

Carpal tunnel syndrome has been linked to a deficiency of vitamin B$_6$, which is found in avocados.

THE CURES

NATUROPATHY

Along with a wholefood diet and exercise, hydrotherapy may be recommended in the form of hand baths, for the effects of both the warm water itself, and the herbal and aromatherapeutic remedies it can bring to the area. Massage might also be suggested, of both the wrists and the upper back, shoulder girdle and upper and lower arms, to tone the muscles and stimulate the circulation.

VITAMINS AND MINERALS

Recommendations include small, regular wholefood meals and snacks, with plenty of fresh, organic fruit and vegetables and their juices for their antioxidant content (which combats the ageing process and the advent of arthritis). Foods rich in B-complex vitamins, such as wheatgerm, wholewheat products, offal, lecithin, salmon and dried beans, should be eaten daily, to prevent or correct the deficiency of pyridoxine (vitamin B$_6$) with which carpal tunnel syndrome has been linked. Specific sources of B$_6$ include avocados, carrots, hazelnuts, salmon, shellfish and wheatgerm.

Specific dietary supplements include pyridoxine vitamin B$_6$ (but do not exceed the recommended dose), general vitamin B-complex, vitamin C with bioflavonoids, vitamin E, selenium and zinc plus the rest of the chief antioxidants beta-carotene, vitamin D, calcium, magnesium.

HERBALISM

Vegetal (as opposed to mineral) silica – also called horsetail – is a

well-known diuretic, and can help dispel excess fluid that aggravates carpal tunnel symptoms. Preparations of the widely available Chinese herb schisandra stimulate the nervous system, increasing the speed of conduction of nerve reflexes and their responses. Nettle leaf preparations are used to treat arthritis (especially gout) and fluid retention.

AROMATHERAPY
Mix 3 drops of pure essence of pepper with 2 tsp (10 ml) sweet almond oil (at room temperature or slightly warmer), and smoothe the mixture into the skin over the affected wrist.

HOMEOPATHY
Take 4 times daily for up to 2 weeks: Natrum mur. 6c for a person who craves salt; Magnesia phos. 4c for pain relieved by warmth and rubbing; and Aconite 30c for pain severe enough to wake the person at night.

OTHER THERAPIES
Acupuncture is often successful in treating chronic neuralgia (nerve pain), whatever the body area. A recommended acupressure point is Big Mound (P7) found in the middle of the inside of the wrist crease.

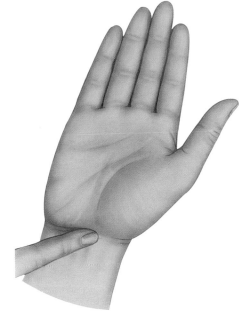

A good place to apply acupressure is the Big Mound, in the middle of the inside of the wrist crease.

MEDICAL TREATMENT
Surgery may be advised, whereby a cut is made in the tough, fibrous roof of the carpal tunnel on the inner aspect of the wrist, releasing the pressure upon the median nerve and other structures that pass through here into the hand. If surgery is not suitable, diuretic (water-relieving) pills and pain killers may be prescribed.

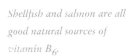

Shellfish and salmon are all good natural sources of vitamin B$_6$.

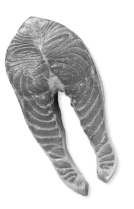

Horsetail has a high content of silica. It was used by Galen, a physician of Ancient Greece, to heal sinews.

carpal tunnel syndrome

Shingles comprises a rash and pain along the route of a nerve as it leaves the brain or spinal cord on its way to the body area it serves. It is caused by infection of the sensory nerve root by the herpes zoster or chickenpox virus. This can lie dormant for decades before breaking out as shingles – often when the immune system is already overtaxed by stress, cancer or by another infectious illness.

shingles

SYMPTOMS

- Feverish for a few days before rash starts
- Pain around the side of the face and eye, the waist, chest or buttocks and genitals
- Small, red spots turn into itchy blisters
- Pain may last for weeks after the rash has disappeared

Propolis, collected by bees, can be used as a treatment for shingles.

THE CURES

NATUROPATHY
Besides a wholefood diet, rest and freedom from unnecessary stress would be recommended, and possibly cool showers and compresses to soothe the prickling discomfort and pain of the rash. Gentle exercise would be reintroduced as an aid to immune system recovery, when the patient is well enough.

VITAMINS AND MINERALS
Small, regular wholefood meals and snacks, with plenty of fresh, organic fruit and vegetables and their juices for their antioxidant, immune-boosting content, will be recommended. Although the person's appetite may be poor, freshly squeezed fruit and vegetable juices offer most of the required antioxidants in a digestible form. A juice combination recommended for shingles sufferers consists of 2 cups of carrot juice to 1 cup of celery, mixed with 1 tbsp (15 ml) parsley juice. Drink three cups of this daily.

Specific dietary supplements include stress-fighting vitamin B-complex, vitamin C with bioflavonoids, vitamin E and selenium, zinc, plus beta-carotene, vitamin D, calcium and magnesium.

HERBALISM
An old country remedy prescribes a compress made by heating a handful each of poppy flowers and their seed capsules, meadowsweet and lime flowers in 3½ pt (2 litres) of water, then allowing to stand until cool. A herbal infusion of chervil, rose, lime flowers or rosemary applied cool to the rash brings relief. In a trial carried out in Yugoslavia in 1978, a 5 per cent solution of propolis tincture was applied daily to a shingles rash in 21 patients. It relieved the pain within 48 hours, and itching persisted in only 3 of the patients.

AROMATHERAPY
Make an oily preparation to be applied three times daily to the rash: 1 tbsp (15 ml) of soya oil, 2 drops of wheatgerm oil (rich in vitamin E, which aids skin healing), and 2 drops each of rosemary, lavender, oregano and/or coriander. If you don't have the last two, just add three drops of the first two – or 6 drops of just one of these – to the carrier oil.

HOMEOPATHY
Take every 2 hours for up to 10 doses: Rhus tox. 6c for red, blistered, itchy skin, especially if affecting the scalp, and if the person is young and finds movement improves symptoms; Arsenicum 6c for burning pain that is worse between midnight and 2am, with a few blisters that increase in number and merge, when the person is restless, exhausted and chilly, and heat relieves symptoms; Mezereum 6c for severe pain, burning, itching skin, brown scabs and when the person is middle-aged or elderly; Ranunculus 6c for nerve pain and itching, when eating and the slightest touch irritate symptoms; and Lachesis 6c when the left side of the body is affected, aggravated by warmth and relieved by cold.

OTHER THERAPIES
Acupuncture may help by boosting immunity; it can also relieve post-herpetic pain that persists after the rash has disappeared. Relaxation, meditation and yoga may improve the lifestyle of, and speed recovery in, tense, anxious, workaholic individuals who claim to have little time to rest.

MEDICAL TREATMENT
Bed-rest, together with some mild pain killers, perhaps calamine lotion to soothe the rash, and the specific antiviral agent acyclovir (Zovirax), a virtually nontoxic medication that should be taken orally for 5–7 days after the rash appears.

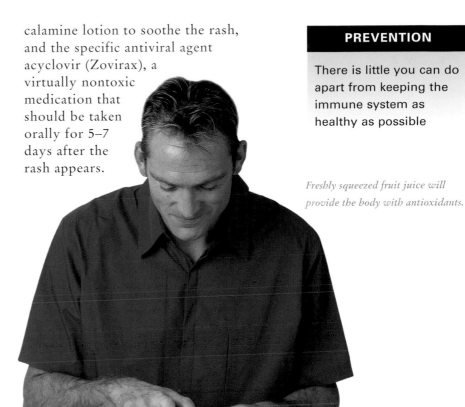

Freshly squeezed fruit juice will provide the body with antioxidants.

Poppy flowers, their seed capsules and meadowsweet can make a soothing compress after being infused with lime flowers.

PREVENTION
There is little you can do apart from keeping the immune system as healthy as possible

CAUTION
• Do not panic if a rash breaking out on both sides of the spine threatens to meet round the front (there is no truth to the old wives' tale that this could prove fatal)
• Shingles is not infectious – there is no need to stay away from babies, the elderly or other susceptible people
• Do not ignore shingles – it is not dangerous unless it affects the ophthalmic nerve supplying the front of the eye, but you need to rest and recover

shingles

Sciatica, another form of neuralgia (nerve pain) caused by compression, affects the sciatic nerve, the largest nerve in the body supplying the whole of the lower body. The sciatic nerve can be damaged or pressed upon by a prolapsed disc or bony outgrowths from arthritic or injured vertebrae. Symptoms arise in the muscles and skin areas of the thigh, leg and foot supplied by the affected fibres.

compressed nerve: sciatica

SYMPTOMS

- Nagging pain anywhere between the buttock and foot
- Pain aggravated by bending, sneezing or coughing
- Standing may be preferable to sitting
- Pins and needles, numbness
- Sometimes, muscular weakness
- Lower back pain often present

Acupressure can provide relief for nerve pain.

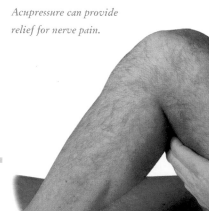

THE CURES

NATUROPATHY

As well as a wholefood diet, gentle exercises may be recommended, together with hydrotherapy in the form of hot showers, a hot-water bottle, and compresses for the lower back. Gentle massage of the lower back and limbs might also be used to tone the muscles, stimulate the circulation and increase the absorption of natural remedies.

VITAMINS AND MINERALS

Recommendations include small, regular wholefood meals and snacks, with plenty of fresh, organic fruit and vegetables and their juices for their antioxidant content (which combat the ageing process and the advent of arthritis).

The high-fibre content of these foods also helps to prevent constipation. Foods rich in B-complex vitamins, such as wheatgerm, wholewheat products, offal, lecithin, salmon and dried beans, should be consumed daily, to prevent or correct the deficiency of pyridoxine (vitamin B_6) with which compressed nerves have been linked. Specific sources of B_6 include avocados, carrots, hazelnuts, salmon, shellfish and wheatgerm. Low levels of thiamine (vitamin B_1) have also been linked to nerve damage and malfunction; sources include beef offal, rye and wholewheat flour, sunflower seeds, pork and salmon.

Specific dietary supplements will include vitamin B-complex, vitamin C with bioflavonoids, vitamin E, selenium and zinc, plus the rest of the main antioxidants (beta-carotene, vitamin D, calcium and magnesium).

HERBALISM

Preparations of scutellariae, turmeric, devil's claw and nettle leaf (among many others) have anti-inflammatory and pain-relieving actions which may be of benefit, as may vegetal silica and schisandra (see Carpal Tunnel Syndrome, page 110). Chamomile tea and American ginseng both produce a calming, relaxing and soothing effect which can benefit anyone confined to bed with sciatica, since muscular tension – a natural consequence of pain – aggravates the problem.

AROMATHERAPY

Add 2 drops of essence of pepper, mustard or juniper to 2 tsp (10 ml) of plain soya oil, warm slightly and massage gently into the lower vertebrae, buttock and lower limb wherever symptoms are experienced. This is most effective after a warm, relaxing bath or shower. You can also add a few drops to an oil burner, and inhale these remedies.

HOMEOPATHY

Specific remedies are to be taken hourly for up to 10 doses, or every 30 minutes if the pain is severe: Colocynth 6c for pain down the right leg, causing occasional numbness and weakness, when the pain is worse in cold, damp surroundings; Ammonium mur. 6c for pain aggravated by sitting but relieved by walking, lying down or sleeping, with difficulty straightening affected leg(s); and Rhus tox. 6c for searing pain relieved by movement and heat but worsened by rest, and the cold and damp.

A traditional remedy is to take a bath to which nettle leaves have been added.

ACUPRESSURE

The Commanding Middle (B54) position, in the centre of the back of the knee crease, is recommended. The suggestion is to lie on your back on a carpeted floor, raise your knees and place your fingertips in the centre of the crease behind your knees. Curve your fingers and use your arm muscles to rock back and forth for a minute, breathing deeply, then place feet flat on the floor and relax.

Right: The correct way to pick up a load is by bending the knees and keeping a straight back.

Left: Picking up a load incorrectly could seriously damage your back.

OTHER THERAPIES

Acupuncture is frequently used to relieve sciatica and lower back pain, as are osteopathy and chiropractic. Regular, gentle exercise should be taken. Dance therapy, yoga and t'ai chi are all likely to be suitable and helpful.

MEDICAL TREATMENT

This depends on the cause of pain, but treatments include physiotherapy, pain killers, anti-inflammatory and muscle-relaxant drugs.

PREVENTION

Seek medical attention for all lower back injuries
Attend physiotherapy if prescribed
Counteract a sedentary lifestyle with appropriate exercise
Learn how to pick up and carry heavy objects safely

CAUTION

• *Do not ignore persistent sciatic pain – more serious causes must be ruled out by your doctor*
• *Follow medical advice – for example, rest flat for however long prescribed, then ease gently back into action*

compressed nerve: sciatica

Stiff, painful joints, back pain and bruised or torn muscles are just some of the problems we can encounter with our bones, tendons and muscles. Strains and sprains occur as we put our bodies through the rigours of daily life and exercise routines. A healthy diet including plenty of protein for the muscles and calcium for the bones can help recovery, and relaxing massages with aromatherapy oils can soothe some of the aches and pains.

bones, tendons and muscles

Most joint pain results from arthritis (joint inflammation), the three main types of which are: rheumatoid arthritis (RA), osteoarthritis (OA) and gout. Arthritis also occurs in various diseases such as Psoriasis (see page 144), rheumatic fever and Sjogren's syndrome (a type of bladder outlet inflammation in men). All arthritis causes pain and stiffness, both of which respond well to alternative treatments.

stiff, painful joints

SYMPTOMS

- Stiff, swollen joint(s)
- Osteoarthritis is mainly in weight-bearing joints at the hips, knees and ankles
- Rheumatoid arthritis often affects smaller joints, e.g. knuckles, wrists, elbows, also knees and shoulders.
- Gout often results in a single inflamed joint and is agonisingly painful

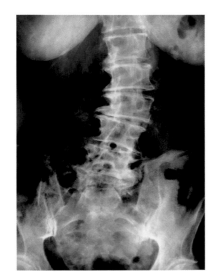

Osteoarthritis is characterised by swollen, painful weight-bearing joints, such as the hips.

THE CURES

NATUROPATHY

A wholefood diet, rest and freedom from stress would be recommended, especially in the case of RA sufferers. Weight reduction can be a priority, as excess weight aggravates joint disorders. Appropriate exercise, especially swimming in a heated pool, is often recommended, to mobilise and support the affected joints. Hydrotherapy (warm showers, compresses and baths) would be used, together with herbal and aromatherapeutic remedies (see below). Applied kinesiology may be used to identify food allergens, and manipulation also prescribed.

VITAMINS AND MINERALS

A vegetarian diet is recommended, with raw foods only for one day a week. Prohibited items usually include salt, sugar, white flour products, cows' milk and its products (use goat-derived substitutes), and red meat, tomatoes, citrus fruit, strawberries and alcohol (the last five being especially applicable to gout sufferers). Protein sources for non-vegetarians include a lightly cooked egg twice weekly, and up to 3 oz (75 g) of fish or poultry on alternate days. Two recommended juice recipes to help relieve acute symptoms include: 1–1¾ pt (500–1000 ml) freshly squeezed celery juice daily; alternatively, 5 fl oz (150 ml) each of carrot, beetroot and cucumber, twice daily.

Specific supplements include antioxidants to boost immunity and reduce inflammation; with extra vitamin B-complex to combat stress.

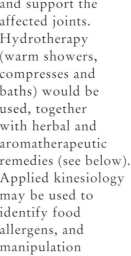

Evening primrose oil and marine fish oil capsules (or cod liver oil) should be taken daily. Extracts of green-lipped mussel also reduce inflammatory arthritis symptoms.

HERBALISM

Garlic, honey, cider vinegar and pollen extracts have all proved beneficial to arthritis sufferers. Preparations of devil's claw counteract inflammation and facilitate the removal of uric acid from the body, thereby being a suitable remedy for gout. Chamomile, in tea or tablet form, has mild pain-relieving properties and relaxes muscular spasm, a common source of pain around arthritic joints. Capsaicin, an active ingredient in cayenne pepper, relieves pain and stiffness when applied (e.g. as a cream) to the exterior of an affected joint.

AROMATHERAPY

A few drops of essence of juniper applied to a painful joint in a warm compress, or added to bathwater, relieves pain and may be effective in cases of gout. Add 2–3 drops of cyprus or pine essence to a bath or massage oil, and apply to affected parts. Inhale any of these essences in steam or from oil in a burner.

HOMEOPATHY

For osteoarthritis, take remedies 4 times daily for up to 2 weeks: Bryonia 30c for severe joint pain aggravated by movement and heat and relieved by cold compresses or cooling showers; Arnica 30c for joint pains resulting from, or worsened by, injury; and Aconite 30c for a severe flare-up in cold, dry weather. For rheumatoid arthritis, take remedies every 2 hours for up to 3 days: Berberis 6c when the knees are stiff and sore, as if from a beating, and any of the remedies mentioned for

OA. For gout, take the following every 15 minutes for up to 10 doses: Arnica 30c when joint(s) feel bruised and painful; Pulsatilla 6c for pains that flit from joint to joint; and Colchicum 6c for excruciatingly painful joints, especially at night or when trying to move, and when the person is depressed, weak, irritable and nauseous.

Raw foods (fresh fruit and vegetables, and juices) might help ease the condition.

OTHER THERAPIES

Any gentle exercises such as yoga, t'ai chi and dance therapy might prove beneficial, especially in the early stages and between acute attacks (when any unnecessary movement should be avoided). Acupuncture is used to great effect in many cases of chronic pain, including all common types of arthritis. Set, deformed joints usually cannot be manipulated, so it is best to start early on with regular massage, chiropractic or osteopathy to keep joints working.

MEDICAL TREATMENT

This consists mainly of painkillers, anti-inflammatory drugs, and steroids by mouth and as injections as required. Surgery is avoided, but replacement hips and other joints can make life more tolerable for those with severe arthritis.

PREVENTION

Maintain healthy immunity – RA is a disorder of the immune system
OA – avoid overuse of weight-bearing joints, e.g. excessive jogging on hard surfaces
Equally, avoid underuse with sedentary lifestyle
Gout – avoid alcohol and other trigger foods

CAUTION

• Seek medical advice for all persistent joint pain
• Seek medical treatment for injured joints – sprains and minor fractures can lead to arthritis later in life
• Rest is vital during an RA flare-up, to strengthen immunity and minimise joint damage

stiff, painful joints

Lumbago (lower back pain) results from lifting or overstrenuous exercise. Strained or torn muscles hurt, then go into spasm, causing further pain. The ligaments that bind the vertebrae together can also become strained or torn, producing severe pain in the spinal joints and muscles. Other causes of lumbago include a slipped disc and arthritis.

backache: lower back pain

SYMPTOMS

- Pain in the small of the back
- Pain may come on suddenly, or overnight
- May be severe and interfere with mobility
- Chronic (longstanding) lumbago is worse in cold or damp weather.

A massage using warm oil made from juniper essence and almond oil will help release muscle tension.

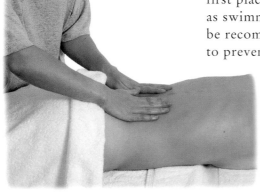

THE CURES

NATUROPATHY

Besides a wholefood diet, rest is a priority for acute lower back pain that starts after lifting or undue exercise, either lying on the floor for maximum support to the lower spine, or in bed with a chopping board or similar placed under the mattress beneath the affected area. Weight reduction where necessary would be recommended as a matter of course, especially since being seriously overweight increases the risks of accident-related back injury in the first place. Appropriate exercise, such as swimming in a heated pool, would be recommended as soon as possible, to prevent further stiffening of the spine and muscle weakness developing from underuse. Further hydrotherapy in the form of warm showers, baths and compresses would be advised, together with appropriate herbal and aromatherapeutic remedies (see below). Manipulation and exercise routines would also be suggested as an integral part of the naturopathic treatment.

VITAMINS AND MINERALS

For chronic lumbago, a wholefood diet with low-fat protein and dairy foods to suit the person's individual tastes would be advised. Although raw food and juice fasts are a healthy approach to dealing with arthritic pain, there is scant evidence that they would benefit either acute or long-standing lumbago caused by physical trauma.

Specific dietary supplements include all the antioxidants to counteract inflammation. Daily supplements of evening primrose oil and marine fish oil capsules (or just plain old cod liver oil) are also recommended to be taken.

HERBALISM

Make a warm compress using a dilute tincture made from angelica, and apply this to the lower back area. Take preparations of devil's claw or willow (containing salicylates, the natural source of aspirin), or sip chamomile or thyme tea for their muscle-relaxing actions.

AROMATHERAPY

Make a poultice with 1 tbsp (15 ml) linseed oil with 5 drops of angelica, juniper, pine or thyme essence, warm gently and leave in place for about 20 minutes – repeat daily as required. Then gently massage the lower back region after placing a warm poultice made with 6 drops of one of these oils added to about 2 tsp (10 ml) of almond oil.

HOMEOPATHY

Take every hour for up to 10 doses for acute lumbar pain that starts suddenly: Aconite 30c for sharp pain aggravated by exposure to draughts and cold dry weather; and Arnica 30c for severe pain following an injury. Specific remedies to be taken 4 times daily for up to 10 days: Rhus tox. 6c for when the lower back feels stiff and bruised, especially after resting and in damp cold weather, and which is relieved by moving around; Aesculus 6c for lower back pain aggravated by walking and stopping; and Sulphur 6c for a violent stabbing pain on stooping, worsened by movement and by the heat of the bed at night.

OTHER THERAPIES

Any activity that involves gentle flexing of the lower spine, such as yoga or t'ai chi, is recommended. Osteopathic or chiropractic manipulation can both prove most useful in this type of spinal problem. Acupuncture may combat the pain of acute or chronic lumbago.

MEDICAL TREATMENT

Painkillers, physiotherapy and non-steroidal anti-inflammatory drugs (NSAIDs) are the recommended treatments.

Swimming in a heated swimming pool will help to keep the spine as loose as possible and prevent back muscles from weakening.

With careful guidance from a qualified instructor, gentle yoga exercises can help soothe lower back pain.

PREVENTION

Learn how to lift items correctly
Do not try to shift heavy furniture unaided
Always exercise safely and under guidance unless you are very experienced
Seek expert help for troublesome symptoms early on, to avoid back pain becoming chronic

CAUTION

• *Pain extending into the buttock and/or down the leg suggests a prolapsed disc – lie on a blanket on the floor and call for medical assistance*

backache: lower back pain

Pain in the upper back is often due to arthritic changes (spondylosis) in the neck and thoracic (chest) vertebrae (spinal bones). The spaces within the joints become narrowed, and small splinters of bone (spicules) develop around the edges of the joints, causing pain and limiting movement. They can also press on the spinal nerves as they emerge from between the vertebrae, triggering pain in nearby muscles.

backache: upper back pain

SYMPTOMS

- The upper back vertebrae are tender to pressure – usually more down one side than the other
- Pain and stiffness upon twisting, turning, stretching or bending the upper spine
- Pain extends up into neck and down towards the lumbar region (lower back)
- The shoulder and lower neck muscles can go into spasm

THE CURES

NATUROPATHY

Along with a wholefood diet, regular stretching and bending exercises would be recommended, possibly under the supervision of an alternative therapist or physiotherapist at first, and later, following improvement, through yoga or other slow movement exercises. Weight reduction where necessary is always applicable to spinal problems, including those in the upper back. Swimming in a heated pool would be appropriate hydrotherapy, to mobilise and support joints and minimise stiffness. Warm showers, baths, compresses and poultices would be prescribed, together with herbal and aromatherapy remedies (see below). Referral would be made for manipulative therapy such as osteopathy or chiropractic, and for acupuncture.

VITAMINS AND MINERALS

A wholefood diet would be recommended, possibly with raw foods only (fresh fruit and vegetables and their juices) for one day a week if there is acute inflammation of the vertebrae. Red meat might be banned initially as for arthritis (see page 118), and the same juice recipes recommended.

Specific dietary supplements include all the antioxidants to reduce inflammation; with extra vitamin

Extracts of green-lipped mussels can help reduce painful inflammation.

B complex to combat physical and emotional stress. Evening primrose oil and marine fish oil capsules (or cod liver oil) should be taken daily. Extracts of green-lipped mussel might also prove useful. Alfalfa, which is extremely rich in antioxidant nutrients, can be added to salads and soups.

HERBALISM

Garlic, cider vinegar, honey and pollen, chamomile and capsaicin are recommended, as for arthritis. Alfalfa herbal tablets, green tea and turmeric extracts all supply antioxidants, and turmeric remedy tablets have similar pain-relieving and anti-inflammatory qualities as orthodox arthritis treatment, without side-effects.

AROMATHERAPY

Add 3-4 drops of aspic (old English lavender) oil, or ordinary lavender oil, to a warm bath and soak your upper back thoroughly. After drying, add 5 drops of either oil to 2 tsp (10 ml) warm soya oil and either massage it gently down the sore, tender sides of the upper vertebrae or, preferably, lie face downwards with a pillow under your stomach to support your back, and get someone to do this for you.

HOMEOPATHIC REMEDIES

These are the same as for osteoarthritis (see page 119). Specific remedies for spondylitis, to be taken 4 times daily for up to 14 days, include: Agaricus 6c for tenderness at the back of the neck and over the backward-pointing spines of the upper back vertebrae, when the chest feels tight, and the person is weak and shaky; Picric ac. 6c for shooting pains up the spine and into the neck and head, and when the spine feels on fire; and Argentum nit. 6c for a tender upper spine, with a headache behind the forehead, when the limbs feel numb and the person has wind.

OTHER THERAPIES

Any regular activity that involves gentle bending and flexing of the upper spine, such as yoga and t'ai chi, is suitable. Osteopathic or chiropractic manipulation can both prove most useful in this type of spinal problem. Acupuncture can be used to combat the inflammatory process as it attacks the vertebrae in the upper spine, and the additional swelling and pain that spondylitis can cause in nerves and adjacent muscles.

MEDICAL TREATMENT

Painkillers, physiotherapy and non-steroidal anti-inflammatory drugs will be recommended; steroids are rarely necessary unless the upper back pain is a symptom of rheumatoid arthritis.

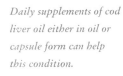

Daily supplements of cod liver oil either in oil or capsule form can help this condition.

backache: upper back pain

Fibrositis describes an inflammation of the small, tough, muscular nodules between the shoulder blades. When these muscles become stressed and tense, small buds of tissue protrude through weak spots in the muscles' membranous capsule, becoming pinched and short of blood. The nodules cause pain locally, and can also press on nerves, sending a toothache-like pain (neuralgia) down the arm.

fibrositis

SYMPTOMS

- Toothache-type pain between the upper spine and one or both shoulder blades
- The seat of pain is a 'nodule' detectable by fingertip exploration of the area
- Pain worse on hot, windy days and after exercise
- Pain can travel down the arm to the elbow

Fibrositis can be experienced as an acute pain between the upper spine and the shoulder blades.

THE CURES

NATUROPATHY

Besides recommending a wholefood diet, a naturopath would examine any exercise regimen being followed, to discover muscle overuse, and would try and find out any sources of tension causing hunching and spasm of the shoulder girdle. (Fibrositis can be a symptom of hunching over a computer in an office, for example.) Exercise, such as swimming in a heated pool, aims at relaxing spasm in the affected muscles. Further hydrotherapy in the form of warm showers, baths and compresses would be used, together with appropriate herbal and aromatherapeutic remedies (see below). Manipulation and further exercise regimens might be suggested if spinal misalignment was thought to be a contributory factor.

VITAMINS AND MINERALS

A wholefood diet would be recommended similar to that advised for arthritis sufferers (see page 118). Raw foods and juice fasts help deal with rheumatic pain, and a useful juice for fibrositis consists of 12½ fl oz (350 ml) carrot juice mixed with 4 fl oz (110 ml) spinach juice and sipped twice daily.

A specific supplement regimen recommended for fibrositis (in addition to the basic multi-vitamin/mineral supplement) comprises calcium pantothenate (a B-complex vitamin): 500 mg daily for 2 days; 1000 mg daily for 3 days; 1500 mg for 4 days; and 2000 mg daily thereafter for 2 months or until relief is obtained. The daily intake thereafter should then be the minimum required to maintain relief.

HERBALISM

Old country remedies include sleeping on fern or a mattress containing it; a poultice of hot cabbage; and a compress using

Acupuncture may be of help to people who are suffering from chronic pain.

PREVENTION

Avoid straining shoulder muscles, e.g. by lifting heavy weights

Maintain shoulder muscle health by gentle upper torso exercises daily

Avoid cramping and spasms in shoulder muscles by stress-relieving measures

Cover up after exercising and avoid perspiration cooling on uncovered upper back

Raw food and juice fasts made up of carrot and spinach juices help with fibrositis pain.

1¾ pt (1 litre) of water in which you have soaked a chopped onion and 1 handful each of lavender, broom flowers, heather and chamomile, and left them to steep until cool.

AROMATHERAPY

Make a massage oil using 2 tsp (10 ml) soya oil plus 3 drops each of lavender and oregano or marjoram essence. Alternatively, try adding 3–4 drops of lavender, marjoram, oregano or chamomile essence to a warm bath or foot bath; or inhale from an incense burner.

HOMEOPATHY

Remedies to be taken every 3 hours for up to 2 days: Aconite 30c for sudden onset of pain in cold, dry weather, aggravated by movement, and when the person is restless and apprehensive; Bryonia 30c for pain in the neck and down the arm(s), aggravated by movement and by cold, dry, easterly winds, but which is

soothed by pressure; and Chamomilla 6c for pain and stiffness, having to get up in the night because of the pain, and when the person feels bad-tempered. In clinical trials, the homeopathic remedy Rhus tox. has been demonstrated to be as effective as NSAIDs in relieving fibrositis pain.

OTHER THERAPIES

Positional therapies such as the Alexander Technique teach healthy deportment, which is aimed at relieving tense shoulder and neck muscles, and how to sit correctly. Simple exercises would also be useful, such as dance therapy, t'ai chi and yoga. Acupuncture can also be used to provide pain relief.

MEDICAL TREATMENT

Anti-inflammatory drugs, simple painkillers and physiotherapy, including infra-red heat and warmth, are standard medical treatments.

CAUTION

• *Seek medical advice for persistent pain in the upper back and shoulders*

• *Fibrositis is sometimes diagnosed by default – it can be relieved with medical and natural treatment*

fibrositis

Everyone loses minerals from their skeletons from around the age of 30 – a loss exacerbated by the fall in oestrogen that affects women at the end of their reproductive years. As many as 3–5 percent of women and around 1 percent of men go on to develop osteoporosis (brittle bones), the biggest cause of serious fractures in elderly people.

brittle bones (osteoporosis)

SYMPTOMS

- Bones fracture following minor injuries
- Fractured neck of the femur at the hip joint is typical
- Loss of height due to crush fractures of spinal vertebrae
- A humped back develops (known as 'widow's' or 'dowager's hump')

Bean sprouts contain plenty of phyto-oestrogens, which help to strengthen bones.

THE CURES

NATUROPATHY
Naturopathic practitioners recommend a wholefood diet and regular, appropriate aerobic exercise for its many health benefits (including excess weight loss). Yoga, relaxation and meditation, and simple stretching exercises as performed in t'ai chi, are also beneficial. Weight-bearing exercises such as walking, gentle jogging, dancing and skipping are specifically recommended to help maintain the mineral density of the skeleton (and reduce the risk of developing brittle bones).

VITAMINS AND MINERALS
A wholefood diet is recommended, with the elimination of all sugar, tea, coffee and cola drinks, and the reduction of alcohol intake to no more than 2 units daily.

Phyto-oestrogens (plant-generated hormones), found in soya products, sprouted seeds and grains, may also be beneficial.

Specific dietary supplements include all the antioxidants to boost the immune system and combat the effects of ageing, both generally and within the bones and joints. Extra calcium, magnesium, phosphorus and copper is recommended to maintain bone strength. A phyto-oestrogen supplement may be advised.

HOMEOPATHY
A specific remedy that should be taken twice daily for up to 3 weeks is Symphytum 6c. This is particularly used for any fracture that is proving slow to heal.

BACH FLOWER REMEDIES
Rescue Remedy would be invaluable for relieving the pain and shock linked to a fracture.

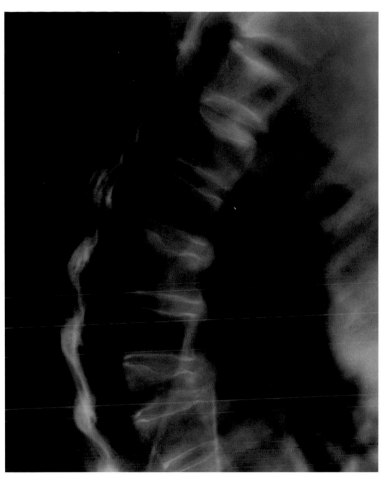

A bone density scan will reveal any serious mineral deficiencies in the skeletal structure.

Below: Doctors prescribe drugs containing calcium and phosphorus to help remineralise weak bones.

PREVENTION

Take hormone replacement therapy (HRT) from the time of the menopause onwards
Maintain bone strength as a young adult through regular weight-bearing exercise
Take vitamin/mineral supplements including calcium and magnesium daily
Have a bone density scan to see whether you are at risk

CAUTION

HRT slightly increases the risk of breast cancer, but more people die from a fractured neck of the femur than of breast cancer

OTHER THERAPIES

Herbal and aromatherapy remedies are essentially the same as for the menopause (see page 84). Dance therapy is an excellent weight-bearing exercise for strengthening bones, and so many forms exist that most people of all ages can find one that appeals to them. Not generally considered for its therapeutic value, ballroom dancing in fact keeps many older people of both sexes trim and nimble (and fracture-free) until well into their nineties.

Yoga and t'ai chi are both invaluable aids to healthy bones – both involve slow, measured movements that stretch and strengthen muscles, thereby enhancing the skeleton's tensile strength. They also balance and calm the mind and the emotions.

MEDICAL TREATMENT

Hormone replacement therapy (HRT) is prescribed to help prevent and treat osteoporosis. The established disease can also be treated with drugs that help to remineralise low density bone with calcium and phosphorus salts.

Bruising is a major symptom of skeletal and soft tissue injury. It is caused by the release of blood into the area surrounding the site of the injury, and the colour changes occur as the blood is broken down and removed by the immune defence system. Torn muscles often result from sporting and other forceful accidents and, like fractures, can also cause bruising.

bruising & torn muscles

SYMPTOMS

Bruising
• Reddened area reflecting impact
• Turns dark blue, greenish-blue, then yellow within days or weeks

Torn muscle
• Acute pain in muscle
• Local swelling
• Bruising, depending on extent of tear
• Restricted use of the muscle until healing is complete

Cream made from arnica is a well-tried remedy for healing bruises or sprains.

THE CURES

NATUROPATHY
Naturopathic practitioners recommend a wholefood diet, and regular aerobic exercise. Yoga, relaxation and meditation, and simple stretch exercises as performed in t'ai chi are also beneficial. Weight-bearing exercises such as walking, gentle jogging, dancing and skipping, are also specifically recommended to help maintain fit and healthy muscles, which are less prone to injury. They will also heal more quickly if there is an injury.

VITAMINS AND MINERALS
A wholefood diet is recommended, with the elimination of all sugar, tea, coffee and cola drinks, and the reduction of alcohol intake to no more than 2 units daily. Phyto-oestrogens (plant-generated hormones) available in soya products, sprouted seeds and grains may also be beneficial for healthy muscles. Eat vitamin C-rich foods to strengthen blood vessels damaged in bruising.

Specific dietary supplements include all the antioxidants – especially vitamin C – to boost the immune system and combat the effects of ageing, both generally and within the muscular system of the body Take extra calcium, magnesium, phosphorus and copper to maintain bone strength, and a phyto-oestrogen supplement.

HERBALISM
Arnica and comfrey creams and ointments help bruises to heal, but should not be used on broken skin. Always keep a clearly labelled ice tray of distilled witch hazel in the freezer and apply a cube directly to

Tackling in aggressive contact sports can lead to muscle injuries or bruising.

a bruise site briefly, or wrap in a cloth and hold in place so that the witch hazel trickles through onto it as the cube melts. A handful of crushed daisies can be held against a bruise in an emergency to reduce pain and swelling, or made into a compress or a poultice. Wintergreen ointment brings relief to torn muscles.

AROMATHERAPY
Five drops of cypress, mint or lavender essential oil mixed with 2 tsp (10 ml) soya oil is good for smoothing gently into bruised areas. They can also be added to bathwater or inhaled from an incense burner. To make a massage oil for sore, torn muscles, add 4–5 drops of rosemary, pine, fennel or thyme (or a couple of drops of any two of these) to 1 tbsp (15 ml) soya oil.

HOMEOPATHY
For bruising, take remedies 4 times a day for up to 3 days: Arnica 30c when bruising is due to injury;

Hamamelis 6c for bruising with broken skin; Bellis 6c for bruises on the breasts. For pulled muscles, take Arnica 30c straight after the injury, hourly for up to 6 doses, then 4 times daily for up to 3 days. If pain persists after a course of Arnica, then take Rhus tox. 6c. 4 times daily for up to 7 days.

OTHER THERAPIES
You can try any of the movement and exercise therapies for pulled muscles when healing is well established. Massage therapy, possibly using the aromatherapy oils mentioned above, might be used in the early stages of healing. Acupuncture is a good standby for promoting healing and reducing the pain of injury.

MEDICAL TREATMENT
Bruising does not generally require medical treatment. Torn muscles may need rest and physiotherapy to heal. Your doctor may also give you advice on strapping the limb in question.

Distilled witch hazel brings relief to the bruised area and helps reduce swelling.

bruising & torn muscles

A sprain occurs when a powerful force is exerted upon a joint from a certain angle. The lateral ligament supporting the outer aspect of the ankle joint may be partly torn (simple sprain); or completely ruptured (severe sprain). Back, torso and limb tendons (and ligaments) are prone to strain, a lesser injury often resulting from inappropriate exercise.

sprains & strains

sprains & strains

SYMPTOMS

Simple sprain
- Joint swells and becomes painful
- Slight bruising

Severe sprain
- Severe pain/swelling
- Intense bruising
- X-ray shows fragment of bone torn from joint

Strain
- Feels bruised and painful to the touch
- Movement hampered until healed

Comfrey has similar qualities to arnica. Both can be used to relieve inflammation and bruising.

THE CURES

NATUROPATHY

Besides a wholefood diet, rest would be recommended for a severe sprain, and some rest together with gently graded exercise prescribed for a simple sprain or strain. Hot and/or cold hydrotherapy (plus swimming where appropriate) would be recommended to deliver other remedies to the painful sites. Weight reduction where necessary would be recommended as a matter of course – serious overweight increases the risks of accident-related injuries in the first place. Manipulation and further exercise regimens may be appropriate if stiffness persists. Acupuncture would be used for persistent pain and also to promote quicker healing.

NUTRITIONAL MEDICINE

A wholefood diet to suit the person's taste, including first-class protein in the form of red meat, chicken, grain and legume combinations to supply the nutrients required in the healing process.

SPECIFIC DIETARY SUPPLEMENTS

All the antioxidants to counteract inflammation. Evening primrose oil and marine fish oil capsules (or just old fashioned cod liver oil daily, now available in 'tasteless' form) because of their overall benefit to joints; and possibly glucosamine and MGM supplements to strengthen and heal damaged tissue.

HERBAL MEDICINE

For both sprains and strains: arnica applied as cream to affected part; or in solution, applied in a compress. Comfrey cream or ointment also reduces swelling and pain, and promotes healing. Thyme tea is an anti-spasmodic and also encourages blood flow to injured area, promoting tissue repair. You can make a warm poultice or compress out of the tea, and apply to area for 20 minutes at a time. A handful of crushed daisies also relieves painful strains and sprains (see page 129).

AROMATHERAPY

For both sprains and strains: a cold compress using essence of cajuput, niaouli or rosemary. Alternatively, add 4–5 drops to bathwater or a basin of water, and bathe the affected area. Chamomile essence reduces painful spasm around injured part, and helps to reduce the pain.

BACH FLOWER REMEDIES

Rescue Remedy straight after accident, to reduce pain and shock; alternatively, Star of Bethlehem (a component of Rescue Remedy) can be used alone.

Increasing the amount of protein-rich foods in the diet helps promote healing for a sprain.

HOMEOPATHIC REMEDIES

Use 12-hourly for up to 1 week, and especially effective for recurrent sprained ankle – Natrum carb. 30c.

OTHER THERAPIES

Gentle exercise via t'ai chi, yoga, or dance therapy, could be individually tailored to enhance bone strength and ligament or tendon healing. Acupuncture might be used to promote healing and relieve discomfort. Alexander technique would be useful, to ensure healthy posture during and after treatment.

MEDICAL TREATMENT

Strains – simple analgesia and rest followed by gentle exercise to regain strength.

Simple sprains – support bandage for up to 2 weeks – patient advised to exercise freely.

More violent sprains – may need a below-knee plaster support for at least 6 weeks, plus painkillers.

Comfrey cream helps reduce localised swelling and helps the bruised area to heal.

PREVENTION

- Take care how you land when playing sports
- Wear supportive boots if you have weak ankles
- Avoid being overweight, which stresses all weight-bearing joints
- Avoid over-taxing exercise that can lead to strains

CAUTION

- *If injured during sports, do not try to play on*
- *If the sprain is severe, do not put weight on your foot before you have received medical advice*
- *Try walking when allowed, for example within a few hours of a simple sprain*
- *Request an X-ray for severe pain and swelling to eliminate the possibility of a fracture*

sprains & strains

Feet hurt for a number of reasons ranging from ill-fitting shoes, excessive walking, and a poor blood supply (see Poor Circulation, pages 52–5), to corns and verrucas (see page 142) and flattened arches. Plantar fasciitis (inflamed connective tissue fascia in the sole), another common cause, is dealt with below.

foot problems

SYMPTOMS

Acute form
- Can affect adults of all ages
- Pain under heel when weight-bearing
- Pain extends along inner edge of sole
- May accompany more generalised inflammatory illness, e.g. gout

Chronic form (also known as 'policeman's heel')
- Affects the 40–60 age group
- Less severe pain, but in the same area as acute
- Not associated with other conditions

THE CURES

NATUROPATHY
Besides a wholefood diet, rest is a priority for plantar fasciitis, although this is sometimes impracticable when it means time off work. However, severe inflammation is unlikely to improve if the feet are persistently

The bog bean plant is known for its anti-inflammatory qualities.

overused, and rest is recommended until anti-inflammatory treatment has started to take effect. Footbaths may help, in the delivery of remedies to the sore area, and cool compresses aid a severely inflamed sole. Weight reduction if necessary would be recommended as a matter of course.

VITAMINS AND MINERALS
A wholefood diet is recommended, with an emphasis upon raw food and juices to supply antioxidants (to boost the defence system and counteract inflammation). This would be especially applicable to the acute form accompanying more generalised inflammatory disease. Specific dietary supplements include all the antioxidants.

HERBALISM
Bog bean preparations, usually available through medical herbalists, are used in many inflammatory

conditions including plantar fasciitis. Preparations of willow, rich in salicylic acid (natural aspirin), are also recommended. Angelica would be used to treat acute fasciitis, while devil's claw (whose anti-inflammatory action has been compared to cortisone – a steroid) would bring relief to the chronic variety.

AROMATHERAPY
Make a massage oil comprising 2 tsp (10 ml) soya oil and 3 drops of pimiento oil: warm slightly then

Ill-fitting shoes and high heals are responsible for many foot problems including corns and bunions.

smooth gently into the painful area. Cover with a hot compress or poultice using this essence, applied for 20 minutes morning and night to relieve acute symptoms.

HOMEOPATHY
Specific remedies to be taken 4 hourly for up to 3 doses: Arnica 30c for feet that ache after too much standing or walking; Graphites 30c for burning soles of feet, worsened by walking; and Muriatic ac. 30c when the soles of the feet are painful to step on, with tightness and pain experienced in one or both of the Achilles tendons.

MEDICAL TREATMENT
Treatment is aimed at curing any inflammatory disease. Pressure-relieving heel pads on an insole, plus an arch support for flat feet (if present) may help, as may NSAIDs (non-steroidal anti-inflammatory drugs) and/or a hydrocortisone injection into the tender area.

PREVENTION

Seek treatment for generalised inflammatory conditions
Check shoes provide adequate support and comfort for long spells of walking and standing

---

CAUTION

• *Seek advice for persistent foot disorders – many can be relieved or cured*

Footbaths can provide some relief, but it is best to reduce the swelling and keep weight off the foot.

foot problems

Skin, hair and nail problems include a wide variety of conditions such as acne, psoriasis, athlete's foot, hair loss and brittle nails. Many of us will encounter some of these disorders at some point in our lives. A healthy diet including plenty of wholefoods containing all the antioxidants, and a stress-free lifestyle, will go some of the way to relieving symptoms for most of these problems.

skin, hair and nails

Acne, affecting mainly adolescents, reflects the hormonal surges of this growth period. Glands in the skin of the face, chest, shoulders and upper back secrete more of the lubricant sebum, the skin's natural oil, than normal, while cells below the skin multiply more quickly. Glands blocked with sebum and dead cells become swollen and infected, forming pus-filled pimples and red spots.

acne

SYMPTOMS

- Painful, red, raised spots
- Spots may be pus-filled
- Painless raised black or white spots (blackheads and whiteheads)
- Spots found on face, neck, upper back and chest

Homeopathic remedies including sulphur may prove effective in combating acne.

THE CURES

NATUROPATHY

A wholefood diet and exercise are considered vital to increase the flow of oxygen to the skin's surface. Exposure to sunlight would be recommended, and hydrotherapy intensively employed as steam (for face and other areas), and as water for bathing affected areas, in addition to poultices and compresses (for their own sake and to deliver other remedies).

VITAMINS AND MINERALS

The naturopathic view is that acne is due not so much to eating junk foods but to the combined effects of emotional stress, hormonal changes, growth fatigue and poor diet. This must be compensated for nutritionally before lasting results can be obtained. Wholefoods rich in all the antioxidants are therefore recommended, especially the fruit and vegetables rich in vitamin A (beta-carotene), and in cis-linoleic acid, an essential fatty acid found in cold-pressed olive and other oils and their products, e.g. margarine, and also in peanut and other nut oils. A freshly squeezed juice combination which helps some acne sufferers comprises 1 pt (570 ml) of mixed carrot, celery and grapefruit juice, which should be taken twice daily.

Specific supplements include garlic, zinc, beta-carotene, vitamin B-complex (especially calcium pantothenate) and vitamin B_6 (pyridoxine), vitamin C and vitamin E, the last-mentioned taken both orally and applied to an acne scar as soon as possible after it has formed.

HERBALISM

Boil a sprig of rosemary and/or thyme in a pint (570 ml) of water and allow to cool. Add a squeeze of lemon juice and bathe the skin with this 2–3 times daily after washing with an unscented pH-balanced soap and warm water. Chamomile tea helps to allay the anxiety and stress that often accompanies or triggers acne, as does orange blossom tea.

AROMATHERAPY
Myrrh, lavender, chamomile, rose, tea tree and thyme are all used in acne therapy. If your skin is normal, mix 2 fl oz (50 ml) soya oil and 1 tsp (5 ml) almond oil with 10 drops of your chosen oil. For extra-sensitive skin, add 5 drops of wheatgerm and 10 drops of your chosen oil. Apply twice daily, and follow with hot compresses to maximise absorption.

HOMEOPATHY
Remedies to be taken 3 times daily for up to 14 days include: Sulphur 6c for longstanding acne, with rough, hard skin, aggravated by washing, especially if the person tends

not to feel the cold and is prone to early morning diarrhoea; Calcarea sulph. 6c for blind pimples and weeping pustules forming yellow crusts, and when spots are slow to heal; and Antimonium tart. 6c when pus-filled pimples are the main symptom of acne.

OTHER THERAPIES
Other therapies are used to control acne. These include acupuncture to boost immunity and promote healing, and perhaps cranial osteopathy for relaxing purposes. Stress-relieving activities include yoga, relaxation and meditation, and t'ai chi.

MEDICAL TREATMENT
Treatment includes antiseptic lotions and creams, antibiotics, skin cleansers, hormones and preparations based on vitamin A (retinol).

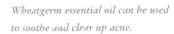

Wheatgerm essential oil can be used to soothe and clear up acne.

acne

Steaming the face with a herbal infusion made from elderflower, chickweed and marigold can help.

This is a highly contagious infection of the skin, most often seen in children. It comes about when germs from an established impetigo lesion, either elsewhere on the body or from another sufferer, invade the outer skin layer (epidermis). These bacteria – usually staphylococci or streptococci – enter via a small crack or cut, causing itchy, scabby lesions on the face and elsewhere.

impetigo

SYMPTOMS

- Small patches of minute itchy blisters on the face, especially at the corners of the mouth and around the nostrils
- Also found on the trunk and limbs
- Blisters burst, producing crusts like brown sugar

THE CURES

NATUROPATHY
A wholefood diet and exercise are vital to increase the flow of oxygen at the skin's surface and help expel toxins. Hydrotherapy would also be used to help detoxification, as water for drinking and bathing affected areas, as well as in poultices and compresses to deliver other remedies.

VITAMINS AND MINERALS
The emphasis is upon boosting the immune system to help overcome the rampant infection impetigo often proves to be. Wholefoods rich in all the antioxidants are therefore recommended, especially fruit and vegetables rich in vitamins A (beta-carotene) and C, and products rich in vitamin E such as wheatgerm, cold-pressed vegetable oils and grain and wholewheat products. Raw juices that work for impetigo include grape juice (1 pint/570 ml twice daily), and 1¾ pints (1 litre) daily of carrot with added spinach, cucumber and garlic.

Specific supplements include garlic, zinc, beta-carotene, vitamin B-complex (especially calcium pantothenate) and vitamin B_6 (pyridoxine), vitamins C and E, the

Add tea tree essence to water for washing. It should help relieve the itchiness.

A variety of raw juices are helpful for impetigo, including grape and carrot, with spinach, cucumber and garlic.

last-mentioned taken both orally and applied to the healing area when the scab has disappeared to help prevent scarring.

HERBALISM

Dab infected lesions 3 times daily with cider vinegar; propolis tincture also prompts impetigo to heal. Steep a handful of fresh rosemary or lavender, basil or eucalyptus leaves, oregano or chamomile in boiling water for 10 minutes, strain and cool. Bathe the lesion 2–3 times daily.

AROMATHERAPY

Add tea tree essence to warm water for washing, and apply to the sores. Mix 1 tsp (5 ml) each of sweet almond and wheatgerm oil, and add 3 drops of essence of benzoin, patchouli or carrot (or 1–2 drops of each) and apply to lesions once a day. Add any of these essences to bathwater, or inhale them from an oil burner.

HOMEOPATHY

Take remedies every hour for up to 10 doses: Antimonium 6c for blisters around the nostrils and mouth, especially in children; Mezereum 6c when the scalp is chiefly affected and oozing a yellow discharge which irritates the surrounding skin; and Arsenicum 6c for blisters accompanied by physical exhaustion, chilliness and mental restlessness. You can also bathe the affected area with a solution of hypericum (St John's wort) and calendula – 5 drops of mother tincture of each to half a pint (285 ml) of cool boiled water. Apply several times a day.

OTHER THERAPIES

Therapies that are suitable for impetigo are the same as those for Acne (see page 137).

MEDICAL TREATMENT

Antibiotics by mouth and as an ointment will be prescribed.

Rosemary steeped in boiling water and allowed to cool can be used to bathe the lesion.

impetigo

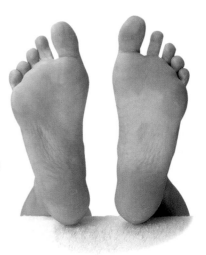

Ringworm is a fungal skin infection, so-called because its red, scaly patches heal from the centre outwards, creating a red ring around a normal-coloured area. Common sites include the scalp, trunk, pubic area, armpits and feet, where it is known as athlete's foot. The fungus, tinea, thrives in warm, moist conditions and is very contagious.

ringworm & athlete's foot

SYMPTOMS

Ringworm
- Red patches of skin
- Patches are ring-shaped, around a pale, healing area
- Intensely itchy

Athlete's Foot
- Inflamed skin on soles and between toes
- Turns white and blistered, or flakes and peels off
- Unpleasant odour

Lemon grass is commonly used in a footbath as a treatment for recurring athlete's foot.

THE CURES

NATUROPATHY
Advice would include following a wholefood diet, and taking exercise to maximise the flow of oxygen to the skin's surface. Exposure of the lesions to fresh air would be recommended, and hydrotherapy to bathe feet or other affected areas twice daily, as well as poultices and compresses to deliver other remedies.

VITAMINS AND MINERALS
As with Impetigo (see page 138), wholefoods with an emphasis upon antioxidant-rich fresh fruit and vegetables will be recommended. A combination of strawberries and fresh dates is recommended by a well-known naturopathic specialist for all skin infections, particularly ringworm – the best way is to juice the strawberries and pulp the fresh dates, then liquidise the date pulp with the strawberry juice because dates have little moisture. Try a combination of 6 oz (150 g) dates and 13 fl oz (350 ml) strawberry juice daily.

Specific supplements include garlic, zinc, beta-carotene, vitamin B-complex (especially calcium pantothenate) and vitamin B_6 (pyridoxine), vitamin C and vitamin E, the last-mentioned taken both orally and applied to the ringworm as soon as possible after it has appeared. Pollen is believed to boost immunity, and comes in tablet form, or you can take your pollen in the form of Cornish saffron cakes.

HERBALISM
Goldenseal kills many infective organisms, including harmful bacteria, parasites and fungi. Practitioners often treat ringworm with a very strong tea made of

goldenseal root, then use the powdered root to dust the area after drying thoroughly. Both procedures should be carried out twice daily. For athlete's foot, an infusion of lemon grass is often used as a footbath. Soak the feet for 20 minutes twice daily and dry thoroughly.

AROMATHERAPY

If you are susceptible to athlete's foot, as a precaution take a footbath twice daily to which has been added 2–3 drops of tea tree oil. To treat attacks of athlete's foot, mix 2 tsp (10 ml) soya oil with 2 drops each of geranium and tea tree, then massage this mixture in between each of the toes and around the nails once every day.

HOMEOPATHY

Take the following remedies every 4 hours for up to 10 doses: Sulphur 6c for a scalp infection, then Sepia 6c afterwards if no improvement has been noted. If infection is confined to the trunk, take Tellurium 6c.

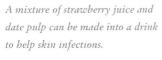

A mixture of strawberry juice and date pulp can be made into a drink to help skin infections.

OTHER THERAPIES

Other therapies are as for Acne, see page 137.

MEDICAL TREATMENT

Treatment will consist of antifungal drugs delivered in an ointment or cream direct to the area, or in tablet form by mouth.

Other therapies are as for Acne, see page 137.

PREVENTION

Avoid close contact with anyone suffering from ringworm
Wash feet at least once daily
Wear pure cotton or wool socks and change them daily
Dry feet thoroughly especially between toes
 Wear flip-flops or similar when walking on poolsides or in changing rooms
 Expose your feet to the air wherever possible; avoid enclosed footwear

CAUTION

• *Seek advice from a pharmacist for early symptoms*
• *Your GP will be able to help if simple treatment fails*

Pollen can be taken in tablet form and should help boost your immune system.

ringworm & athlete's foot

Warts and verrucas are small, coarse, benign growths arising from the skin's outer layer. They vary from match-head size to around ⅕ in (0.5 cm) across. Verrucas are usually below the skin, and hurt because of the pressure upon them; warts elsewhere are more of a nuisance than anything else. They look unsightly and bleed when damaged or picked.

verrucas & warts

SYMPTOMS

- Warts are small, tough skin growths on the hands, feet or elsewhere
- Verrucas are often just a painful swelling on the sole of the foot, with a wart-like growth visible in the centre
- Genital warts grow in clusters of fleshy pink, finger-like growths up to about ⅖ in (1 cm) long, and are found on the genitals, around the rectum and on the perineum (the area between these two)

THE CURES

NATUROPATHY
A wholefood diet and exercise to boost immune defences will be recommended. Hydrotherapy may be

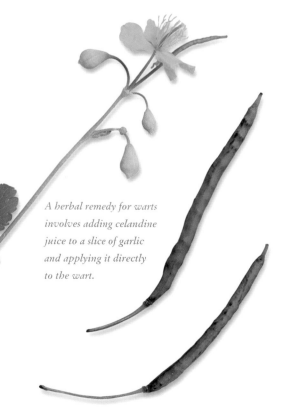

A herbal remedy for warts involves adding celandine juice to a slice of garlic and applying it directly to the wart.

used to bathe affected areas, e.g. cool water for stinging genital warts, warm water soaks for thickened skin over verrucas. Poultices and compresses might be recommended (for an infected or bleeding wart), and plant remedies added to water where applicable.

VITAMINS AND MINERALS
Wholefoods rich in all the antioxidants are recommended, especially fruit and vegetables rich in vitamin A (beta-carotene), vitamin C with bioflavonoids and vitamin E. Green tea is extremely rich in antioxidants. Try the date and strawberry juice combination suggested on page 140.

Specific supplements include vitamins A (beta-carotene), C with bioflavonoids and E (the last-mentioned taken both orally and applied to the wart or verruca then covered with a plaster); vitamin

B-complex (especially calcium pantothenate) and vitamin B$_6$ (pyridoxine).

HERBALISM
Apply celandine juice on a slice of fresh garlic directly to the wart, and protect the surrounding area by a little Vaseline or a plaster. Dandelion sap – the milky liquid that exudes from fresh-cut dandelion stems – is corrosive and can be used effectively against warts. Apply directly from the stem, protecting the surrounding area as above.

AROMATHERAPY
Tea tree oil is active against wart-causing viruses – apply a little neat or in a cream, twice daily directly to the wart or verruca. Tincture of thuja applied directly, or in an ointment, is also effective.

HOMEOPATHY
Take remedies every 12 hours for up to 3 weeks: Thuja 6c for soft, fleshy, cauliflower-like warts, especially on the back of the head, which ooze and bleed easily; Causticum 6c for warts on the face, especially on the eyelids and fingertips, and for painful verrucas; Kali mur. 6c for warts on the hands; and Natrum mur. 6c for warts on the palms, which tend to be sweaty. You can also apply thuja mother tincture twice daily and cover with a plaster. For facial, genital and any extra-large warts, seek a qualified opinion and treatment.

OTHER THERAPIES
Treatments are as for Acne (see page 136). There is abundant anecdotal evidence that warts can be charmed into disappearing; they may therefore be especially susceptible to other forms of subtle healing, and acupuncture (which is known to boost immunity) may be successful.

MEDICAL TREATMENT
Various applications can be painted onto warts and verrucas, aimed at killing the virus and allowing the growth to come away naturally. They can also be frozen off, or surgically removed, but both these treatments tend to hurt, without guaranteeing that the warts will not return.

Thuja mother tincture applied twice daily and covered with a plaster should relieve symptoms.

Never share flannels or towels with wart or verruca sufferers
Wear cotton socks while swimming, especially if you have verrucas
Use condoms during sexual intercourse
Attend to small cuts and grazes as they appear (to prevent the entry of bacteria and viruses)

Garlic is well known for its properties as a booster for the immune system.

CAUTION
• *Genital warts may increase the risk of cervical cancer – consult your GP about these*
• *See your doctor if you are diabetic and have verrucas (foot care is most important)*
• *Seek a diagnosis for any strange lesion – moles may need early identification and treatment*

verrucas & warts

Psoriasis has several forms, the most common being bright red raised areas shedding dead skin flakes. It can only occur in people predisposed to the condition. Believed to be caused by a disorder of skin biochemistry, dead (outer) epidermal skin cells are replaced more quickly than necessary, with consequent thickening of the underlying skin. Stress is a known trigger.

psoriasis

SYMPTOMS

- Raised, inflamed areas with whitish scales
- Usually occurs on thicker skin, e.g. the elbows, knees, hands and nails
- Also found in the genital area, on the buttocks, scalp and eyebrows
- Discoloured or pitted nails

Lecithin is a natural fat emulsifier found in wheat, eggs, liver and nuts.

THE CURES

NATUROPATHY

A wholefood diet and exercise are considered vital to increase the flow of oxygen to the skin, and combat the effects of both depression and anxiety. Hydrotherapy would also be employed for bathing affected areas, in addition to the use of poultices and compresses. Acupuncture is often used to bring relief to the sufferer.

VITAMINS AND MINERALS

The naturopathic view is that psoriasis is linked closely to an error of fat metabolism. Various studies have shown that many psoriasis sufferers tend to have raised levels of cholesterol, and many have recovered from their skin condition through nutritional therapy that has included the natural emulsifier lecithin. Found in unrefined plant oils, wheat, eggs, liver and nuts, lecithin also has the advantage of lowering the blood cholesterol level, in some cases where orthodox drugs have failed to do so. Raw juices can also help this condition. A recommended raw juice for psoriasis consists of 1 pint (570 ml) carrot and apple in equal proportions, once or twice daily. Fish oils also help combat psoriasis – good sources include salmon, sardines, tuna, mackerel, kippers and whitebait.

Specific dietary supplements include garlic, zinc, fish liver oil, beta-carotene, vitamin B-complex (especially calcium pantothenate) and vitamin B_6 (pyridoxine), vitamins C and E, and lecithin (you need to take the maximum dose recommended on the label of the packet in order to get the best results).

psoriasis

HERBALISM
Make an infusion with 2 pinches of each of the following added to a cup of water – sage, lavender, thyme, chamomile and lime flowers – and drink 3 cups daily. Alternatively (or in addition), bathe affected areas in warm water and pat dry. Apply calendula or comfrey ointment.

AROMATHERAPY
Make up an oil using 2 tsp (10 ml) sweet almond oil plus 10 drops of essence of cajuput. Apply twice daily.

HOMEOPATHY
Take remedies 4 times a day for up to 2 weeks: Arsenicum 6c when the affected area is burning hot, and the person is physically exhausted although mentally restless, and feels chilly; Sulphur 30c to treat dry, red, scaly, itchy patches that are worse after baths, especially if the person often feels too hot; Graphites 6c when areas behind the ears are affected, and there is honey-coloured pus; Petroleum 6c when psoriasis is aggravated by the cold and is much worse in winter; and Kali ars. 6c when affected areas are excessively scaly, and aggravated by warmth.

OTHER THERAPIES
Like eczema, psoriasis is undoubtedly influenced by tension and stress, and may, therefore, be greatly helped by relaxation and meditation techniques, and exercise such as dance therapy, t'ai chi and yoga, which harmonise body, mind and spirit.

MEDICAL TREATMENT
Treatment includes skin preparations to help remove the encrusted scales and plaques, ultraviolet (UV) light therapy and tar baths. Steroid skin preparations and tablets are sometimes prescribed for very severe psoriasis.

Fish oils, taken as dietary supplements, help to combat the symptoms of psoriasis.

PREVENTION

This condition is hereditary and can only be controlled, not cured

Avoid known triggers such as poor diet and excessive stress

Take supplements as advised below

CAUTION

• Psoriasis sufferers are at risk of depression
• Avoid scratching – patches of psoriasis easily become infected

Since psoriasis is brought on by episodes of stress, one of the best methods of controlling the condition is stress management, which can be achieved by meditation.

psoriasis

This irritating condition, also called heat rash or miliaria, tends to affect people from temperate climates on first visiting the tropics. The overworked sweat glands become blocked by sebum (the skin's natural lubricant), trap perspiration and then burst. Inflammation causes the characteristic itching, prickling sensation, and the rupture of large numbers of sweat glands can lead to heatstroke.

prickly heat

SYMPTOMS

- Moist, inflamed itchy patches in armpits, groin and between rolls of body fat
- Occurs in a tropical or subtropical hot, wet environment
- More common in fair-skinned people
- Triggers include being overweight, using soap too often and overproduction of sebum

Try a juice made from freshly squeezed apple and carrot, with some cucumber added, as a dietary supplement.

THE CURES

NATUROPATHY
A wholefood diet, exercise and relaxation will be recommended. To discourage further perspiration, air needs to flow freely over the skin's surface – wear cool, loose, cotton clothing. Use fans, drink plenty of water, go swimming and bathe affected areas. Cold poultices, showers, compresses and skin lotions are also recommended. Regular exercise might be rescheduled if carried out in a hot, moist climate.

VITAMINS AND MINERALS
Wholefoods for general and skin health, rich in all the antioxidants, especially the fruit and vegetables rich in vitamin A (beta-carotene), and in cis-linoleic acid, an essential fatty acid, will be recommended. Drink plenty of cool fluids and herbal teas, such as green tea. A freshly squeezed juice combination to help restore lost fluids and salts consists of equal volumes of apple and carrot, with a little cucumber.

Specific supplements include zinc, beta-carotene, vitamin B-complex (especially calcium pantothenate) and vitamin B_6 (pyridoxine), and vitamins C and E.

HERBALISM
Bathe the affected area with cold chamomile and/or tea tree infusions. For a quick, relief-bringing compress, wring out a flannel that has been soaked in a basin of ice-cold water

Neroli essence can be inhaled from an oil burner to relieve inflammation.

containing 4 tsp (20 ml) distilled witch hazel, and apply directly to the prickly heat rash.

AROMATHERAPY

Add 2–3 drops of chamomile or calendula essence to 8 fl oz (200 ml) cold water and spray the rash liberally. Mix 3–4 drops of myrrh or lavender with 2 tsp (10 ml) soya oil and spread on gently to relieve the inflammation; use neroli essence similarly, or add to bathwater, to relieve the knotted inner tension that can accompany a persistent itch.

HOMEOPATHY

Take Apis 30c every 2 hours for up to 10 doses, as soon as the prickling sensation starts, and if necessary, repeat the dose daily. As a preventative, take Sol 30c three times a day during exposure to hot, wet conditions, for 3 weeks out of every 4. Aconitum napellus is also sometimes prescribed.

OTHER THERAPIES

Prickly heat is usually a transient condition and does not tend to last, but for frequent outbreaks, stress-beating therapies such as yoga, t'ai chi and relaxation and meditation may be helpful. Cranial osteopathy and/or acupuncture may also be used as a means to harmonise the various body systems and boost the immune cells.

MEDICAL TREATMENT

This consists of cold compresses, cool showers and cooling skin lotion.

PREVENTION

Keep as cool as possible
Wear loose, cotton garments
Avoid hot baths and showers
Avoid highly spiced food, hot drinks and meat extract (it is very salty)
Drink plenty of cool fluids
Reduce the use of soap

CAUTION

Follow self-help advice as soon as prickly heat appears – salt and water loss can trigger heatstroke

A cooling compress made from iced water and witch hazel can provide instant relief.

prickly heat

Possible causes for hair loss or poor condition include hormonal changes, inherited male pattern baldness (MPB), an underactive thyroid gland, long illness and skin infections. Other triggers include stress, the contraceptive pill, steroids, antibiotics and barbiturates, and cancer therapy (drugs and radiotherapy).

hair problems

SYMPTOMS

- Shedding more hair than usual
- Hair comes out in clumps
- Bald patches appear
- Poor condition manifests in dullness, dry or coarse texture and split ends

Avocados and olives provide a good source of essential fatty acids, which can help this condition.

THE CURES

NATUROPATHY

A wholefood diet and exercise to increase the flow of oxygen to the scalp, coupled with head massage to improve blood flow to the area, removing toxins and supplying nutrients, will be recommended by a naturopathic therapist. There is no doubt among experts that stress and stress-related conditions, such as nervous tension, upset hormonal balance and seem to act directly upon the hair's condition, too. Yoga and relaxation could prove very beneficial in this context. Hydrotherapy will be recommended, in washing hair carefully, and in bringing plant remedies into contact with the hair and scalp.

VITAMINS AND MINERALS

Cutting out animal fats, found in butter, cream and full-fat dairy products, would be recommended – a high intake can weaken the hair follicles and lead to hair loss. The intake of essential fatty acids should be maintained or increased: salmon, herrings, tuna, sardines, and cold-pressed plant oils, wholegrain products and nuts and seeds, as well as olives and avocados, are excellent sources.

Specific supplements include zinc, beta-carotene, B-complex vitamins, vitamins C and E, and selenium. Fish liver oil capsules, evening primrose oil (see Eczema, page 174) and silica are recommended.

HERBALISM

Burdock root is excellent for hair that is falling out: put a handful of washed fresh roots in 1¾ pt (1 litre) of water, simmer for 20 minutes and use the

Horseradish essential oil is a well-known aromatherapy treatment for hair loss.

liquid (after straining and cooling) to massage directly onto the scalp. This liquid can also be used as a rinse after washing the hair with a mild herbal preparation. Nettles are recommended for their cleansing and toning quality and as an astringent both internally and externally: pick a saucepanful of the fresh green leaf tops (the best time for this is in spring, but it is possible at any time of year), wash and cook with a tablespoonful (15 ml) of water as you would spinach. Drain carefully, eat the vegetable (which is absolutely delicious) with a very little olive oil and sea salt, and massage the juice gently and thoroughly into the scalp.

AROMATHERAPY

Essential oils of pimiento, clary sage and horseradish are all recognised treatments for alopecia (hair loss). To 4 tsp (20 ml) coconut, soya or grapeseed oil, add 6 drops of pimiento or horseradish essence; or 5 drops of clary sage plus 5 drops of rum. Massage gently into the clean scalp, leave for a few hours or overnight, then rinse off.

HOMEOPATHY

Take every 12 hours for up to a month: Lycopodium 6c for hair loss following childbirth, or for premature baldness and greying; Fluoric ac. 6c when hair is brittle and falls out in little tufts; Selenium 6c for a tender scalp, combined with loss of body hair; and Sepia 6c for hair loss related to hormonal changes, either after childbirth or around/after the menopause, especially if these factors are combined with an indifference towards loved ones.

OTHER THERAPIES

Stress-beating therapies such as yoga, t'ai chi, and relaxation or meditation therapies, may be helpful for hair problems.

MEDICAL TREATMENT

Dietary advice, vitamin supplements and hair replacement treatments may be given, depending on the needs of the patient.

A gentle massage preparation made from nettles will help cleanse and tone the scalp.

hair problems

Nail problems often result from nutritional deficiencies, particularly a shortage of fatty acids. Cis-linoleic acid, obtained from cold-pressed vegetable oils and converted into gammalinoleic acid, may be in short supply, or the body may simply not be manufacturing GLA efficiently (see Eczema, page 174). Weak nails may also be due to a shortage of calcium, zinc, silicon and other nutrients.

brittle nails

SYMPTOMS

• Finger (and, perhaps, toe) nails repeatedly flake and split
• Hangnails appear
• False fingernails fail to disguise the nails' weakness
• Fingernails break or flake without provocation

THE CURES

NATUROPATHY

Recommendations include a wholefood diet and exercise. Massaging the arms, hands and fingertips is advised to improve and maintain blood flow, and remove toxins and supply oxygen and nutrients. The condition of the nails often deteriorates when a person is affected by illness, stress or poor diet. Yoga and relaxation could prove beneficial. Hydrotherapy will be recommended for hygiene and for delivering remedies to the nails and the hands.

VITAMINS AND MINERALS

Follow a wholefood diet with plenty of vegetables and fruit rich in antioxidants. Calcium-rich foods such as low-fat milk and its products, and soy substitutes, are also recommended. Drink plenty of water to remove toxins and maintain a good state of hydration. Eat the bony bits in tinned salmon and sardines, which contain bone- and nail-strengthening nutrients in suitable proportions.

Specific supplements include zinc; beta-carotene, B-complex vitamins, vitamins C and E, and selenium. Take fish liver oil capsules, evening primrose oil (see Eczema, page 174), and silica.

The bony parts found in tinned fish such as sardines provide essential nail-strengthening nutrients.

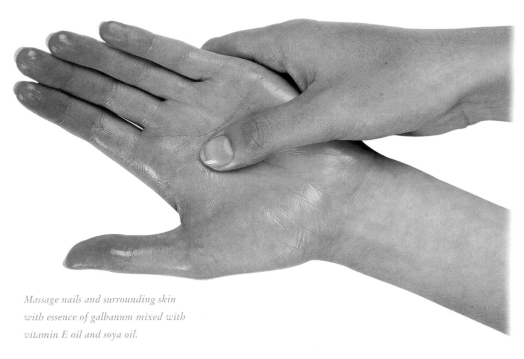

Massage nails and surrounding skin with essence of galbanum mixed with vitamin E oil and soya oil.

HERBALISM

Oil of evening primrose is usually recommmended as a herbal remedy. Vegetal silica is also useful in strengthening weak or brittle nails. Calendula is also a good herb to counteract nail brittleness: rub a little calendula cream around and onto the nails twice a day, in the morning and at night, or alternatively soak the nails in a tea made using the fresh or dried herb.

AROMATHERAPY

Add 2–3 drops of wheatgerm or pure vitamin E oil to 1 tsp (5 ml) soya oil, and 2 drops of essence of galbanum, frankincense or myrrh. Smooth gently onto and around the edges of nails about once a week in order to strengthen brittle or flaking nails.

HOMEOPATHY

Take remedies 4 times daily for up to 3 weeks: Silicea 6c for deformed nails with white spotting; Antimonium 6c for brittle nails with horny thickening; Thuja 6c for brittle nails with red and swollen skin at the base of the nail; and Graphites 6c for nails that are thickened, deformed, brittle or crumbly, inflamed and painful with blackening.

MEDICAL TREATMENT

In a consultation with a doctor, advice may be given to the patient about essential fatty acids that could be included in the diet, and vitamin/mineral, calcium and/or zinc supplements may also be prescribed to help deal with this condition.

Find a nail polish remover that is gentle on the nails and does not strip them of vital nutrients.

Evening primrose oil capsules taken regularly can help to prevent the symptoms of brittle nails.

brittle nails

Two main types of infection affect nails – fungal: for example, tinea (see Ringworm, page 140); and whitlows (paronychia), bacterial infections down the side of the nail. Toenails can also be infected by tinea, and ingrowing toenails by bacteria after botched attempts to cut them away from the fleshy toe side.

nail infections

SYMPTOMS

- Fungal infections thicken and discolour nails
- May separate them from the underlying nail bed
- A whitlow appears as painful swelling down one side of a fingernail, and often follows a minor injury, for example, with scissors or a needle
- An infected ingrowing toenail is very painful and may ooze pus

Preparations made from dried root of goldenseal can be used to make a hand bath.

THE CURES

NATUROPATHY

A wholefood diet and exercise, plus additional relaxation if necessary, will be recommended to optimise the health of the immune defence system. Hydrotherapy provides soothing baths and showers, opportunities for exercise (swimming and water sports), poultices and compresses, and hand and footbaths transport plant remedies as required.

VITAMINS AND MINERALS

Recommendations include wholefoods with plenty of vegetables and fruit rich in antioxidants, calcium-rich foods such as low-fat milk and its products, and soy substitutes. Drink plenty of water to remove toxins and maintain a good state of hydration.

Specific supplements include zinc beta-carotene, B-complex vitamins, vitamins C and E, and selenium. Take fish liver oil capsules, evening primrose oil (see Eczema, page 174), and silica.

HERBALISM

Boost the immune system with preparations made from alfalfa, cat's claw, echinacea and astragalus. Take preparations of goldenseal root (which can be extremely anti-infective and also helps boost immunity), either by mouth, or steep the crushed fresh or dried root in boiling water, then strain, cool, and use the liquid as a foot or hand bath. Dust the fingers and toes with powdered goldenseal root before putting on socks or gloves.

nail infections

AROMATHERAPY

Dab an ingrowing toenail with tea tree oil or whitlow, or make up a poultice, adding a few drops of tea tree or oregano essence. Make a massage oil using 1 tsp (5 ml) soya oil with 2–3 drops of eucalyptus, basil, lavender, geranium or clary sage essence, and blend around the nails and around or on sore spots.

HOMEOPATHY

To strengthen repeatedly ingrowing nails, take Magnetis austr. 6c every 12 hours for up to a month. For whitlows, take hourly for up to 10 doses: Belladonna 30c in the early stages, when the skin over the whitlow is painful and throbbing; Hepar sulph. 6c when the base of the nail yields pus when pressed, and the surrounding skin is very painful; and Silicea 6c when the infected area is slow to heal.

OTHER THERAPIES

If poor posture is causing foot strain and crushing of toes within shoes, the Alexander Technique may be beneficial. In addition to this, general relaxation and stress-management

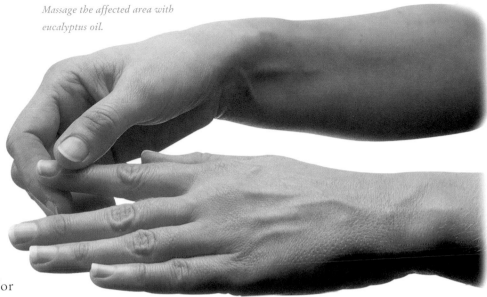

Massage the affected area with eucalyptus oil.

measures to boost immunity and promote healing are recommended.

MEDICAL TREATMENT

Antibiotics will be prescribed for whitlows and infected ingrowing toenails. Part of the (toe)nail may be removed under local anaesthetic to prevent further ingrowing; and a large or persistent whitlow may be lanced under local anaesthetic and drained of pus.

Foods that are rich in calcium, such as low-fat milk products, can help combat nail infections.

PREVENTION

Seek treatment for fungal skin infections before they attack the nails

Wash and cover even the smallest wound and apply antiseptic cream or its herbal equivalent

Seek treatment from a podiatrist (chiropodist) for ingrowing toenails

Maintain a healthy immune system

CAUTION

• *Do not ignore minor fungal or bacterial infections*

• *A red streak rising up the arm (or leg) from an infected nail denotes lymph vessel inflammation – seek medical attention without delay*

nail infections

The ears and eyes are very sensitive organs, and we have to look after them carefully. Our ears not only allow us to hear what is going on around us, but they also affect our sense of balance. Problems to do with the eyes include soreness and itchiness, and the presence of foreign bodies such as dust. This tends to cause further discomfort, making the eyes tired and irritated.

the ear and the eye

Defective hearing can be caused by inadequate conduction of sound waves through the outer or middle ear to the inner ear, where they are converted into electrical impulses and transferred to the brain by the auditory nerve. Ear wax, ageing and disorders such as Menière's disease can all impair hearing.

poor hearing

SYMPTOMS

- A sudden reduction in hearing
- The ear feels blocked – probably due to ear wax (or a foreign body in small children)
- High-pitched sounds become gradually harder to pick up, from middle age onwards (an age-related problem)
- Attacks of deafness with dizzy spells and buzzing sounds may indicate Menière's disease

Menière's disease can make the patient feel dizzy or nauseous. Ginger and clove essences can help.

THE CURES

NATUROPATHY

A wholefood diet and exercise, plus additional relaxation if necessary, will be recommended to optimise the health of the immune defence system and combat the ageing process. Inhaled steam as a form of hydrotherapy can be used to relieve catarrh, which can temporarily clog the Eustachian tube leading from the middle ear to the throat, impairing hearing, and to provide a means of transport for plant remedies to the throat, head and neck.

VITAMINS AND MINERALS

Ample supplies of fresh fruit and vegetables and their juice will be recommended for their antioxidant properties and nutrient content. A beneficial juice combination consists of 6 fl oz (150 ml) each of carrot, celery and apple.

Specific supplements include stress- and age-combating antioxidants such as vitamin C with bioflavonoids, B-complex vitamins, vitamin E, zinc and beta-carotene and the trace element selenium.

HERBALISM

Korean ginseng and echinacea help to combat free radical activity, which is instrumental in the ageing process. Ginkgo biloba improves the delivery of oxygenated blood to the brain, and thereby to the ear (and eye), which is useful when infection is present. Cayenne preparations are especially good for upper respiratory tract infections. For earache, medical herbalists often prescribe a tincture of pasque flower, which acts directly on the ears, perhaps combined with anti-catarrhal preparations such as goldenseal and eyebright.

AROMATHERAPY
Essence of clove and ginger help to relieve the nausea and dizziness of Menière's disease. Hardened ear wax can be softened using a little warmed almond oil, containing a single drop of tea tree oil. Plug the ear with cotton wool and after a few days the wax should come away naturally.

HOMEOPATHY
For ear wax, use Causticum 6c 4 times daily for up to 7 days, to combat copious production of wax with intermittent hearing loss. For Menière's disease, take remedies 4 times daily for up to 7 days: Salicylic ac. 6c for muffled hearing and dizziness, followed by Chininum sulph. 6c in the same dosage; and Lachesis 6c if attacks begin on waking.

MEDICAL TREATMENT
Ear wax solvents will be prescribed for hardened wax prior to syringing the ear gently with warm water or removing the wax using an auriscope and a fine curette. Hearing aids will be advised for age-related deafness. For Menière's disease, drugs such as prochlorperazine (Stemetil) act upon the inner ear's balancing mechanism.

PREVENTION

Do not poke soapy fingers (or anything else) down the ears – this encourages wax formation

Combat ageing free radicals with exercise and dietary measures

Maintain the blood supply to the head and ears with dietary supplements, yoga and scalp massage

Children sometimes experience loss of hearing because of glue ear, a build-up of sticky fluid in the middle ear. Strengthening the immune system may prevent it.

A tincture of pasque flower may be used to calm the symptoms of earache.

CAUTION

• Seek medical advice for diminished hearing whatever your age

• Symptoms such as those that occur in Menière's disease can nearly always be treated

poor hearing

Motion sickness – manifested by nausea and vomiting – is caused by a disturbance of the inner ear's balance organ by the movement of a vehicle. It can be aggravated by visual irritation, such as gazing at the swiftly approaching road, an expectancy of feeling sick, a hot, stuffy atmosphere, petrol and other smells, and fear of vomiting in public.

motion sickness

SYMPTOMS

- Churning stomach
- Increased sensitivity to smells
- Desire to vomit or actual vomiting
- Relieved by ceasing, aggravated by continuous motion

To calm a queasy stomach or remove the aftertaste of vomiting, mint tea is recommended.

THE CURES

NATUROPATHY

Recommendations include wholefoods and exercise plus additional relaxation, if necessary, to combat the nerves and dread of travelling that often generate motion sickness. Fresh air and exercise prior to a long journey would help to boost the spirits and produce a healthy tiredness, enhancing the chances of sleep during the trip. Smelling salts combat motion nausea.

VITAMINS AND MINERALS

Ample supplies of fresh fruit and vegetables and their juices will be recommended; a small glass of ginger wine for adults, or organic ginger ale (non-alcoholic) can help keep nausea at bay. Snacks of crystallised ginger, boiled glucose sweets, ginger- or fruit-flavoured glucose drinks sipped slowly, are also beneficial.

Specific supplements include calcium and magnesium to calm the nerves, in addition to the usual nutritional supplement advised.

HERBALISM

Ginger, fennel and aniseed teas all combat nausea, while lime flower or melissa teas can ease symptoms where there is emotional upset as well. Mint calms the stomach and removes the unpleasant aftertaste of vomiting. Powdered ginger capsules can prevent and treat both motion and morning sickness.

AROMATHERAPY

To combat nausea, try essential oil of marjoram, lemon or thyme inhaled from a burner, or added to bathwater or plain massage oil.

HOMEOPATHY

Take remedies every 15–60 minutes depending on the severity of

Eat a small, dry meal before travelling

Sip glucose drinks or mineral water to avoid dehydration

Old-fashioned smelling salts counteract nausea and vomiting

Open windows, and arrange regular stops where possible

Close your eyes or avoid watching passing traffic or objects

Take medicines or natural remedies before travelling

Acupressure applied to the point just above the wrist can relieve symptoms of nausea.

symptoms, beginning 1 hour before starting a journey: Aconite 30c where the person fears death and disaster (as is the case with most aerophobes – those who fear flying); Tabacum 6c when the person is nauseous, giddy, faint, pale, cold, sweaty, and finds cigarette smoke especially nauseating; and Cocculus 6c when the sight of food causes nausea, and the person feels giddy and worn out, and wants to lie down.

ACUPRESSURE
Press the acupoint Inner Gate (P6) – in the middle of the inner side of the forearm, two and a half finger-breadths above the wrist crease. (Seasickness bands stimulate this point.)

It is not uncommon for people to experience motion sickness on a boat, when the horizon feels as if it is constantly moving.

OTHER THERAPIES
Relevant therapies for motion sickness include those such as exercise, t'ai chi, yoga and dance therapy which, when practised on a regular basis, help calm the mind and combat the symptoms of nervous tension.

MEDICAL TREATMENT
This is unlikely to be required unless the person has vomited so much that a state of dehydration occurs. A doctor may prescribe drugs such as Avomine that control nausea.

• *Do not give children fizzy drinks to make them vomit while travelling – motion sickness is very distressing and preventive measures are effective*

• *Beware of dehydration or potassium loss due to repeated vomiting: children are especially prone to this*

motion sickness

Itchy, red eyes are usually due to an allergy such as Hayfever (see page 32), an airborne pollutant, or infection. With allergy or chemical irritation, the white of the eye (sclera) can become intolerably itchy, but does not exude pus. Bacterial infection makes the eyes very sore, but invariably produces pus as well, which helps doctors to identify the underlying cause.

itchy, red eyes

SYMPTOMS

- An irritant such as pollen or an airborne chemical causes itchy, watery sore eyes and bloodshot sclera (whites)
- Pus produced by the conjunctiva (membrance inside the eye) indicates bacterial infection

Eyebright, with its well-documented astringent properties, is often recommended for sore, tired eyes.

THE CURES

NATUROPATHY
Wholefoods, exercise and relaxation maintain a robust immune system, which will help to combat eye and other infections, and also minimise the allergic response to harmless substances such as pollen and fungal spores. Immune defence cells are also responsible for 'healthy' inflammatory reactions such as bloodshot sclera (caused by the blood vessels bringing extra white cells to the area) and watering eyes, which occur when a noxious substance is encountered. Hydrotherapy would provide eye baths and cold compresses to relieve the discomfort and carry other remedies to the eyes.

VITAMINS AND MINERALS
Recommendations include wholefoods and a particular effort to eliminate any suspected personal allergens which further tax the immune system. Fresh fruit and vegetables and their juices will be recommended, and carrot juice, in particular, for its high content of beta-carotene, which helps heal mucous membranes, and citrus juices, which contain vitamin C with bioflavonoids, a potent immune system booster and membrane-healer.

Specific supplements include the whole range of antioxidants, with extra beta-carotene and vitamin C with bioflavonoids.

HERBALISM

Cover tired, sore eyes with slices of cucumber or fresh rose petals, lie down and relax for a while. Chamomile, cornflower and marigold infusions are useful for making cool compresses to place on the eyelids and on the forehead. Eyebright, the best-known herbal remedy for eyes, is often recommended by herbalists and treats eye irritations primarily through its powerful astringent properties. Preparations of bilberry extract are used to prevent and treat eye disorders, chiefly macular degeneration (which can be a cause of blindness), glaucoma and cataracts, but the active flavonoids naturally present in bilberries also strengthen the integrity of eye tissues, improve the blood circulation and increase oxygen and energy levels in the eye tissues.

AROMATHERAPY

Add a drop or two of essence of fennel, chamomile or parsley to water and use for making cool compresses for the eyes.

HOMEOPATHY

Take remedies hourly for up to 10 doses: Aconite 30c when symptoms arise after injury or exposure to cold; Argentum nit. 6c for copious discharge; and Euphrasia 6c when there is little or no discharge. You can also bathe sore, inflamed eyes with the Euphrasia remedy – add 10 drops of the mother tincture and a level teaspoon (5 ml) of salt to half a pint (290 ml) of warm water. Use every 4 hours, no more than 4 times a day.

OTHER THERAPIES

Recommendations include all those that boost the immune defence system, combating the allergic response and fighting infection.

MEDICAL TREATMENT

For hayfever treatment, see page 32. Antibiotic drops or ointment will be prescribed for bacterial eye infections. First-aid measures and painkillers (including local anaesthetic drops) may be recommended for corneal damage or irritation.

For hayfever treatment, see page 32.

PREVENTION

Wear sunglasses in hot, windy weather if you are prone to hayfever

Wear an industrial mask if dealing with noxious substances

Keep your flannel, sponge and eye make-up scrupulously clean – never borrow or lend these

CAUTION

• Seek medical attention for allergic eye irritation

• Learn and apply first-aid measures for any chemicals you handle

• Seek medical attention urgently for suspected chemical irritation or damage

• Untreated eye infections can damage the cornea (the transparent part of the sclera in front of the iris and pupil)

Strong sunlight and windy weather can make eyes feel sore and uncomfortable. Sunglasses will protect them.

itchy, red eyes

Foreign bodies affecting the eye range from grains of dust and sand to tiny metal particles produced during industrial work. All can cause pain, but many are impossible to find. The danger lies in the damage they can cause to the sensitive cornea, the transparent outer coat of the front of the eye. If the cornea becomes scarred, it can interfere permanently with sight.

foreign body in the eye

SYMPTOMS

- Sharp pain in the eye, usually of sudden onset
- Pain is intensified by movement of the affected lid
- The eye waters (in attempt to remove the irritant)
- The eye is adversely affected by light

Preparations made from agrimony will make an effective, soothing eyewash for sore eyes.

THE CURES

NATUROPATHY

Wholefoods, exercise and relaxation will be recommended to boost the immune system, to reduce the risks of infection from the foreign body and/or its removal, and to help neutralise and possibly wash the particle out. Hydrotherapy would enhance the eye's natural watering ability, providing eye baths with the hope of dislodging the object, and cold compresses to relieve the discomfort and carry other remedies to the painful eyes.

VITAMINS AND MINERALS

Recommendations include wholefoods, and fresh fruit and vegetables and their juices: carrot juice, in particular, for its high content of beta-carotene, which helps heal mucous membranes; and citrus juices, which also contain vitamin C with bioflavonoids, a potent immune system booster and membrane-healer. Milk, especially as a night-time drink, will be recommended to help soothe frazzled nerves.

Specific supplements include the whole range of antioxidants, with extra beta-carotene and vitamin C with bioflavonoids. Calcium and magnesium are recommended to calm the nerves (which are typically set on edge by acute eye pain), in addition to the usual recommended supplement.

HERBALISM

Soothe pain and soreness with an agrimony eyewash, made from a strained infusion, using ⅓ oz (10 g) herb to 18 fl oz (500 ml) water. Eye preparations of purple coneflower (echinacea) are effective when infection is likely to develop (due to the nature of the foreign body, or because the eye has been rubbed a lot). Preparations of bilberry extract

Wear protective goggles where applicable
Avoid sandstorms, dust storms, and windy weather in dry, dusty areas (protect your eyes with sunglasses if you have to venture forth)

In situations where metal, sand or grit are likely to be blown about, protect your eyes with goggles.

CAUTION

• Do not rub the eye – wash only with cool water
• Seek medical attention for a foreign body you cannot remove yourself
• Seek medical attention for pain that persists despite home remedies

would also be useful in cases of infection – their active flavonoids would strengthen damaged, weakened eye tissues, and, by improving the circulation, oxygen and energy levels in the area, promote healing.

AROMATHERAPY

A drop or two of essence of fennel, chamomile or parsley can be added to water and used for making cool compresses for the eyes.

HOMEOPATHY

This is especially useful when a foreign body has become embedded in the eye following an accident or injury: take remedies every 5–10 minutes for up to 10 doses in an emergency: Arnica 30c after injury for shock and pain; Symphytum 6c when the injury is caused by a blunt object, and pain is felt deeply in the eyeball; and Hypericum 30c for pain that persists despite medical treatment. If Hypericum does not ease the pain, then take Aconite 30c.

MEDICAL TREATMENT

Foreign bodies often become trapped under an upper eyelid. A doctor may gently raise the lid by its lashes and fold it back over a wooden cotton bud stick. The lid and underlying sclera (the protective outer layer) can then be examined with a torch and magnifying glass. Corneal scratches are identified with a drop of fluorescein dye, often with the help of an ultraviolet torch. Metal fragments may be removed with a specially designed magnet. Antibiotic drops or ointment are then instilled and a patch placed over the eye, to avoid friction of the lid against the damaged area, and promote healing.

foreign body in the eye

Childhood ailments tend to be particularly distressing, as your child may have difficulty expressing the problem verbally. Common ailments in children include teething problems, croup, tonsillitis and earache. Most children experience these conditions at some point, and they are relatively easy to clear up. More serious disorders covered here include asthma, eczema and attention deficit hyperactivity disorder (ADHD).

ailments of childhood

Babies start teething at six months and have usually cut all milk teeth (eight incisors, four canines and eight molars) by the end of their third year. The little flaps of skin that are pushed aside by the arrival of the molar teeth (larger teeth at the back) are normal, and come away from the gum. Teething symptoms respond well to alternative treatments.

teething

SYMPTOMS

- Sore, red gums
- Dribbling more than usual
- Child crying and irritable
- Stomach upsets are common
- Child may develop mild fever

Fruit and vegetables such as apple or carrot are soothing on the gums.

THE CURES

NATUROPATHY

For nutritional advice, see Vitamins and Minerals. Bathe the child's face and dab inflamed gums with cool water (which can also be used to transport remedies to the mouth and jaws). Rest and relaxation, a suitable prescribed remedy to aid sleep if very fractious (see below), and gentle massage to the scalp and back of head, can soothe screaming attacks.

VITAMINS AND MINERALS

Either breastfeed your child or give natural, homemade wholefoods suitable for his or her age, such as puréed vegetables and fruit, freshly squeezed juices, soft, mashed chicken and fish, pasta mashed with grated or cottage cheese, mashed potato, custard and soups. A suitable juice would be 4–5 fl oz (100–125 ml) fresh lettuce juice, with equal quantities of apple and/or carrot juice. Specific supplements are not applicable unless the child is severely malnourished, in which case a qualified practitioner should be consulted.

HERBALISM

Give your child a chilled piece of carrot, apple or marshmallow root to gnaw on. Make up some chamomile

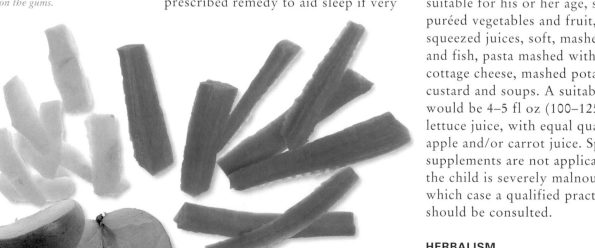

Homeopathic remedies for a child who is particularly distressed may be repeated at thirty-minute intervals.

for teething accompanied by constipation and ineffectual straining to open the bowels; and Mercurius 6c for a child with sore gums and diarrhoea or copious salivation.

MEDICAL TREATMENT
A doctor may recommend a gum preparation such as Bonjela, which counteracts any inflammation and promotes healing. Otherwise, any treatment would be directed at specific constitutional upsets that might or might not have been brought on by teething problems, such as diarrhoea, sleeplessness, fever and general discomfort. Calpol (liquid paracetamol) soothes away the pain and often quietens the child, too.

Puréed foods are helpful when your child is teething. Fruit and vegetables both purée successfully.

or catnip tea, and give the child a few teaspoonfuls, or rub a little into the sore gum. Medical herbalists sometimes prescribe a weak infusion of linden, which you can put in your child's bottle.

AROMATHERAPY
Make a cold compress using a square of clean gauze wrung out in chilled water to which you have added a drop of clove, catnip or chamomile essence. Hold gently but firmly against the red, sore gum area.

HOMEOPATHY
Give remedies every 30 minutes or more often if the child is very distressed, for up to 10 doses: Chamomilla 30c for an irritable child who fusses about being put in his or her cot, wants to be carried around, has one hot, red cheek and the other is pale and chilly; Belladonna 30c when the child is flushed and hot, with eyes wide and staring; Nux 6c

teething

Croup is acute inflammation and narrowing of the respiratory tract in young children, characterised bý stridor – the grunting, wheezing or high-pitched crowing noise made when the larynx (voice box) is infected or obstructed (e.g. with a foreign body). Similar to croup, and also causing stridor, is epiglottitis – inflammation of the epiglottis, the tissue that covers the entrance to the larynx and prevents food from going down the wrong way.

croup

SYMPTOMS

- Wheezing, whistling sound (i.e. stridor) on breathing
- Child may have (or have had) a fever, cold, or sore throat
- A whistling, high-pitched cough may indicate croup
- Pronounced stridor and cough, when the child is more unwell than with a normal cold, and high fever are all indicators of bacterial infection, and possible epiglottitis

THE CURES

NATUROPATHY

For nutritional advice, see Vitamins and Minerals. Use cool water to bathe a child with fever, and allow him/her to dry off naturally or use an electric fan. Steam inhalations reduce the inflammation and swelling of the vocal cords in the larynx – use several times a day and add herbal or aromatherapy remedies. Bed-rest and sleep will promote healing once the child has ceased to panic over breathing difficulties.

VITAMINS AND MINERALS

Give the child natural wholefoods prepared to suit his/her age, such as puréed vegetables and fruit, freshly squeezed juices, soft, mashed chicken and fish, pasta mashed with grated or cottage cheese, mashed potato, custard and soups. A suitable juice would be 4–5fl oz (100–125ml) fresh apple, carrot and celery juice.

Specific supplements are not applicable unless the child is severely malnourished, in which case a qualified practitioner should be consulted immediately.

HERBALISM

Make an infusion of rose petals – colour with a little red food dye and add a fresh petal or two to make the drink more attractive. Flavour with honey and/or lemon if liked, and try to persuade the child to drink a little several times daily (rose attacks catarrhal mucus and combats

A steam inhalation with some anise essential oil should help to clear breathing passages.

An older child recovering from croup may eat a little cinnamon toast. Cinnamon has a pleasant flavour and cough-relieving properties.

laryngeal inflammation). Also make herbal teas of chamomile (for its calming influence), hyssop (a decongestant and expectorant), lavender (for its calming effect and lovely perfume), rosemary (antibacterial) and cinnamon (for its pleasant flavour and cough-relieving properties). When recovering, an older child may eat a little cinnamon toast (powdered cinnamon on toast with a sprinkling of sugar).

AROMATHERAPY

Tea tree, hyssop and anise essential oils are all useful. Add a few drops of any or all of these to a steam inhalation, or to a little sweet almond or soya oil and use as chest rub. A tissue soaked in eucalyptus, tea tree, hyssop or anise oil, and placed under the child's pillow or close to the head of the cot, can aid clear breathing during sleep.

HOMEOPATHY

For a child who wakes coughing at night, breathless and scared, give Aconite 30c immediately and again after 30 minutes if the child is still awake. If the symptoms persist, give Spongia 6c and Hepar sulph. 6c alternately every hour for up to 3 doses each.

MEDICAL TREATMENT

This consists of cough linctuses, antibiotics where applicable, and directions to ease breathing with steam inhalations, adding possibly friar's balsam or tea tree oil. Acute epiglottitis is regarded as life-threatening, and a child suspected or diagnosed with this condition will be admitted to hospital because he/she may need assistance with breathing.

A few drops of tea tree essence added to sweet almond oil makes an effective chest rub.

croup

Asthma is an example of reversible airways obstruction (for irreversible obstruction see Persistant Cough, page 40). The lungs' small air tubes (bronchioles) narrow and their linings become inflamed, which interferes with breathing. Proneness to asthma is inherited, and the many triggers of attacks include allergy, pollution, anxiety and infection.

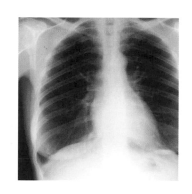

asthma

SYMPTOMS

- Persistent cough
- Shortness of breath
- Laboured breathing (expenditure of much energy inhaling and exhaling)
- Person sometimes restless and panicky
- Skin may be sweaty and pale, with bluish lips and tongue

A mixture of cider vinegar and runny honey has been known to give relief to asthma sufferers.

THE CURES

NATUROPATHY

Recommendations could include a wholefood diet, relaxation methods, the banning of pollutants (including smoking in teenagers), steam inhalations, ionisation therapy and stress reduction. Allergy testing (see Hayfever, page 32) by applied kinesiology or other natural method would also be carried out if relevant. The wholefood diet would be geared to weight reduction if necessary.

VITAMINS AND MINERALS

Consumption of raw juices for all their energising and antioxidant nutrients would be advised; especially recommended juices for asthma include carrot (with a little spinach), carrot and celery (any proportions), and grapefruit.

Specific dietary supplements include live yoghurt, which can be taken to eliminate the possible presence of Candida yeast (thrush) as a cause, especially if the child has to take many courses of antibiotics. The antioxidants beta-carotene, and vitamins C, B and E plus selenium and zinc, will be recommended. Propolis taken as medicine or lozenges boosts the immune system, too; and cider vinegar is said to have brought considerable relief to asthma sufferers. Mix 2 tsp (10 ml) each of cider vinegar and runny honey with a tumbler of water, and drink 3 times daily.

HERBALISM

Herbal practitioners may treat asthma with a tea made from a clove of garlic mashed with pinches of poppy petals, thyme, aniseed and lavender (only use poppy derivatives under advice from a qualified practitioner). Other useful herbal products include cat's claw, green tea, licorice and kava kava.

AROMATHERAPY

Try these essential oils: eucalyptus, savory, thyme, marjoram, lime or linden flowers and hyssop. Hyssop is a decongestant, expectorant and stimulant, and is very pleasant to smell. Savory (which the ancient Greeks called after the word 'satyr' because of its reputed aphrodisiac properties) also has very useful antiseptic properties.

It is not considered safe for asthmatics to have inhalations, so it is best to either breath these oils from a tissue or handkerchief, or vaporise them in an oil burner. Electric vaporisers are widely available and much safer to use.

BACH FLOWER REMEDIES

These can be helpful in cases of asthma because of the link with tension, anxiety and dispositional triggers. Heather, for example, helps people obsessed with their own troubles and experiences. Agrimony suits people who hide worries behind a brave face. Elm is the Bach flower remedy for someone who is overwhelmed by inadequacy and responsibility (e.g. children with little belief in themselves).

HOMEOPATHY

Specific remedies can be taken every 15 minutes for up to 10 doses: Arsenicum 6c for an attack starting between midnight and 2am, when the child is chilly and restless, wants sips of water and feels better sitting up; Antimonium tart. 6c for exhaustion and weakness, and when the child is unable to cough up phlegm, has rattly breathing, and cold, clammy skin; and Aconite 30c for an attack coming on suddenly after exposure to a cold, dry wind, when the child is anxious and fears dying, particularly if the attack starts at night.

MEDICAL TREATMENT

This focuses on relieving attacks with bronchodilator drugs, which expand the narrow airways, and helps to prevent them with steroids, among other measures. Chest or other infections would be treated with antibiotics, and any anxiety treated with an appropriate antidepressant or counselling. Studies have shown that the slight reduction in growth curve that some children experience when treated with steroids for asthma is often made up for later, before growth ceases.

Heather is the Bach flower remedy suitable for children who are always worrying about their own experiences and troubles.

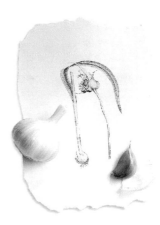

Garlic has been used traditionally to reduce attacks of allergic asthma and hayfever.

asthma

Most sore throats are due to pharyngitis – inflammation of the pharynx. Pharyngitis often accompanies a head cold or a post-nasal drip (when nasal mucus drips down the back of the throat). Inflamed tonsils (tonsillitis) appear as two red swellings at the back of the throat. Tonsillitis is more common in children and young adults, and it is often caused by bacterial infection.

sore throat & tonsillitis

SYMPTOMS

- Prickling sensation in the throat
- Pain or difficulty in swallowing
- Glands below the jaw may be swollen and tender
- Feeling of being under the weather
- Fever, especially in bacterial infections
- Stomach ache and/or vomiting in tonsillitis sufferers under 12 years of age

THE CURES

NATUROPATHY

Advice includes warm baths and mustard footbaths (make these fun for small children by bringing their bathtime toys into play). Fairly young children can sniff warm water up the nose – teach older ones to gargle. Practitioners of naturopathy might prescribe a 2–3 day fruit and fruit and vegetable juice fast for the acute stage of tonsillitis for older children, and suggest a rest built into a child's daily routine to counteract excessive stresses and strains.

VITAMINS AND MINERALS

Let your child drink freshly squeezed fruit and vegetable

Give your child citrus fruits that are packed with vitamin C, such as oranges, lemons and limes, or their juices.

juices, suck frozen juice ice cubes, take a little broth or vegetable soup if hungry (spare your child's body heavy meals while it is trying to fight infection). Fresh fruit jellies and ice-cream made from wholefood ingredients such as soya milk, flavoured with fruit juice or purée, are other popular choices. To help prevent recurrent attacks of tonsillitis (or pharyngitis), institute a wholefood regimen rich in natural vitamin C and bioflavonoids, found in citrus fruit, berries, peppers, broccoli, green leafy vegetables, tomatoes, potatoes and sweet potatoes.

Specific dietary supplements include the antioxidant vitamins A (beta-carotene), C and E to boost immunity (see Mouth Ulcers, page 10), and help to repair the inflamed mucous membranes covering the throat and tonsils. Junior zinc lozenges sucked close to the sorest throat area ease stinging pain.

HERBALISM

Fenugreek, horehound and marshmallow are popularly prescribed by medical herbalists in the form of teas and gargles. Aloe vera juice or gel (see Herbalism, page 190) mixed with tepid water makes an excellent gargle for an acutely sore throat. Propolis, a substance produced by bees to reduce the risks of infection in their hives, is a most effective remedy for tonsillitis and pharyngitis. Suck a propolis lozenge, or a teaspoon (5ml) of brown sugar containing 4–5 drops of the tincture, 3 times a day for rapid relief. Alternatively, just add the juice of a freshly squeezed lemon or lime to half a tumbler of hot water, and stir in a heaped teaspoonful (5ml) of organic honey.

AROMATHERAPY

Hoarseness or loss of voice can follow throat irritation caused by talking or shouting too much. Other causes include a dry, smoky atmosphere, and infection or inflammation of the larynx (voice box). Steam inhalations of aromatherapy essences reduce the swelling and inflammation and soothe the pain. Useful essences for this, and for sore throats in general, include niaouli, rosemary, lemon, cajeput, hyssop or myrrh (see Aromatherapy, page 202).

HOMEOPATHY

Take remedies every 2 hours for up to 10 doses: Gelsemium 6c for a horrible taste in the mouth, pain in the neck and ears, when the child is unwilling to drink because swallowing is so painful, and is hot and cold in turns; and Baryta mur. 6c for pain and soreness on the right side of the throat and neck, when glands are swollen and tender, and the child is thirsty and has dry lips.

Children under the age of twelve with tonsillitis may have further symptoms, such as stomach ache.

MEDICAL TREATMENT

Doctors usually advise a healthy diet, plenty of exercise and vitamin supplements to reduce the risk of colds and sore throats. Antibiotics are normally prescribed only for tonsillitis, and for sore throats that are caused by bacterial infection.

PREVENTION

Steer clear of those with colds or sore throats
Avoid kissing and facial contact, and other sufferers' dirty tissues
Avoid crowded, poorly ventilated areas full of smoke and fumes, and encourage children to play outside
Boost immunity with antioxidant nutrients

Soft foods such as fresh fruit jelly and soya milk ice-cream will not aggravate an already sore throat.

CAUTION

• *Do not panic at the sight of a streak of blood in nasal or throat discharge (inflamed tissues easily bleed)*
• *However, do not ignore repeated bleeding, even in tiny amounts*
• *Increase fluid intake, especially in children (fevers produce sweat, leading to dehydration)*
• *A youngster with tonsillitis may complain only of stomach ache or sickness, due to swollen lymph glands in the abdomen (though many seem not to experience throat pain at all)*

sore throat & tonsillitis

Also known as dermatitis, eczema consists of red, itchy areas on the skin, plus blisters, weeping sores and the loss of dry skin scales. Several varieties exist, reacting to at least one irritant. Emotional factors aggravate the condition, especially childhood eczema, which is linked with atopic (allergy-related) conditions such as asthma, hayfever and urticaria (nettle rash or hives).

eczema

SYMPTOMS

- Red, dry, cracked skin
- Clusters of blisters that break down and weep yellow fluid
- Crusty scabs following blisters
- Severe itching
- Atopic eczema is commonly found inside elbows, knees, and around the neck
- Contact eczema is usually due to metals in jewellery

Evening primrose. The oil is available in capsule form from health food shops.

THE CURES

NATUROPATHY

Recommendations will include following a wholefood diet, and taking exercise to increase the flow of oxygen to the skin's surface and provide an outlet for negative emotions and tension. Hydrotherapy for bathing affected areas, in addition to poultices and compresses, may be recommended for their own sake and to deliver other remedies. Acupuncture may be recommended to boost the immune system.

VITAMINS AND MINERALS

Wholefoods rich in all the antioxidants and cis-linoleic acid are emphasised, possibly following a carefully monitored exclusion diet to identify and eliminate personal allergens (for older children). A broad selection of fresh, preferably organic fruit and vegetables and their juices would be recommended, including many eaten raw as salads; cold-pressed vegetable oils and their products (for cis-linoleic acid); wheatgerm; and unrefined wholewheat breads and cereals for vitamin E.

Specific supplements include zinc, beta-carotene, vitamin B-complex, vitamin C with bioflavonoids and vitamin E. Vitamins A, C and E are especially appropriate, because they decrease the permeability of cell walls (as does cis-linoleic acid), thereby keeping out many potential allergens. Evening primrose oil is a rich source of gamma-linolenic acid (GLA) into which cis-linoleic is transformed after absorption. For a variety of reasons associated with our modern diet and lifestyle, we lose some of our facility for making this conversion, and supplying GLA directly helps to ensure that the final products of this

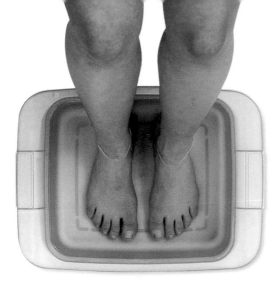

Footbaths using the appropriate herbal essences should be given twice a day.

pathway – the much needed prostaglandins E-1 – are still manufactured in adequate amounts.

HERBALISM

Evening primrose oil is most effective when taken orally or applied directly to the lesions. Medical herbalists recommend foot and hand baths, twice daily, made from a handful of each of the following added to 1¾ pints (1 litre) of water: elecampane leaves and flowers, celandine leaves, artichoke leaves and cabbage leaves.

AROMATHERAPY

Foot and hand baths, poultices or compresses can be applied as appropriate to the area of the body affected with eczema, using Borneo camphor or chamomile essential oils. Or make up this therapeutic oil and apply twice daily: 2–3 drops of either of the aforementioned, or of cedarwood or niaouli essence, mixed with 2 tsp (10 ml) soy and 2–3 drops of wheatgerm or pure vitamin E oil.

HOMEOPATHY

Take remedies 4 times a day for up to 14 days: Graphites 6c for eczema that mainly affects the palms and the areas behind the ears, oozing a honey-like discharge; Alumina 6c for dry and itchy skin, and when the child is

constipated; and Sulphur 6c when skin is dry, red, rough and itchy, aggravated by heat and washing, especially if the child has diarrhoea which is worse in the morning.

OTHER THERAPIES

See Acne, page 137, for other therapies. Stress often plays a major role in eczema, which may be greatly helped by relaxation and meditation techniques in older children. Exercise such as dance therapy, t'ai chi or yoga, geared to the child's interests, age and aptitude, will harmonise body, mind and spirit.

MEDICAL TREATMENT

Bath preparations and soap substitutes moisturise skin and allay itching. Steroid creams and ointments of various strengths relieve symptoms and encourage affected areas to heal. Evening primrose oil has been shown to be so effective in treating childhood eczema that it has for some years held a product licence under the name Epogam, allowing it to be prescribed on the NHS like any other officially recognised medicine.

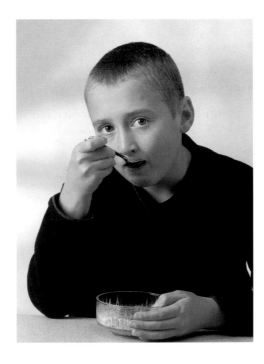

Vitamin E is a well-known skin supplement, which can be found in cereals.

PREVENTION

Identify and avoid your child's personal eczema triggers – e.g. soap, detergent used for nappies or clothes, play-paint, or shampoo
Take measures to reduce stress if applicable
Keep the skin well lubricated with suitable oils and creams
Give your child an evening primrose oil supplement

CAUTION

Seek urgent medical advice:
• *If eczema seems infected*
• *If it spreads rapidly, bleeds or is painful*
• *If your child has a high fever and/or is severely distressed with eczema*

eczema

Earache is usually caused by infection of the middle ear, the small chamber on the far side of the eardrum. Known medically as otitis media, it can start for no apparent reason or follow an upper respiratory tract infection such as a cold. Common in childhood, the eardrum becomes painful and may burst, due to a build-up of pus, if left untreated.

earache

SYMPTOMS

- Sharp or throbbing pain deep within the ear
- Fever
- May be accompanied by headache or sore throat
- Discharge from ear if the drum perforates

As with most illnesses, boosting the immune system with vitamin C is a good idea.

THE CURES

NATUROPATHY

A wholefood diet and exercise, plus additional relaxation if necessary, will be recommended to optimise the health of the immune defence system. Children often need regular relaxation to combat the stresses of their lives, though on a different level from adults. Inhaled steam as a form of hydrotherapy can be used to relieve catarrh and inflammation in mucous membranes, and to provide transport for plant remedies to the throat, head and neck. Warm baths (keeping the ear dry) also ease the discomfort of upper respiratory tract infections.

VITAMINS AND MINERALS

Breastfeeding provides babies with significant immunity to otitis media for the first six months, and some heightened degree of immunity thereafter. For older children (and adults), ample supplies of fresh fruit and vegetables and their juices for their antioxidant (and other) nutrient content are recommended. Consume plenty of cooling drinks to prevent dehydration and help reduce temperature. A beneficial juice combination would be 6 fl oz (150 ml) each of carrot and grape juice.

Specific supplements include vitamin C with bioflavonoids, B-complex vitamins, vitamin E and the trace element selenium, zinc and beta-carotene.

HERBALISM

Boost immune defences with preparations of echinacea, alfalfa, astragalus and cat's claw. Make an infusion of chamomile or calendula using a handful of the fresh herb or a commercially prepared teabag, dip a small wad of cotton wool into it while still warm, wring out the excess moisture and insert gently into the ear.

If you can breastfeed your child for the first six months, it will help to build up the baby's immunity against infection.

restlessness and anxiety, and the attack has been brought on by exposure to severe cold; Pulsatilla 6c for pain resembling pressure behind the eardrum pushing it out, and when the child is weepy; and Belladonna 30c for a flushed, hot face and fever, especially in children, when they have staring eyes, accompanied by excited and incoherent behaviour and unusual sensitivity to touch.

OTHER THERAPIES
Yoga and t'ai chi will calm the body and mind, boost your child's immune system and help combat tension and irritability. Exercise also enables a child to let off steam.

AROMATHERAPY
Dip a cotton bud in warm almond oil mixed with a drop or two of calendula or chamomile essence, and insert in the ear. (Do this very gently and do not insert the cotton bud deep into the ear canal.) Mix a drop of clove or marjoram oil with 1 tsp (5 ml) of warm almond oil and massage gently. Where a head cold is the problem, help the child to inhale any of these oils from a burner or in steam: cinnamon, clove, pine, ginger, lavender or eucalyptus. For a chest rub, add 1–2 drops of eucalyptus, pine or geranium oil to 2 tsp (10 ml) warm soya oil and apply twice daily.

HOMEOPATHY
Take remedies half-hourly for up to 10 doses: Aconite 30c when there is

MEDICAL TREATMENT
Treatment includes antibiotics, painkillers, and medication such as aspirin (paracetamol for the under-12s) to combat fever.

Calendula has been used for centuries for its anti-inflammatory and antimicrobial properties and is a useful remedy.

PREVENTION

Dry ears thoroughly after swimming and bathing
Wear a woolly hat, cap or ear muffs in cold weather
Seek medical attention for a child's persistent catarrh or sore throats, which can predispose to otitis media
Breastfeed your baby during the first few months of life

CAUTION

• *Do not ignore severe earache – a perforated eardrum can seriously affect hearing*
• *Infection can also spread into the air spaces of the mastoid bone, felt as a smooth knobble behind the ear lobe. Mastoiditis is a serious condition, often requiring surgical treatment*

earache

Rickets occurs worldwide, but it is more common in developing countries. The cause of rickets is a deficiency of vitamin D, made in the skin under the influence of sunlight and essential for the proper absorption of calcium and phosphorus. The parathyroid glands step in, excreting parathormone which maintains the blood calcium level at the expense of the skeleton, which becomes weak and deformed.

weak bones in childhood

SYMPTOMS

- Usually occurs in children at around one year
- The child may seem unwell, with swollen wrists and bowed lower legs
- Head may be enlarged
- Chest may be deformed
- Blood tests show raised level of parathormone

THE CURES

NATUROPATHY
A wholefood diet would be recommended, along with rest and gentle exercise while the child's metabolic problems were being treated. Deformed bones and joints would require some sort of splint or support bandage, but may also benefit from warm and cold water applications delivering herbal and aromatherapy remedies to alleviate pain. Acupuncture and/or cranial osteopathy might be recommended to help restore balance to the various body systems. Appropriate weight reduction may be encouraged.

VITAMINS AND MINERALS
A wholefood diet with low-fat protein and dairy foods to suit the child's tastes would be advised, while raw food and juice fasts would be included to obtain a wide range of essential nutrients in a highly absorbable form. Goat's milk and its products may suit children who are lactose-intolerant (cannot take cow's milk); soya yoghurts and cheeses also supply calcium.

Horsetail provides a rich natural source of silica, the trace element responsible for strengthening bones.

PREVENTION

• Protect children from the damaging effects of too much sun but encourage healthy exposure to sunlight
• Give vitamin and/or mineral supplements to faddy eaters

CAUTION

• *Dark-skinned children are especially at risk of developing rickets*
• *Seek medical advice if you suspect any of the symptoms listed opposite*

As long as your children are adequately protected from the harmful ultra-violet rays of the sun, allowing them to play outside increases their production of vitamin D.

Specific dietary supplements include all the chief antioxidants, with an individually recommended dose of vitamin D. Evening primrose oil and marine fish oil capsules (or cod liver oil) should be taken daily.

HERBALISM
One herbal remedy is treatment with vegetal silica, a very rich source of the trace element silicon, which strengthens bones. Its diuretic effect (it increases the volume of urine passed) would also help to reduce swelling due to injury. Nettle-leaf preparations are also rich in silicon, and have both diuretic and anti-inflammatory actions.

HOMEOPATHY
Specific remedies for bone pain (as would occur in this complaint) can be taken 4 times day for up to 3 days:

Ruta 6c when bones feel bruised, especially after a knock; Calcarea phos. 6c when limbs ache and feel numb and chilly, and when the child is very tired after climbing stairs; and Fluoric acid 6c to combat swift, stabbing pains.

OTHER THERAPIES
Gentle exercise through other therapies such as t'ai chi, yoga and dance could be individually tailored to enhance bone strength and healing. Acupuncture might be used to promote healing and relieve discomfort. The Alexander technique would be useful, to ensure healthy posture during and after treatment. Note that there is no particularly relevant aromatherapy remedy for nutritional rickets.

MEDICAL TREATMENT
Vitamin D and calcium may be all that is required, although surgery is sometimes necessary to correct significant deformity.

Calcium-rich, low-fat dairy products are useful supplements for children with rickets.

weak bones in childhood

A childhood complaint, the symptoms of ADHD first appear in infancy and continue into adolescence. Affected babies seem to need no sleep – they remain awake, crying and demanding attention. Once mobile, they constantly run around, wanting one toy or activity after another and never paying much attention to any of them.

ADHD
(attention deficit hyperactivity disorder)

SYMPTOMS

- A crying, disruptive baby
- May have been unusually active in the womb
- Tendency to suffer from atopic (allergy-linked) illnesses such as eczema or asthma
- Uncontrollable when older and able to move around freely
- Given to temper tantrums and disruptive behaviour

Ensure your child has small, regular wholefood meals and snacks.

THE CURES

NATUROPATHY
Recommendations include a strictly wholefood diet and stress reduction techniques. Hydrotherapy may include swimming to work off steam and excess energy. Swimming with dolphins, helpful to some autism sufferers, may have a place in treatment of ADHD.

VITAMINS AND MINERALS
Regular wholefood meals, with fresh fruit and vegetables, are recommended.

Hypoglycaemia should be avoided by never allowing too long between eating. Additives, such as the yellow food colouring tartrazine, should be avoided, as these aggravate ADHD symptoms. Dietary supplements include multivitamins and minerals. Applied kinesiology or another alternative technique such as dowsing may be used to identify any food allergies present because these also worsen the symptoms of ADHD. Evening primrose oil capsules, which can be opened after immersing in a little warm water and squeezed into food or drink, help to restore the balance of helpful prostaglandins which many ADHD sufferers have been shown to lack. Zinc as a separate supplement can also prove most helpful, as it increases the effectiveness of the essential fatty acids in evening primrose oil, and many ADHD sufferers are found to lack this mineral.

ADHD

Art therapy can be tailored to meet the specific needs of a child and can be an effective treatment.

HERBALISM

Herbal remedies include evening primrose oil as described above. To help induce calm, chamomile tea may be acceptable to the child if it has been sweetened first with a little honey, and flavoured with some freshly squeezed lemon or orange juice. Mint also has a calming effect, and most children will sip a little warm mint tea, as long as it has been suitably sweetened in the same way.

AROMATHERAPY

A gentle massage of the chest, stomach and back, using 2 tsp (10 ml) plain massage oil and 2 drops of marjoram, lavender, mandarin, orange, rose or ylang-ylang, can help to induce sound sleep.

HOMEOPATHY

Expert homeopathic treatment by a qualified practitioner is recommended for this complaint.

OTHER THERAPIES

Art, music, dance and colour therapy can all be adapted to a child's needs, and can be useful in the treatment of disruptive and aggressive behaviour under the careful guidance of a trained therapist.

MEDICAL TREATMENT

This is based upon the paradoxical effect of known central nervous system stimulants such as ritalin and other amphetamine-related compounds. In children with ADHD these stimulants tend to have the opposite effect of calming them down. Psychological therapy and child-oriented counselling for the child and his or her family, can be helpful.

Regular massages just before bedtime can have a calming effect on your child.

ADHD

two: therapies

Interest in alternative therapies has grown rapidly in recent years. Many people are now choosing to supplement any treatment they receive from conventional medicine with further therapies in order to take a more holistic approach to their illnesses. More people are taking an active role in improving and maintaining their own health and general well-being through alternative therapies.

Naturopathic medicine developed during the 19th century and is based upon the simple, natural principles of leading a healthy lifestyle to enable the body to heal itself. Naturopathic practices centre around the belief that we know instinctively how to eat, rest, exercise, combat stress and provide for our intellectual and spiritual needs, but lose touch with this ability because of our modern lifestyle.

naturopathy

naturopathy

THEORY

The basic theory of naturopathy is our bodies' search for and adoption of a natural way of living. It helps to rekindle this awareness, and also releases the power of a vital or 'life' force (referred to in Traditional Chinese Medicine as ch'i or qi: see Acupuncture, page 208).

As with yin and yang in Traditional Chinese Medicine, balance is central to naturopathic principles.

THE FACTS

THREE MAIN PRINCIPLES
The first of the three principles of naturopathic philosophy states that, once our life force has been re-established through a natural way of living, our vitality helps us to heal ourselves.

The second principle states that the symptoms of a disorder are proof of the life force at work. Our state of health reflects the interplay of three main factors: mechanical structure (e.g. body weight, the state of muscles and bones); biochemistry (metabolic processes such as digestion and breathing); and psychological state. When these factors are balanced, we are physically, mentally and emotionally well. When equilibrium is disrupted, for example

by injury or excessive stress, our self-healing powers come into play, triggering symptoms that remind us that something is amiss.

Suppose, for instance, you are basically quite healthy, but eat very few fruit and vegetables, put off going to the lavatory because you are too busy, get bombarded all day at work with pop music, and relax with the TV and newspaper at home instead of taking exercise. You are likely to suffer from constipation and bloating (indicating that you need fibre for healthy bowel habits), headaches (your body's protest at noise stress), weight gain (piling on fat against lean times in the future), and colds and sore throats (due to a lack of antioxidant nutrients).

The third principle is the holistic perception of humans as whole beings with physical, emotional and spiritual needs, rather than as, say, someone with a sore throat needing antibiotics.

Because the aim of naturopathy is to identify and eliminate root causes, many aspects of a client are considered during a consultation, including inherited weaknesses or tendencies, previous medical history, present general health, and lifestyle and nutrition.

TREATMENT

Practitioners of naturopathy play a preventive health role by promoting sound nutrition, exercise, relaxation and spiritual awareness as fundamental to well being, and base prescriptive treatment for disorders on adaptations of healthy living to suit an individual's needs. Fasting, nutritional measures, hydrotherapy, natural hygiene, and structural measures such as postural adjustment are commonly included.

Recommending other forms of therapy, such as acupuncture, homeopathy and herbal medicine, spiritually oriented yoga, relaxation and meditation, music, dance, colour or art therapies, is a further important aspect of naturopathic practice.

FASTING

Supervised fasts or 'detoxes' may be prescribed, lasting for 3–7 days. Care is normally taken to monitor the client's response to a process designed to rid the body of accumulated toxins via the liver, kidneys and skin.

Permitted liquids include boiled water, fruit and vegetable juices. Possible side effects include exhaustion, and feelings of faintness, irritability, impaired concentration, a bad taste in the mouth and bad breath. Small quantities of organic foods are then introduced, and a nutritional plan worked out with the client to suit his or her lifestyle.

Eating plenty of naturally produced, organically farmed vegetables without any chemicals is part of a healthy, balanced diet and lifestyle advocated by naturopathy.

Other therapies, such as meditation and relaxation, are also recommended as part of the naturopathic approach.

naturopathy

naturopathy

VITAMINS AND MINERALS

Certain foods are widely used to treat disorders, many examples of which appear in the ailments section of this book. Balance is the key, achieved by including as wide a variety as possible of natural, unadulterated foodstuffs. Care is taken to minimise the client's intake of both processed foods containing synthetic additives, and refined items from which wholesome ingredients have been extracted, such as white flour and its products, white rice and white sugar.

Typically low in sugar (even the natural brown variety), this diet obtaines sweetness from dried and fresh fruit and their juices, and vegetables such as sweet potatoes, carrots, sweetcorn and parsnips. It is also low in salt due to the link between sodium and high blood pressure, and in alcohol (no more than 2 glasses of organic wine or beer daily), tea and coffee, although green and herbal teas are recommended. The fibre content is high, because of the high content of fresh fruit and vegetables, and unrefined grains and cereals and their products.

The total fat content level is carefully monitored, using reduced-fat milk and

The naturopathic diet derives sweetness from additive-free fruit and vegetables such as carrots, parsnips and sweetcorn.

dairy products, and mono- and polyunsaturated oils such as olive, soya, corn oil, and butter substitutes formed from them.

Protein is obtained from poultry, offal, fish (the oily type especially, because it offers protection against heart disease and arthritis), eggs, low-fat cheese, and lean cuts of lamb, pork and beef trimmed of all fat. Food is cooked by stir-frying, grilling with lemon juice, microwaving and steaming in preference to frying and roasting. Many naturopaths advocate the high-raw diet, popularised by Leslie and Susannah Kenton in *Raw Energy* (1984), although this was used worldwide for centuries before industrialisation. The high-raw diet is based upon raw fruit and vegetables, nuts, seeds and sprouts, and the cheeses, breads, biscuits, sweets, drinks and sauces which can be made from them. It boosts the immune system against the effects of ageing, infection and cancer, and contains a wide spectrum of the essential nutrients we all need to stay healthy.

A wide variety of wholesome, raw, unadulterated vegetables are a crucial part of the naturopathic diet.

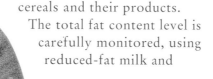

SPECIFIC SUPPLEMENTS

Controversy has continued for decades over our need (or otherwise) of vitamin and mineral supplements. Those against maintain that a balanced diet should satisfy our nutritional requirements. However, the operative word is 'should'. For most of the time, our diets are anything but balanced; and even if they are, the fruit, vegetables, dairy products, cereals and fish we buy may not be in peak condition, providing a full quota of every vitamin, mineral and trace element that they are meant to contain. Many of the RDAs (recommended daily allowances) of nutrients, drawn up by the World Health Organisation (WHO) and other authorities, are now regarded by nutritional experts as woefully low; nor do they cater for high-risk groups such as vegetarians, older people, smokers, pregnant and nursing mothers, and the chronically ill. The RDA of vitamin E, for example, is 10mg or IU (International Units). Yet an intake of 100mg (IU) daily has been suggested in a number of studies to ensure the minimum vitamin E blood concentration for protection against cancer and heart disease.

For these reasons, naturopathic practitioners are generally in favour of vitamin and mineral supplementation, and in many instances recommend an increased intake to overcome particular disorders. Many examples appear under specific disorders, including calcium to promote relaxation and sound sleep, the B-complex vitamins for stress-related complaints, and iron when anaemia is present.

HYDROTHERAPY

The ancient Greeks, Romans and Egyptians (among others) enjoyed the benefits of hydrotherapy, the use of

A Roman spa. Hydrotherapy has long been used for its healing powers.

water in healing, as we know from contemporary art, and from the archaeological remains of baths, fountains and spas. Far from being outdated, however, hydrotherapy in some form is practised all over the world, and by none more than the French; an impressive sight in the costal town of Dieppe is the large Hydrotherapie centre on the edge of town, and colonic irrigation (an enema to cleanse the large bowel) has long been fashionable.

The main forms referred to in this book include water for drinking; hot and cold baths and showers for cleansing, pain relief and comfort; hand, foot and general baths to deliver plant remedies; steam inhalation with and without plant extracts; and in making teas and other herbal medicines, poultices, and hot and cold compresses, usually with the addition of other natural remedies.

Recommended daily allowances for vitamin supplements do not take into account the needs of high-risk groups such as pregnant women.

naturopathy

The literal meaning of Ayurveda is the science (veda) of long life. Like Traditional Chinese Medicine, it covers all aspects of health care. Ayurveda is the main traditional holistic healing system in use on the Indian subcontinent. Practitioners believe that well-being is affected by constantly fluctuating vital energies, or doshas, and treatment aims to restore the doshic balance.

ayurvedic medicine

USE

Ayurveda is used to treat a range of illnesses including: arthritis, asthma, liver and heart disease, diabetes, epilepsy, stress, skin disorders and depression.

If the tongue has a white coating, it indicates that the body is out of balance.

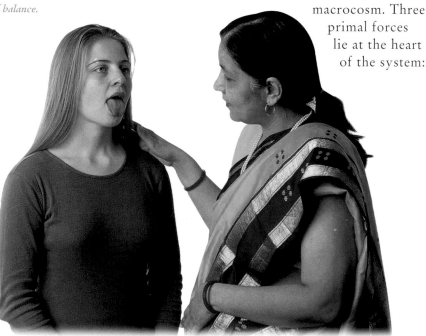

THE FACTS

THEORY

Like the medicines of Ancient Greece, upon which much of Western medicine was founded, Ayurveda sees humankind as the microcosmic equivalent of the universe, or macrocosm. Three primal forces lie at the heart of the system: prana, the breath of life; agni, the spirit of light or fire; and soma, which is love, harmony and cohesiveness. Five elements combine to form all matter: air, earth, fire, water and ether. These elements are converted by agni, the digestive fire, into three 'humours' or doshas, which influence a person's physical, mental and emotional make-up, but are also regarded as the waste products of digestion. Vata, or wind, is formed from ether and air; pitta comes from fire or bile; while kapha, phlegm, comes from earth and water. With perfect digestion (which does not exist) the doshas would be perfectly balanced; in reality, imbalance and ill health ensue. The dominant dosha controls the person's character – vata people are melancholic, pitta people are easily irritated, kapha people are calm and phlegmatic. Aspects of yoga, alchemy and sexology are also embraced.

DIAGNOSIS

A practitioner will identify your doshic constitution and imbalances by asking about your health and lifestyle. Pulse diagnosis is important; there are three points on the wrist that correspond to each one of the doshas and reflect the health of specific organs. Other tests include examining the tongue, the eyes and palpating the abdomen.

TREATMENT

Before treatment, the body is cleansed and detoxified using massage oils, saunas, enemas or laxatives. Health problems are treated by supplying elements thought to be deficient due to doshic imbalance. Catarrh or water retention, for instance, with excess phlegm, is treated with warm, light, dry foods, fasting, and the absence of cold drinks, which would augment kapha. Herbal medicines such as head-clearing gotu kola, warming cayenne and cinnamon, and pungent saffron might be chosen to combat a water-logged condition. Treatment might also include massage with warm aromatic oils, burning incenses such as frankincense and myrrh, and surrounding the individual with fire-coloured clothes and belongings in bright crimsons and yellows.

Ayurvedic philosophy maintains that most of us are born in a state of balance, which is disturbed sooner or later by poor nutrition and an inappropriate environment. Great emphasis is placed upon diet as a means of realigning the humours and maintaining their balance. Ailments are treated by specific dietary recommendations.

Ayurveda also draws on herbal medicines and simple massage techniques. Advice to patients embraces many aspects of their lifestyle, from posture, relaxation and exercise, to stress control, dietary changes, and the attainment of a balanced outlook and physique through yoga and transcendental meditation (TM).

The condition and appearance of the eyes are examined during the assessment.

FOOD TASTES

The taste of foods is all-important in Ayurveda. There are six main classes of food tastes that are recognised; sweet, salty, bitter, astringent, pungent and sour:

Sweet This includes foods such as chocolate and sugar

Salty This taste group includes seaweeds and mineral salts

Bitter Foods such as globe artichokes, chicory and burnt bread or toast fall into this category

Astringent This group includes lentils, beans and spinach

Pungent Foods that are categorised as pungent include horseradish, garlic and cloves

Sour This group includes foods such as fermented foodstuffs and mustard

ayurvedic medicine

Herbalism – also known as herbal medicine and phytomedicine – refers to any medical treatment in which plants and/or their extracts play the dominant role. Strictly speaking, herbalism includes aromatherapy and Bach flower remedies, and crosses the dividing line between therapies through its involvement in homeopathy.

herbalism

THEORY

Herbal preparations are used both in the form of patent remedies (available from health food stores and pharmacists), and as herbal prescriptions to treat symptoms. Familiar examples include valerian tablets to help cure insomnia, and cranberry extract tablets for the relief of cystitis. Medical herbalists do not, however, regard this as their main function, but in common with other holistic therapists consider that disease stems from an imbalance between a person's physical, psychological and spiritual aspects, and it is the aim of plant remedies to rectify this.

THE FACTS

HISTORY

The need to reinstate harmony and thereby treat diseases remained a major goal during the evolutionary stages of modern herbalism. In about 420BCE, the ancient Greek physician Hippocrates classified foods into categories of hot, cold, dry or damp, to correspond with the widely held notion of 'man's four humours'.

Centuries later, the physician Galen and his followers extended Hippocrates' original list, describing herbs and foods in such a way, based chiefly on their likely action on the humours. Cold, moist foods, such as apples, were thought to increase phlegm and lead to catarrh, while an excess of hot foods (e.g. mustard seeds, onions and almonds), or dry foods (asparagus, millet and coriander, for example) evoked the choleric humour (yellow bile), leading to skin or liver problems.

Our discrimination between foods and herbs is of relatively recent origin – in the 17th century carrots, cabbage and cucumbers were all referred to as 'herbs' alongside what we now recognise under this name, such as parsley, marjoram and thyme.

Culpeper believed astrology had an impact on the efficacy of herbal preparations. Some gardeners today take account of the moon's cycles when planting.

herbalism

Nicholas Culpeper, one of the best-known English herbalists, practised as an apothecary in London's East End over four hundred years ago. His published work, *Culpeper's Herbal*, is still regarded as the definitive herbal in English, and is constantly referred to for its exquisite drawings of plants and detailed descriptions of their attributes, despite the author's conviction of a close relationship between astrology and the efficacy of herbal preparations.

It is easy from our privileged and sophisticated vantage point to mock the beliefs held in the seventeenth century, but the profound effect of the moon on the tides, winds and weather is beyond dispute, and more and more gardeners nowadays are taking the moon's waxing and waning phases into account when planning their planting programmes. Also beyond dispute are the plant-based origins upon which so much of our modern pharmacopoeia is founded. It is common knowledge that the original aspirin (salicylic acid) came from willow bark, that opium (and all the opiate pain killers to which this gave rise) stemmed from the opium poppy, and that digitalis comes from foxgloves. We have also to thank the coca plant for the pain-numbing properties of cocaine, used in dentistry until recently, and from which the local anaesthetics lignocaine and xylocaine are derived.

Pharmaceutical products have often used the properties of plants. Digitalis comes from foxgloves.

Vegetables, such as carrots, cucumber and cabbage, were classified as herbs in the 17th century, and were treated as such.

herbalism

herbalism

One fundamental way in which herbal remedies differ from pharmaceutical medicines (which are usually synthetic molecules modelled on original plant extracts) is in their preparation from plants in their natural state. This is because of the belief that the whole plant organism is in a state of balance, and that using it as it developed in nature provides both buffering action (counteracting possible unwanted effects) and synergistic action (enhancing the desired effects).

DIAGNOSIS

Like naturopaths, herbal practitioners take a case history, asking questions about stress, family weaknesses, inherited tendencies and emotional well-being, exercise habits, diet and recreation. Their examination and diagnostic aids are similar to those used in general practice, but they are more likely to employ alternative diagnostic methods as well, such as pulse examination (see Acupuncture, page 208) and perhaps Applied Kinesiology (see page 230). A herbalist's diagnosis also tends to be expressed in terms of the symptoms of the disease: chronic inflammation of the bladder, for instance, rather than infective cystitis, or muscular spasm rather than irritable bowel syndrome.

In making a diagnosis, herbal practitioners establish a patient's case history, determining their well-being and diet, as well as conducting a pulse examination.

herbalism

PREPARATION OF HERBAL REMEDIES

INFUSIONS:
Used for the tender parts of plants such as flowers and leaves. Pour boiling water onto fresh or dried herbs, and leave for up to 10 minutes before straining. Bruise fresh herbs first by pounding them with a pestle and mortar.

MACERATIONS:
Bring plant material to the boil in a saucepan of water, remove from the heat, cover the pan and allow the mixture to infuse for several hours. Strain. This method can be used to make a more concentrated and potent medicine.

DECOCTIONS:
Used for tougher roots, bark, seeds and stems. Bruise the herb thoroughly first with a hammer, then gently bring to the boil in water for 3–4 minutes. Cover the liquid and leave it to infuse for 15 minutes. Strain.

TREATMENT
Treatment is chosen according to the aspect of health considered most in need of adjustment: dietary measures are extremely likely to be included, the overall aim being to help the body to help itself – to enable the body's self-healing mechanism to function properly. Herbs are carefully selected with this view in mind, their main features for this purpose being described in one of the following ways:

CHALLENGING: These qualities provoke protective responses from the body. For example, slippery elm preparations soothe an inflamed stomach lining, easing pain and facilitating improved digestion. Other common examples include senna preparations, which irritate the bowel lining, encouraging it to move (and therefore relieve uncomfortable constipation), and diuretics, which stimulate the kidneys to produce more urine.

BODY PROCESS-DIRECTING: Hawthorn preparations, for example, increase the blood flow in the coronary arteries and slow the heart-rate, thereby proving invaluable in cases of heart failure. Another example is Korean ginseng, which helps the body respond healthily to stress through its effects upon the adrenal glands (these manufacture the various stress hormones).

ELIMINATORY: These encourage the excretory functions of the skin, lungs, large intestine and bladder, and the healthy functioning of the heart and blood vessels.

PREPARATION OF HERBAL REMEDIES
Some recipes (the original name for medical prescriptions) simply tell you to take a handful of this or that herb and add it to bathwater, or a basin for hands or to footbaths. Other common preparations include tinctures (concentrated herbs soaked in alcohol) and hot or cold compresses.

Herbal preparations such as this one can be used with other types of alternative complementary therapies, including aromatherapy or hydrotherapy.

herbalism

Twenty safe and useful healing herbs and the ailments and conditions they can be used to treat

For centuries many healing herbs have traditionally been used in the home to treat a variety of minor ailments and injuries. Some of those most commonly used and their effects are described below.

RASPBERRY

SLIPPERY ELM

3. NETTLE

Tonic, diuretic and astringent, nettles are known as a blood tonic and cleanser and are a good source of iron. They can be drunk as an infusion or cooked like spinach. (Do not inhale the steam as it contains the formic acid that gives nettles their sting.) They are also thought to be good for the scalp and hair.

5. FEVERFEW

This is widely used for severe headaches, migraines and period pains. Research is being done to test its effectiveness in treating rheumatism. The leaves are made into a sandwich to make them palatable.

6. CHAMOMILE

A favourite calming herb, chamomile tea soothes the digestion and can help to cure insomnia. Chamomile cream or lotion is useful for inflammatory skin conditions and it is a good herb for children's complaints.

1. SLIPPERY ELM

Knowledge of this herb comes to us from the Native Americans. It soothes the mucous membrane lining of the digestive tract and is useful for people convalescing from gastric complaints and in the treatment of gastric and duodenal ulcers.

2. RASPBERRY

Raspberry leaf tea is traditionally taken during the later stages of pregnancy and during labour to help with the birth. The fruits are also a good source of vitamin C.

4. COMFREY

Known for its soothing and healing properties, comfrey is used for bruises, wounds and painful joints. It is also prescribed for gastric complaints and for the troublesome skin disorders psoriasis and eczema.

FEVERFEW

ELDERFLOWER

9. ELDERFLOWER
Elderflower tea taken at bedtime can treat feverish conditions by helping the body to sweat, and can safely be given to children with feverish colds or flu. Drunk regularly three times a day for twelve weeks before the season it can help to prevent hay fever.

10. CINNAMON
Long used as a ready remedy for nausea, vomiting and diarrhoea, cinnamon is also prescribed to treat rheumatism. It is a warming remedy for coughs, colds and fevers.

7. ROSEMARY
This herb is a tonic and an anti-inflammatory. Rosemary infusion is good for headaches and low spirits, and for colds and colic. It can be applied to the scalp for dandruff.

8. PEPPERMINT
Refreshing and cleansing, peppermint tea is used for colic, indigestion and flatulence, nausea, and headaches linked to indigestion. It can also be helpful for period pains, and may be applied to the skin for hot and itchy skin conditions.

11. CALENDULA
Marigold, pot marigold or calendula is good for inflamed skin, sores, bruises and fungal infections of the skin, used as a wash, or in tincture or ointment form. The infusion can safely be given to children for mumps, tonsillitis, swollen glands and fevers generally.

12. MARSHMALLOW
This herb soothes the lining of digestive, respiratory and urinary tracts and is used to treat gastritis, bronchitis and cystitis. Drinking an infusion is said to alleviate dry skin.

13. GARLIC
A powerful antiseptic, garlic also improves the circulation and protects the heart and arteries, preventing high blood pressure. Eating garlic helps to prevent coughs and colds, and it may be helpful in treating bronchitis, asthma, hay fever and sinusitis.

14. ALOE VERA
The gel from this plant can be applied neat for burns, sunburn, bites, eczema, dermatitis and skin rashes, and to treat athlete's foot. It can be taken internally as a digestive aid.

MARSHMALLOW

15. FENNEL
Fennel tea is made from the seeds and is good for colic and flatulence. It is taken by breast-feeding mothers to promote the flow of milk and prevent colic in babies. It is also used as an eyewash for sore eyes.

16. ECHINACEA
This herb is widely used today to help to boost the immune system. It will also help to treat infections of the upper respiratory tract and is a well-known aid in the treatment of skin diseases.

17. THYME
Thyme is an expectorant which brings up phlegm and is also antiseptic. It is useful for the treatment of coughs and bronchial infections. Herbalists will also prescribe it for infections of the urinary tract.

18. DANDELION
As a diuretic and tonic this well-known weed is used to boost the action of the kidneys and liver. It acts as a general spring tonic. The leaves contain large amounts of vitamin A and can be eaten in salads.

19. ST JOHN'S WORT
This sunny herb has long been used to help the healing of wounds. Taken internally it seems to help to allay feelings of anxiety and to be beneficial in dealing with symptoms of the menopause.

20. LEMON BALM
This herb, also known as bee balm or melissa, is mild but effective in treating feverish conditions, colds and flu, as it gently encourages perspiration. It is also pleasant to taste and gently sedative so good to drink at bedtime.

herbalism

Of all the alternative therapies, homeopathy has probably evoked the most ridicule. It can be difficult to understand exactly how the principles of homeopathy work, so many orthodox doctors remain sceptical. A common comment is: 'If reducing a substance's concentration increases its strength, then it should be possible to get roaring drunk on a teaspoonful of whisky.'

homeopathy

THE VITAL FORCE

Homeopaths believe we all have our own energy or 'vital force', which can be disrupted by poor lifestyle and diet, pollution or stress. The remedies stimulate this force, enabling the body to heal itself.

THE FACTS

A MEDICAL FOLLOWING

Although the majority of UK homeopaths are not medically qualified, nearly a thousand orthodox GPs and hopital doctors have studied to become members of the Faculty of Homeopathy in Britain and include homeopathy in their repertoire of treatments. Consultations in homeopathic medicine are available on the NHS, and the remedies can be prescribed on ordinary EC10 prescriptions forms. There are also five homeopathic hospitals in the UK, where patients receive both homeopathic and orthodox ('allopathic') treatment.

HISTORY

The main incentive appearing to guide patients and therapists towards homeopathy is the need for safe treatment which is also effective, accessible and suitable for people of all ages. It was his perception of this which first motivated homeopathy's founder, Dr Samuel Hahnemann, to seek out and establish a new system of medicine in the late 18th century. A German physician and chemist,

Calendula is a popular herbal medicine, used for its anti-inflammatory and antimicrobial qualities. It is a common first-aid treatment for cuts and grazes.

Hahnemann was appalled by the overt brutality (and uselessness) of many contemporary treatment methods. Purging people already weakened by fluid loss, diarrhoea and vomiting, cupping (letting blood) to treat, for example, fainting or epilepsy, and noxious medicines containing powerful poisons such as arsenic, mercury and lead, all took a toll reflected in the high mortality rates of that period.

Hahnemann was convinced of the body's ability to heal itself and, like naturopaths, he interpreted symptoms as evidence of the body's self-curing action. He was also convinced that disease resulted from the 'vital force'

becoming unbalanced, and that the aim of treatment was the restoration (rather than the further disruption) of harmony and balance.

THEORY

Adopting a holistic approach focused upon the patient as a complete and individual being, Hahnemann began to experiment with an extremely wide range of natural remedies, which were derived from animal, plant, mineral and biological raw material. During this process, Hahnemann discovered the truth of the ancient dictum of 'like curing like' (also known as the law of similars).

REMEDY TYPES

Tablets – these are sucked for about five minutes in the mouth, and then chewed

Triturated tablets – these dissolve easily under the tongue

Sugar pillules – no dairy elements mean that these are good for dairy-allergic people

Ailments such as colds, diarrhoea and allergies can all improve with homeopathic treatments. More serious conditions such as arthritis, psoriasis and depression can also be helped.

Powders – these are tipped under the tongue and allowed to dissolve

homeopathy

homeopathy

Mother tinctures are often made from the extracts of plants such as sea sponge.

What this means is that taking small quantities of a substance, which in far larger doses would produce the symptoms from which the person is suffering, can cure them. An analogy with vaccination makes this clearer, since this technique injects tiny quantities of the harmful organism against which immunity is sought, with a view to stimulating the production of protective antibodies. In a similar manner, homeopathy stimulates the person's latent vitality, causing it to set the healing process in motion.

Hahnemann's findings were described in detail in his famous work, *An Organon of Rational Healing* (1810), and at this point he discovered that the smaller the dose of an active substance used, the more powerful its effect. In preparing the remedies, mother tinctures (extracts of plant or other material used) are made and repeatedly diluted one hundredfold. The first hundredth dilution is termed 1c; the second – 2c – is a hundredth dilution of the first, and so on. The dilution process (known as trituration) is followed by an episode of vigorous shaking hundreds of thousands of times over by specially designed machinery. This was vital to the 'potentising' of the remedy in Hahnemann's view, and it is still integral to the preparation process today.

The explanation of how and why remedies prepared in this way are so potent has still not been finally settled; but the consensus of opinion focuses upon the molecular energy which is built up during the grinding,

diluting and trituration stages. Electromagnetic waves constitute solid objects rather than hard material masses of atoms, and homeopathic theory holds that the molecular blueprint of an active substance can be impressed upon inert carrier material such as lactose (of which the remedies are constituted) by successive stages of grinding and shaking. The more the

Homeopathic remedies are perfectly safe to give to babies and small children, and will cause no side-effects.

Frail and elderly people can benefit from homeopathic remedies, which are entirely safe.

original active molecules are diluted and processed in this manner, the greater the electromagnetic potency (healing capacity) of the final remedy.

TREATMENT

Remedies are prescribed according to personality type; physical appearance; individual responses to common conditions such as heat, cold, light, noise and movement; reactions (such as irritability, anger, fear, despair) towards illness; and the way in which symptoms vary with the time of day or night. Prescribing the remedies is a highly complex art, requiring experience, keen observation and assessment, and the ability to read between the lines of, for example, a simply presented family history or

Prescribing remedies is a complex process. Assessing a person's personality type and their emotional responses to illness are crucial.

account of the patient's past or present illnesses.

Various potencies are prepared, the most common being 6c and 30c (i.e., the tincture is diluted a hundred times, then six times and then thirty times over respectively). Serious or persistent disorders ought always to be diagnosed and treated by a qualified homeopathic practitioner, but over-the-counter remedies are available from healthfood stores and pharmacies.

THE REMEDIES

The remedies, the main ones of which are listed overleaf, are safe for use on babies and elderly, frail people, pregnant and nursing mothers, and the chronically ill. Some are prepared as liquids or as creams to be applied topically, but the majority are in the form of slightly sweet lactose tablets that dissolve readily on the tongue.

REMEDY POTENCY

Mother tincture – this is the pure, undiluted form of the remedy

Diluting – the tincture is diluted to reach 1c potency

Potentising – the mixture is potentised by vigorous shaking

Adjusting dose – the process is repeated to gain 6c or 30c potency

Tablets – lactose tablets are soaked in the remedy for easy use

homeopathy

Twenty useful homeopathic remedies and the ailments and conditions they can be used to treat

Homeopathic remedies are matched to the patient and the way the individual is responding to an ailment as well as to the type of ailment. At home the remedies are particularly useful for mild infections and minor ailments.

NATRUM MUR.

BELLADONNA

3. BELLADONNA

Deadly nightshade provides this remedy for violent pains that arise and subside quickly. It is suitable for migraines and for sudden feverish symptoms in children's illnesses. The patient may be hot with a great thirst.

4. PULSATILLA

Useful for when a patient is tearful and feels low. Try it for colds with heavy mucus or that affect the ears, and coughs that come on in the night. Also for any illness where the person feels moody.

7. NATRUM MUR.

This may relieve bad headaches that start in the morning, where the person needs to sleep and may feel unexpressed grief. There may be great thirst, the head feels hot and the face is red. It is also taken for sunstroke and for indigestion with belching and bloating.

8. SYMPHYTUM

This is derived from comfrey and is thought to promote the healing of broken bones. It is also used for an injury to the eye and surrounding area.

1. NUX VOMICA

Derived from a poison nut tree, this is often the remedy for a hangover, nausea and headaches. It may also help catarrh, colds and flu. Good for people who wake up worrying in the middle of the night and prefer to be left alone when ill.

2. ARNICA

This is the remedy for accidents and emergencies, especially for stoical people who pick themselves up after a fall. Good after falls, sprains, surgery and dental treatment.

5. APIS MELLIFICA

This remedy is produced from bees and may be useful for insect bites that swell and are sore; also for allergic reactions, and stinging, burning rashes in infectious diseases such as chickenpox. Some people may prefer not to use it because of its source.

6. BRYONIA

A remedy for complaints that seem to have developed slowly following exposure to cold and wind. For dry coughs, headaches accompanied by constipation and flu.

ACONITE

homeopathy

HEPAR SULPH.

13. CHAMOMILLA

A calming remedy for teething infants and for childhood illnesses where the child has temper tantrums and needs calming. Also indicated if the child is screaming in pain, such as with colic. In adults it is used for PMS and digestive disorders.

14. GELSEMIUM

This remedy may be useful in disturbed, excited states, either after an accident or before an ordeal such as an interview. There may be trembling, a dull headache, or a dull, heavy feeling.

9. RHUS TOX.

Based on poison ivy, this remedy may treat conditions affecting the skin, ligaments and joints. It may also help colds with a dry cough, a feeling of cold and cold sores. Try it for shingles and for joint pain improved by exercise.

10. ACONITUM (ACONITE)

Treats intense symptoms such as panic attacks and sudden-onset illnesses and suits people who are normally strong and energetic. Good for colds and chills with a fever and thirst, headache, earache and coughs.

15. HEPAR SULF.

For colds that affect the ears and throat accompanied by a sore throat with swollen glands. There may be sharp pain and sour sweat, irritability and oversensitivity. Also for headaches that affect the right side and are worse for cold and draughts.

16. HYPERICUM

For painful haemorrhoids (piles), and emergency treatment for severe cuts or puncture wounds, falls followed by concussion and dizziness, bangs to the fingers or toes, and animal bites.

11. ARSENICUM

For illness such as colds and flu accompanied by anxiety and chilliness, especially when followed by fever, and with watery nasal discharge. Treats stomach cramps and diarrhoea or vomit that burns.

12. DROSERA

Derived from an insectivorous plant, drosera can be tried for tickling sore throats, spasmic coughs where the chest feels constricted and where coughing takes the breath away and may be followed by retching.

17. HAMAMELIS

This remedy is from witch hazel bark and is used for similar complaints as the herb: bleeding and bruising from injuries, including nosebleeds; haemorrhoids (piles) and varicose veins, especially during pregnancy.

18. CALENDULA

An essential remedy for the first-aid kit, Calendula is given to anyone who has just received a wound of any kind. Naturally, conventional first-aid treatment should be given as well but this remedy helps to prevent infection and aid healing.

19. EUPHRASIA

Derived from eyebright, this is used help watery eyes. This condition may be caused by hay fever, conjunctivitis or coughs and colds. The eyes may be sore and the eyelids puffy.

20. SILICA

A remedy to help the body expel splinters and other foreign bodies. It may also help with headaches, especially caused by hunger and accompanied by ringing in the ears, and is taken for sore nipples and pain during breastfeeding.

CAUTION

Concussion and dizziness following head bangs are serious and should always be treated by a medically qualified practitioner.

CALENDULA

homeopathy

Aromatherapy is a popular alternative therapy, used widely due to its feel-good factor. People buy a vast range of products, from scented candles and bubble baths to shampoo and deodorisers for the home. While it is not necessary to learn about its origins and mode of action to enjoy its benefits, understanding the healing potential of the essential oils does expand our choices for treating common ailments.

aromatherapy

USES

Aromatherapy oils can be used in various ways including:
- Massages
- Mouthwashes and gargles
- Inhalations
- Compresses
- Oil burners
- Baths

Using the essential plant oils for their properties is not a new idea. Saints, healers and magicians have relied on plants such as lily of the valley for centuries.

THE FACTS

HISTORY

The term 'aromatherapy' was coined in the early twentieth century to describe the use of essential oils of plants for their medicinal and wider therapeutic properties. However, the

use of plant essences dates back to ancient times. Ancient Egyptians used them in embalming, Greeks and Romans used them both therapeutically and for pleasure, and the biblical wise men are said to have brought gifts of precious frankincense (olibanum) and myrrh (sweet cecily) to the infant Jesus. Distillations of plants were used in ancient Persia, Turkey and India, and the distillation process was perfected by the Arabs of the Middle Ages. The use of plant essences in perfumery grew during the period and by the sixteenth century a large perfume industry was centred in Provence in southern France.

Aromatherapy has two-fold but intertwined benefits – purely sensual to uplift, calm, stimulate and revitalise, and medicinal. Modern aromatherapy has developed mainly in France, where clinical research has revealed many of its bactericidal uses as well as exploring its possibilities for the mind.

HOME USE

While essential oils can be used at home in many ways, it must be remembered that although the oils are completely natural substances they are also potent chemicals that should be used with care. They should never be taken orally except under the guidance of a medically qualified practitioner, and with few exceptions they should not be used undiluted on the skin. Many commercially available preparations sold as aromatherapy contain synthetic perfumes or are diluted and mixed with preservatives. Pure, undiluted essences are naturally more expensive than artificial substitutes, but nothing else will do. Read labels carefully and buy your oils for home use from a reputable source.

BATHS AND BURNERS

To enjoy the perfume of your favourite oils add a few drops to an odour-free carrier oil such as soya and warm the mixture in a specially designed burner. Even through inhalation the molecules of the oils can enter the bloodstream. Another simple way to enjoy the benefits of essential oils is to add up to ten drops to the bath water. Used this way the oils act on the sense of smell and also penetrate the skin. A sense of well-being can be induced using oils such as mandarin, rose, rosemary or frankincense. Relaxation is enhanced with ylang ylang, lavender, neroli, sandalwood or clary sage.

MASSAGE

Massage encourages the absorption of plant essences through the skin by increasing the blood flow. Oils for massage are blended with a bland carrier oil, using five drops per 15 ml. To treat colds and coughs, rub diluted oils such as hyssop, cinnamon, eucalyptus, lavender and geranium into the chest. Their vapours will be released by the warmth of the body and absorbed into the bloodstream through the skin.

STEAM INHALATION

A treatment for colds, sore throats and chest infections is to sprinkle oils on steaming hot water and breathe in the steam with a towel over your head. You can continue the treatment by sprinkling a few drops of the same essential oil/s onto your handkerchief and onto a pillow at night.

CAUTION

Massage can be harmful in some circumstances. Do not massage over injuries and broken skin, recent scar tissue, or varicose veins, or on anyone with inflammatory conditions, thrombosis, a heart condition or any other serious medical condition. Avoid massage immediately after a meal, when there is an acute infection or high temperature, and during the ten days immediately after vaccination. If in doubt consult your doctor or medical adviser.

Aromatic baths can be taken to help enhance the mood, relax or stimulate various body systems, treat certain skin disorders and ease musculo-skeletal pain.

Aromatherapy oils are used to treat the whole person, helping the person to regain overall balance and restore his or her energy potential.

aromatherapy

Twenty safe and useful aromatherapy oils and the ailments and conditions they can be used to treat

The oils listed in this table are among the most widely used and readily available. Essential oils should not be applied to the skin undiluted or taken internally unless specifically prescribed by a medically qualified adviser.

EUCALYPTUS

YARROW

1. PEPPERMINT

This refreshing, clean-scented oil is beneficial for the digestive and respiratory systems. It is also reviving, and can help cure fatigue, headache and migraine.

2. YARROW

This balancing, healing oil is good for any form of inflammatory skin condition, and for indigestion and flatulence. Aromatherapists also use yarrow essential oil for its tonic, restorative and psychologically strengthening effects.

3. EUCALYPTUS

In a steam inhalation, eucalyptus is an excellent remedy for catarrh, sinusitis and throat infections. Diluted in carrier oil it can be dabbed on the skin as an insect repellent and to treat head lice.

4. FRANKINCENSE

Also known as olibanum, this deeply scented resinous oil makes a good inhalation for asthma as it calms the feeling of panic that goes with the attack, as well as soothing the mucous membranes. It is also a well-known beauty treatment for older skins.

5. GERANIUM

This oil has a lovely minty-rosy scent and is widely used in skin care. It treats a range of problems from acne, bruises and cellulitis to menopausal problems, PMS and nervous tension, and also repels mosquitoes.

6. GINGER

Ginger oil is warming and drying, and good for conditions involving phlegm, such as catarrh and an unsettled digestive system. It can be used in massage for arthritis and muscle pain. It is helpful for any form of nausea.

7. JASMINE

This luxurious oil is a perfect skin balancer. A few drops of the oil in the bath water counteract stress, fatigue and the effects of PMS, and calm dry skin as well as aches and pains, leaving you feeling uplifted and relaxed.

8. MANDARIN

A gentle, cheering oil, this is a tonic for the digestion and good for restoring appetite after illness. Can have a reviving and strengthening effect on the mood and is often liked by children.

GERANIUM

MANDARIN

11. NEROLI
Used in perfumery this orange-flower oil is soothing and uplifting, useful for anxiety, emotional problems and PMS. It is also good for dyspepsia of nervous origin and is used in skin care.

12. LAVENDER
One of the most widely used of all oils, lavender is healing and refreshing. It soothes sunburn, aids the healing of burns and skin injuries, and is used to treat eczema, fungal infections and irritated, flaking scalp. It can be used neat.

17. ROSE
Richly floral and feminine in scent, rose oil is good for female problems. It can help all kinds of menstrual irregularity and sexual problems, relieves anxiety and stress and is used by aromatherapists to treat liver congestion.

18. SANDALWOOD
Relaxing and comforting, sandalwood oil is used to treat dry coughs, and dry skin conditions such as eczema. It can also be helpful in cases of cystitis and diarrhoea.

9. ROSEMARY
This invigorating oil revives flagging energy and used in massage it will soothe tired, stiff muscles and menstrual pain. Inhalation helps to clear the head and cure headaches.

10. JUNIPER
Refreshing and cleansing, juniper treats water retention and can be helpful for cystitis. Aromatherapists use it for gout and rheumatism and a juniper bath has a reviving tonic effect. This oil should not be used during pregnancy.

13. CLARY SAGE
Many people find this a most uplifting scent that relieves anxiety and tension. The oil is good for itchy scalp, inflamed skin and muscular aches and pains.

14. LEMON
Antiseptic and refreshing, lemon oil can help to treat infectious diseases, especially feverish colds. It is good for the circulation and can also be helpful for migraine. In skin care it is a tonic for oily skins. Lemon juice can be inhaled for nosebleeds.

19. TEA TREE
Strongly antiseptic and antifungal, this is one of the most useful oils of all, and can be used undiluted. Treats cold sores, vaginal thrush, athlete's foot, boils and infected wounds, can be helpful in cystitis, and is used for infectious diseases.

20. YLANG-YLANG
Has a balancing influence on emotional disturbances and a sedative effect. Reputedly a powerful aphrodisiac and, with its balancing action, is beneficial for all kinds of skin in beauty treatment.

15. ROMAN CHAMOMILE
An ultra-soothing, warming and calming oil for eczema, skin rashes and insect bites, as well as joint and muscle pain, indigestion, and all kinds of headache or migraine. This oil is useful for children.

16. GRAPEFRUIT
Cheering and mind-clearing, grapefruit oil is used mainly as a mental and physical tonic. It is said to counteract jet lag and travel tiredness generally. It stimulates the digestive and lymphatic systems and is good for oily skin.

JASMINE

NEROLI

aromatherapy

This therapy was devised by **Dr Edward Bach**, a doctor, bacteriologist and homeopath who believed that illness derived from psychological and emotional conflict, and that remedies should be directed inwards rather than outwards at physical symptoms. In the 1930s he produced these remedies from plant material infused in springwater and they are popular today to take in times of stress.

bach flower remedies

USE

Bach Flower Remedies are intended for self-treatment of negative emotions to restore the equilibrium between mind and body necessary for good health. They are not intended to directly relieve any specific physical symptoms.

THE FACTS

THEORY

Dr Bach recognised that persistent stress resulting in negative emotions lowers our resistance to disease. Experience and studies have demonstrated that prolonged stress impairs the strength of the immune defence system and increases the risks of suffering from shingles, infectious illnesses and cancer. Bach also observed that a person's attitude to their illness had an effect on its progress and duration. Patients with different complaints yet with similar temperaments and outlooks would all respond to a particular remedy, while others suffering from the same physical complaint but differing dispositions needed different treatments. Thus Bach came to formulate the axiom: take no notice of the disease, think only of the personality of the one in distress.

Dr Bach left a lucrative private London practice to return home to Wales in search of a new healing system without any side-effects.

To take a remedy, simply place a couple of drops onto your tongue. If you prefer you could add a drop or two to a little springwater.

Except for Rescue Remedy, Rock Water (collected from a rocky stream) is the only other remedy that is not made from a wild flower.

While convinced that it was wrong to use poisonous animal, plant or mineral substances even in minute quantities, Bach remained aware that very dilute medicinal substances can stimulate the body's healing process.

A born healer, Bach believed that the key to genuine cures lay within the plant kingdom among special wild plants. He became so sensitive to nature that he was able to detect the effects of a flowering plant on the body, mind and spirit by placing a single petal on his tongue. Bach deduced that certain flowers were of a higher order, with greater curative power than 'ordinary' medicinal plants which heal the body at a biochemical level. True healers of the plant kingdom rectify imbalance within the psychological and spiritual spheres, catalysing negative emotions such as rage, apathy, fear and self-centredness into placidity, motivation, courage and awareness of the needs of others, thereby correcting the causes of disease at their fundamental source.

STATES OF MIND AND REMEDIES

Bach identified seven negative emotional states, subdivided into 38 negative feelings, each associated with a particular plant. He made up his flower remedies by floating fresh blossoms on the surface of bowls of fresh water for three hours, while being irradiated by sunlight. The water, he believed, picked up the essence of the plants. The vitalised liquid, carefully strained using twigs from the remedy plant to avoid other contaminants, formed the remedies' 'stock'. An equal volume of brandy was added, forming the mother tincture, and this in turn was diluted in a further quantity of brandy. The resulting liquid, the stock concentrate, is the form in which the remedies are sold.

There are 39 remedies – 37 from wild flowers, one from Rock Water (pure water from a rocky stream), and Rescue Remedy. It is usual to place a drop or two (dropper provided) on your tongue, or add to springwater. Examples include Beech Remedy for people who are critical and intolerant of others; Willow for those suffering from feelings of resentment or self-pity; and Gentian for anyone whose predominant emotion is one of despondency.

HOW THE REMEDIES WORK

Precisely how Bach Flower Therapy works is not fully understood, but the remedies seem to act at the vibrational level, on disturbances within the electromagnetic wave formation of our systems (see Homeopathy, page 196) that have been found to occur during mental and physical illness. The flower remedies can have a beneficial and remedial effect, and that this is not 'all in the mind' is evidenced by the response of injured or clinically shocked animals to Bach's Rescue Remedy, the only remedy made using more than one flower type (Cherry Plum, Clematis, Impatiens, Rock Rose and Star of Bethlehem).

Olive Remedy is often recommended for people who are exhausted, lethargic and drained of energy.

bach flower remedies

Acupuncture has been practised in China for thousands of years and is part of Traditional Chinese Medicine (TCM), which embodies important differences from, and similarities to, Western medicine. In common with the philosophies underlying holistic therapies already described in this book, TCM recognises an elemental 'life force' that it terms ch'i or qi (pronounced as 'chee').

acupuncture

QI

Qi runs freely through the body when a person is in a state of harmony (healthy). It becomes obstructed when their biological, mental and spiritual faculties are unbalanced – when the two opposite, complementary principles, yin and yang, are out of synchrony with one another, due to poor diet, stress or lifestyle.

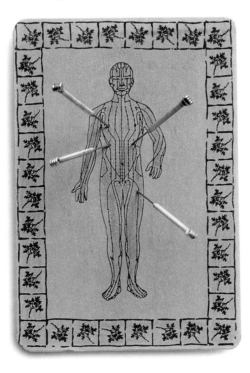

This meridian map shows the main meridians along which the acupuncture points, high energy sites of the human body, are located.

THE FACTS

OBJECTIVE
The art and objective of acupuncture is to restore a person's natural balance by removing the blockages that impede the free passage of qi energy, believed to run throughout the body along invisible lines called meridians, until disharmony triggers symptoms. Fifty-nine meridians are recognised in acupuncture, and there are around 1500 acupuncture points – specific high-energy-potential sites along the meridians where qi is most likely to become obstructed, and where stimulation with specially designed needles is most likely to reinstate the free flow of qi.

YIN AND YANG
Western medicine does not appear to have an equivalent of the polar opposites yin and yang, unless it is the theory of humours (see page 190). The latter, however, tend to be identified only within living organisms, in contrast to yin and yang, which the experienced therapist can identify everywhere he looks, in both animate and inanimate objects.

Examples of their manifestation include male and female, darkness and light, night and day, heat and cold, dryness and wetness, activity and passivity, and heaven and earth. Within a healthy person, neither yin-ness nor yang-ness holds sway: they coexist in a state of dynamic equilibrium, forever active, potent and fluctuating slightly, but each, at all times, the other's perfect counterpoint.

Their harmonious interplay is disrupted when, for instance, yin – regarded as female, dark and cold, is inadvertently encouraged to gain ascendancy over yang, which is male, light and hot. Dietary imprudence is a common cause for this, although it differs from the Western concept of overindulgence in salt, sugar or animal fat, or too little water or fibre; rather, it consists of eating, for instance, too many cool, bitter and salty foods at the expense of hot, sweet, pungent yang foods.

In a hot, dry climate, the strength of yin may be weakened, and eating extra fruit would be a possible way of rectifying the problem. Someone from a cold northern country, however, spending Christmas in Australia would be predominantly yin to start off with, because he/she originates from a cold, damp climate. But in the hot, moist environment, he/she may be tempted to eat large quantities of melons, paw paws or mangoes, pushing yin energies into excess and triggering the cold, moist diarrhoea that mars so many holidays.

THE FIVE ELEMENTS
The correspondences between yin and yang are, in fact, extremely complex, and balanced by the other important theory in TCM, that of the elements. Five of these exist – wood, fire, earth, metal and water – in contrast to the four underpinning Western (Greek) philosophy, namely, earth, air, fire and water. Each element has many associations, ranging from organs of the body to human sounds, the seasons, colours and tastes.

Water, for instance, relates to winter, a salty flavour, fear, and the body parts ear, hair, bone, kidney and bladder. TCM practitioners often look for the cause of illnesses in a related element: weakness of the liver (wood), for example, may be caused by deficiencies in the kidneys (water); a weak stomach (earth) may be caused by over-exuberant wood (liver) failing to be controlled by deficient metal (lungs).

DIAGNOSIS
Treatment, of course, has to be preceded by diagnosis, which is arrived at in a manner equally alien to the Western mind, related as it is to five basic colours and five smells.

acupuncture

acupuncture

The five elements of TCM, wood, fire, water, metal and earth, are balanced against the theory of yin and yang to provide an appropriate diagnosis.

acupuncture

Pulse diagnosis is also a highly sophisticated art; six pulses are identified in each wrist, one for each of the twelve main meridians and each associated with a vital organ. Each of the 12 pulses is held, in turn, to have 24 different qualities, which collectively supply information about which meridians are blocked (preventing the free flow of qi), and whether yin or yang is in excess.

The initial consultation may last about an hour or perhaps longer. The therapist is likely to enquire about the person's past and present medical history, family history, lifestyle and stress factors. He/she will also note the condition of the person's hair, and finger and toenails, his or her skin colour, timbre of voice, body odour, and the state of the tongue, eyes, respiration, emotions and posture.

TREATMENT
Students of TCM may devote many years to the study of acupuncture, not least to the location of the meridians (which tend to be far easier to find on certain people than on others), and of the many acupuncture points, all of which have to be learned by heart until memory and experience makes them become second nature. The acupuncture points themselves are located by touch or by an instrument that measures the Chinese inch, which actually differs from one patient to another.

The sterile needles (2–6 of them) are inserted and left for 20–30 minutes, during which time they may be left undisturbed, pumped gently up and down, or twiddled around to increase the potency of the stimulation.

Alternatively, a low-frequency electric current may be used, administered via a blunt pointed instrument that does not puncture the skin. This is especially likely to be used by Western doctors who have been trained in aspects of TCM, and in the case of patients who are terrified of needles. Interestingly, though, many recipients of traditional acupuncture claim not to have felt a thing while the needles were being inserted. This may be linked with attitude to the disorder and general (optimistic or pessimistic) outlook on life, for those who feel nothing when the needles are used often make the best recovery.

When further treatment reinforcement is required, moxibustion may be performed. After the needles have been inserted, a small cone of moxa (dried mugwort) is placed on top of the needles' heads (which are small blocks offering a ready platform for this practice). Small card discs are arranged around the insertion points to protect the skin from falling ash, and the moxa is then ignited, which generates enough heat down the needle for a pleasant warmth to be felt.

The number of acupuncture treatments required depends upon both the nature of the disorder and the responsiveness of the patient. Six is a common number, but one is sometimes sufficient and as many as 20 or 30 may be required to help relieve a long-standing condition in

The heat of a moxa stick is used to relieve pain in an injured shoulder by moving blood and qi from the affected area.

someone in poor health. The immediate effect of treatment varies between great relaxation and drowsiness and a feeling of increased alacrity.

USE
Conditions for which acupuncture is helpful include arthritis and both upper and lower back pain (except where severe structural damage has occurred), recurrent headaches and migraines, recovery from a stroke, trigeminal neuralgia and the nerve pain that can follow shingles (see page 112). Others include high blood pressure, addictive disorders such as smoking, drinking and drug dependency, asthma and eczema, hiatus hernia and stress-related indigestion.

Acupuncture can be used to treat a broad range of serious conditions, such as migraines, arthritis and nerve pain.

acupuncture

Also known as compression massage and zone therapy, reflexology is a system of diagnosis and treatment based upon the understanding that the human body is divisible into energy zones corresponding with sensitive areas of the feet. Today, reflexology is one of the most popular of all the available complementary therapies.

reflexology

PRECAUTIONS

- Ensure that you see a qualified practitioner
- Avoid reflexology if you have heart or circulation problems
- Do not visit a reflexologist if you have a severe viral or fungal infection, especially on the feet

Reflexology can be especially helpful if you suffer from stress or anxiety.

THE FACTS

HISTORY

Foot massage has been practised for thousands of years. However, the concept of zone therapy was developed by a physician, Dr W Fitzgerald, and his colleagues in the United States during the 1920s. It was elaborated into an alternative system of diagnosis and treatment by a therapist named Eunice Ingham, who mapped out the distribution of representative body areas on the soles, sides and tops of both feet. An English nurse, Doreen E Bayley, studied under Eunice Ingham and later set up the Bayley School of Reflexology in the UK.

THEORY

Reflexology describes ten discrete energy pathways in the body – reminiscent of the meridians of Traditional Chinese Medicine (TCM). After running throughout the body delivering energy (the 'life force') to every area and organ, the pathways end in energy terminals in the feet, where they are examined by palpation (pressure) of the therapist's fingers. As in TCM, illnesses are attributed to blockages of these channels, mainly due to inner tension and chronic anxiety, anger, despair, jealousy, hatred and other negative emotions.

Areas requiring work are identifiable at the time of examination by both the patient, who finds pressure on affected energy terminals very uncomfortable, and the therapist, who detects a crystalline or granular feel to the flesh in the affected areas.

TREATMENT

The therapist normally takes a case history, although some prefer to diagnose 'feet first' and do not seek details of symptoms before making their diagnosis. It is normal for the feet generally to feel tender when health is poor, but a grainy feel to certain areas indicates blocked energy channels, and poor circulation of the life force. They also pinpoint the areas in which stimulation is needed.

The therapist compresses the tender foot areas and gently but firmly breaks down the crystalline deposits by massaging the areas with the fingertips. He/she may first encourage the patient to relax by gently rotating the feet round and round, clockwise and then anticlockwise, then repeating this motion with each large toe in turn. He/she then works on each foot, starting always with the left, partly because the main vessel of the lymphatic system, the thoracic duct, is stimulated by this manoeuvre to release toxic residues. Once the deposits have been worn away, they are absorbed by the body and, being water soluble, disposed of in sweat and/or urine.

The massage may be gentle and superficial, or very strong and aimed at the deep tissues of the foot, inevitably causing some discomfort and sometimes sharp pain. The nature of this pain is often described as similar to that felt when a strained muscle in spasm is massaged into a state of relaxation.

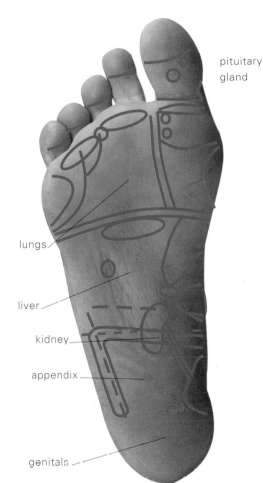

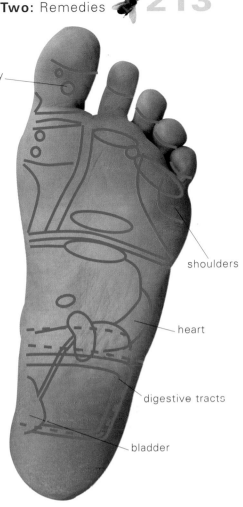

pituitary gland

lungs

liver

kidney

appendix

genitals

shoulders

heart

digestive tracts

bladder

Each part of the reflex map on the feet relates to a particular part of the body.

USE

How reflexology achieves its results is not understood; but practising therapists claim that massage manipulates the body's complex stimulus-response system, and that its effects are mediated by electrical impulses generated by pressure upon the foot. Reflexology is said to be able to relieve most disorders; it is not, however, a panacea for all ills, and does not aim solely at the relief of symptoms. Reflexology is holistic in its approach, because it controls and harmonises the energy flow throughout the entire body, producing increased well-being and vitality. Conditions for which reflexology has proved especially helpful include backache, hayfever, sinusitis, certain kidney disorders, hiccups, menopausal hot flushes, arthritis and asthma.

reflexology

Osteopathy, from the Greek *osteon* (bone) and *pathos* (disease), is a manipulative therapy and a total healing system. In common with other holistic therapies, osteopathic theory recognises the body's innate self-healing powers. While other therapies consider illness to be triggered by nutritional or psychological defects, osteopathy centres upon structural defects in muscles, nerves and bones.

osteopathy

PRECAUTIONS

- Check that your osteopath is qualified and registered with the appropriate organisation
- Osteopathy is not for some disorders: cancer, bone diseases, fracture, nerve or spinal cord damage

Certain problems, such as headaches, can be relieved by manipulation of the neck joints.

THE FACTS

HISTORY

Like Dr. Hahnemann, the inventor of homeopathy, and Dr. Bach, who developed the flower remedies, Andrew Taylor Still, an army doctor in the American Civil War, was deeply disillusioned with the shortcomings of contemporary medical practice. What concerned him most were the unrefined medicines then in use, many of which caused toxic side effects and left the sufferer worse than ever. He had to stand by helplessly as his three young children died of spinal meningitis – suggesting to him the important role of the spinal cord in health.

The realisation that physical manipulation could achieve better results in non-structural complaints (than current medical practice) without harming the patient occurred to Dr. Still after he managed to save the life of a child suffering from dysentery, an illness characterised by profuse diarrhoea and dehydration, which, at the time, claimed many lives. While examining his patient, Dr. Still noticed that the child's lower back and the back of his neck and head were hot, while his abdomen, forehead and nose were cold. In common with other doctors at the time, Dr. Still knew very little about 'flux' (as dysentery was then known), and not a lot more about the spinal cord or how it worked. Instinctively, however, he began to press and rub the area around the base of the child's skull, in an attempt to 'push some of the heat back into the cold places', as he put it.

As he did this manipulation on the sick child, Dr. Still discovered that there were rigid and loose places throughout the child's spine, and much congestion in the lumbar region. After some gentle physical manoeuvres aimed at correcting these problems, Dr. Still left the child overnight in the care of his mother, who reported the following morning that the boy had turned the corner: whereafter he made a full recovery.

Remembering how he had relieved his own headaches as a child by cracking his neck joints, Dr. Still began to manipulate his patients' spinal and other joints instead of prescribing them potions. He later claimed to have cured a further 17 cases of flux, all without drugs, and spinal manipulation is still used with considerable benefit in many infectious illnesses.

THEORY

Through research, trial and error, Dr. Still discovered that similar spinal lesions existed in many conditions, convincing him that understanding the structure of the body in relationship to its use was the only viable foundation for understanding disease. He came to believe that good health depends upon the unhampered, normal functioning of the spinal column, and that all disorders originate from one or more areas in misalignment.

Dr. Still explained this by pointing out that the spinal column encloses the spinal cord, which is inevitably affected when part of the bony cage around it is displaced in some way. The spinal cord, in turn, works in close association with the autonomic nervous system (ANS), which is responsible for regulating many of our bodily functions such as respiration, digestion, urination and heartbeat.

Dr. Still formulated the idea of identifying trouble areas within the vertebral column, and correcting any misalignment by manipulation. In so doing, he maintained, he was freeing the body's innate self-correcting mechanism to solve the problem.

This relating of the liberation of the 'life force' to the mechanical relief of pressure upon the ANS is the closest holistic therapists came for decades to identifying concrete links between their innovative, somewhat esoteric practices, and the basic facts of anatomy and physiology (how the body works) as deduced from observation and experience.

NATUROPATHIC OSTEOPATHY

Some osteopaths combine the treatment with naturopathy, using its main principles of a wholesome diet, drinking plenty of water and ensuring the body gets lots of clean, fresh air, and paying attention to a person's emotional and mental state.

Osteopaths aim to identify problem areas in the spinal column and correct them through manipulation.

osteopathy

osteopathy

A newborn baby's skull plates are soft enough to be manipulated easily by a cranial osteopath.

One form of treatment used by osteopaths includes soft tissue manipulation.

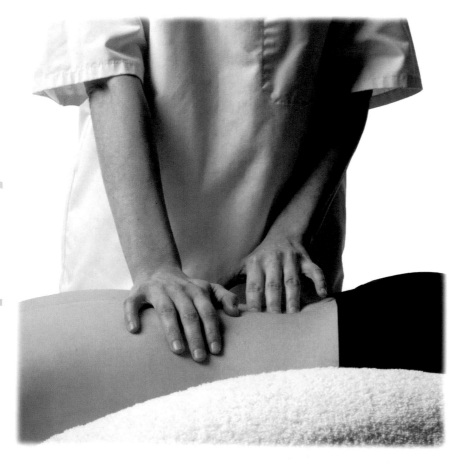

However, the concept of such changes in the spine – originally described as 'osteopathic lesions' – evoked such vitriolic ridicule from both medical and non-medical critics that they were eventually renamed 'areas of somatic (i.e. body-related) dysfunction'.

Like many innovators who have lastingly benefited humankind, Dr. Still was an eccentric and a visionary who weathered a perpetual shower of contempt and abuse from colleagues who were jealous of his success and growing reputation. But by the time he died in 1917, there were more than five thousand osteopathic physicians practising in the US.

TREATMENT

During the course of diagnosis and treatment, osteopaths utilise a wide variety of techniques, some gentle and others more vigorous, which, when properly applied, should have no side effects. Compared with nutritionally and psychologically oriented therapies, osteopathy often brings rapid results, since it is generally easier to correct a structural problem located in the neck, for example, than deep-seated malnutrition requiring months of corrective nutritional medicine and dietary change.

In practice, osteopathy fulfils two quite different roles. The first, comparable to physiotherapy, supplies limited care to patients with back and joint injuries or disorders, working to relieve sciatica, for instance. The second supplies total patient care, helping to maintain health and treating any disorder from which the patient may suffer.

USE

In theory osteopathy can be used to relieve and/or cure any illness, but it is particularly suitable for the following disorders: asthma, hyperventilation and panic attacks, many long-standing infectious illnesses, palpitations and other causes of an irregular pulse, chronic fatigue syndrome, irritable bowel syndrome, nervous colitis and gastric hyperacidity (note: osteopathy can help reduce the amount of hydrochloric acid released by the stomach lining – an important factor in peptic ulceration – and possibly relieve ulcer symptoms, but cannot remove a hiatus hernia once one has formed).

Osteopathy also helps alleviate numerous problems such as migraines, tension headaches, stress-related symptoms, painful and heavy periods, lumbago, sciatica, arthritis, frozen shoulder, carpal tunnel syndrome and various other forms of neuralgia.

CRANIAL OSTEOPATHY

This specialised form of osteopathy includes the bones of the cranium, the part of the skull that surrounds the brain, in its assessment and treatment of mechanical defects. It attempts to normalise the bones of the skull (which fit together in a tongue-and-groove fashion), and the tough bands of fibrous tissue named fascia that divide and support the brain within. As it does so, it influences the flow of the cerebrospinal fluid found in the hollows of the brain and around the spinal cord.

At the end of the 19th century, William G. Sutherland, a pupil of Dr. Still, discovered a degree of movement between the interlocked skull bones. He also demonstrated a rhythmic expansion and contraction occurring all over the skull, independent of heartbeat and respiration but comparable to the expansion and contraction of the chest and diaphragm during breathing. This 'primary respiratory mechanism' involves the skull bones, connective fascia, the spinal column and also the sacrum (the thick, wedge-shaped bone forming the back of the pelvis).

Slight movement within these structures facilitates the circulation of the blood and cerebrospinal fluid throughout intricate channels in the fascia and can be felt by a sensitive, trained hand. As it traverses these channels, the cerebrospinal fluid transports vital hormones both to and from the body's master gland – the pituitary gland, located at the base of the brain – which relies upon the efficiency of this mechanism for normal function.

Osteopaths maintain that trauma to the skull and spine, such as whiplash injury, dental extraction, bumps on the head or base of the spine, even new dentures, can interfere with this mechanism and cause local disorders such as Menière's disease (see page 156), tinnitus (ringing in the ears), visual disturbance, migraine and other headaches and difficulty in chewing. Remote effects can include sudden changes in the body due to hormonal dysfunction.

Treatment is carried out by gentle pressure, which is applied to the skull and areas of the pelvis. Disorders that have responded positively to cranial osteopathy include multiple sclerosis, rheumatoid arthritis, fluid retention, asthma and allergies, as well as distortions to the skull sometimes suffered by newborn babies. Some practitioners also claim a degree of success in cases of autism and many other childhood mental disorders.

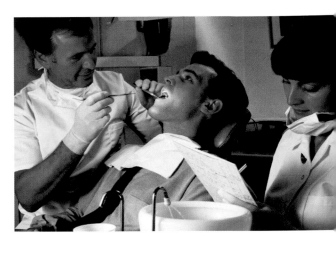

Osteopaths believe that any trauma to the skull or spine, including some forms of dental treatment, could cause localised disorders.

Disorders such as behavioural problems in children may be relieved by cranial osteopathy.

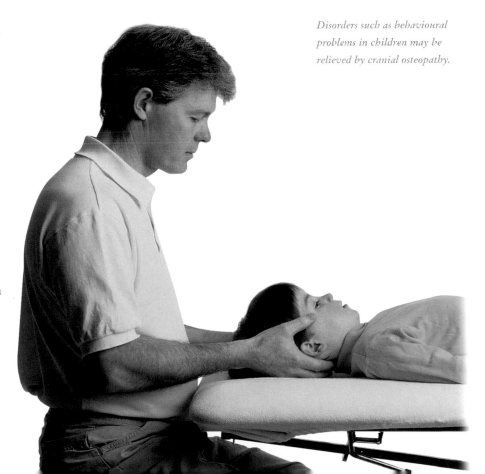

osteopathy

The word 'chiropractic' comes from the Greek *cheiro* (hand), and *praktikos* (manipulation). Although superficially having much in common with osteopathy, chiropractic is defined by the British Chiropractic Association as 'an independent branch of medicine specialising in the diagnosis and treatment of mechanical disorders of the joints, especially those of the spine, and their effects on the nervous system'.

chiropractic

chiropractic

PREVENTING LOWER BACK PAIN

- Exercise regularly.
- When lifting, keep objects close to the body.
- Put work tables at a comfortable level.
- Use a chair with good lower-back support.
- Wear comfortable, low-heeled shoes.
- Place a pillow or rolled-up towel behind the small of the back when driving long distances.

THE FACTS

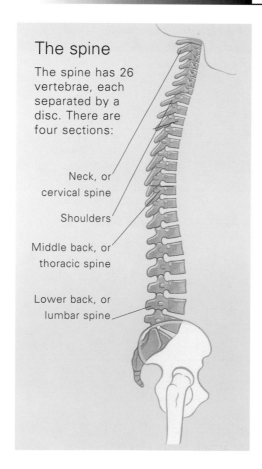

The spine

The spine has 26 vertebrae, each separated by a disc. There are four sections:

Neck, or cervical spine

Shoulders

Middle back, or thoracic spine

Lower back, or lumbar spine

HISTORY

Like osteopathy, the practice of chiropractic healing was developed in the United States towards the end of the 19th century, being founded in 1895 by Daniel D Palmer. A holistic therapist, Palmer had investigated the new science of osteopathy, but differed from Andrew Still in his opinion about the roles of the spine and nerves in health and disease. Daniel Palmer's first inkling that manipulation bore any relevance to non-structural defects came after he managed to restore the hearing of a man who had been deaf for many years. A janitor in the building in which Palmer practised mesmerism (the forerunner of hypnotherapy) and magnetic healing (which later became therapeutic touch), Harvey Lillard's difficulty in hearing manifested itself after he had been bending over awkwardly and felt something 'go' suddenly in his back. Palmer located the trouble spot, which he identified as an incorrectly positioned vertebra, repositioned the bone, and – apparently miraculously – cured Lillard's problem. He devoted the rest of his life to researching and developing the therapy that resulted from this event.

THEORY

Chiropractic theory identifies joint lesions called 'subluxations' – partial dislocations involving biochemical malfunction such as poor blood and oxygen supply, nutritional deprivation and inefficient nervous control. It acknowledges vitality or the 'life force' in terms of a 'universal intelligence' which directs the self-healing ability present in all living organisms. It considers the spine and nervous system to be the vehicles of this intelligence, so that even the most minute misalignment of a vertebra can compromise the operation of a nerve, interfering with the correct function of the organ or body area it supplies. Chiropractors see their task essentially as the liberation of trapped nervous tissue, thereby removing obstacles to the freely flowing universal intelligence.

The scientific explanation for chiropractic's efficiency is that misaligned vertebrae may impinge upon and adversely affect normal neurological functioning. Studies have suggested that chiropractic may influence neurohormonal control of the body. In other words, malfunctioning nerve impulses (triggered in an area of the central nervous system close to a misaligned joint) may reduce brain signals regulating the manufacture and release of endorphins and other 'mood chemicals'. These elevate the mood and raise our pain threshold, thereby making us less perceptive to pain at a particular level.

Pain is the body's SOS signal and, identified early enough, it can and will respond to chiropractic manipulation aimed at freeing the body's own life force. Chiropractic is generally considered to be most useful for pain and other disorders that arise before the body has lapsed into a state of identifiable disease, and conservative practitioners hold that when an identifiable pathological condition develops, patients benefit most from the swift intervention of an orthodox medical practitioner. More liberal chiropractors, however, are willing to treat certain acute conditions just after they start, looking beyond the symptoms to the root causes extant before the underlying problem generated the disease proper.

TREATMENT

A chiropractor will take a full case history from his patient, including a history of the symptoms, past medical history including all injuries, the amount and types of exercise taken, stress factors, occupation and relaxation techniques. This is followed by a physical examination, paying particular attention to posture to pick up hints of malpositioned joints. The history of muscular and bony injury from falls, strains and sprains is important, as are job-related and postural defects that may be causing abnormal joint action or muscle tone. Pain in a body area can indicate neurological disturbances, congestion (of blood vessels and their supply), mechanical faults and physical or psychological ailments.

The chiropractor tests the patient's reflexes, assesses his or her tissue tone and moves and rotates all relevant joints. Tests are then performed to elicit signs of nerve inflammation, and finally X-rays are arranged if relevant.

POSTURE

Posture is important to chiropractic diagnosis:

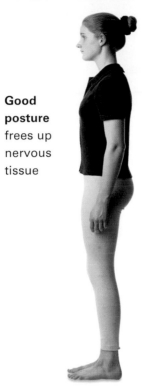

Good posture frees up nervous tissue

Bad posture can lead to pain later on

chiropractic

chiropractic

Before deciding upon a treatment, a chiropractor will assess a person's weight, exercise regime, diet and posture.

Advice is also offered on weight reduction if applicable, suitable exercise, diet, posture, beneficial lifestyle changes and relaxation. Where massage is included in the treatment picture of either chiropractic or osteopathy, aromatherapy oils are frequently employed, and referrals made as appropriate to other holistic practitioners.

USE

Although most patients visiting a chiropractor are seeking treatment for a bad back, many have other complaints such as neck pain, headaches, sciatica and other leg pain, hip and knee problems, shoulder, wrist and arm pain, pins and needles, numbness, and pain and stiffness in the elbows, ankles and feet. Migraine, sinusitis, catarrh, digestive disorders, menstrual problems and constipation are also frequently treated.

With regard to infection, chiropractic does not contradict the received wisdom that illnesses such as flu, colds and cystitis are due to bacteria and viruses, but it does stress the idea of a 'susceptible host' – i.e. an individual predisposed to catch a disease (as we would say, due to an impaired immune defence system). Heredity, environmental pollution, poor nutrition, subluxations (see page 219), inherited weaknesses, stress factors and learned responses to stress all contribute to enhanced susceptibility.

CHIROPRACTIC AND OSTEOPATHY

Chiropractic is well recognised in the UK and US, and is far more widely established than osteopathy in Australia. Both are holistic therapies regarding man as an individual with physical, spiritual and psychological needs, and aim to cure causes rather than simply alleviate symptoms. Practical differences between them include the chiropractors' greater inclination to include X-rays in their investigations of a patient's disorder, and their using possibly fewer joint mobilising and soft tissue techniques (manipulation of the soft skeletal structures such as fibrous connective tissue).

Chiropractic also utilises less leverage than osteopathy, with therapeutic force generally being applied close to the mechanical fault. It has no equivalent of osteopathy's high velocity thrust, a dramatic and superficially alarming manoeuvre involving a quick 'hugging' motion applied to the patient's torso as he lies curled up on his side on the treatment couch. Although, like the simplest procedure, this can be dangerous and/or painful in the hands of an amateur, it causes no pain whatever when performed by an experienced professional. Chiropractic is indisputably less dramatic, and is likely to be applied, for example, to two adjacent vertebrae, utilising a swift pushing movement to alter their relative positions.

Chiropractic theory emphasises the nerves and the organs they supply, while osteopathic theory focuses ultimately upon the blood vessels and the circulation as these are affected by structural malpositions. Practitioners of each therapy adhere closely to the traditional explanations of how these systems work, while others relegate these to the realm of

historical interest. Concessions have of course been made to the traditional scientific explanations of disease, in order to expand acceptance of each of these therapies, but many GPs in Britain study and practise them without bothering too much about the fundamental theories as long as they continue to achieve effective results in their patients.

Chiropractors believe that environmental pollution, poor nutrition and stress factors all contribute to making people susceptible to various diseases.

Chiropractic healing uses much less force than osteopathy, focusing on the nerves and the organs they supply.

chiropractic

Massage was used for healing purposes up to 15,000 years ago, according to the evidence from rock paintings, papyri and oral traditions. It was integral to ancient Greek medicine and it was enjoyed by the Romans as part of hydrotherapy (see Naturopathy, page 184). According to the historian Plutarch, Julius Caesar indulged in frequent sessions.

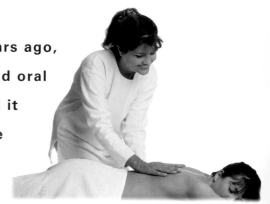

remedial massage

USES

Massage helps with a range of problems, including:
- Asthma
- Circulatory problems
- Musculo-skeletal disorders
- Stress

Petrissage is performed with the pads of the thumbs and the palms of the hands. It is especially effective for relieving muscular tension.

THE FACTS

AN UNDESERVED REPUTATION
Massage is effective both as a reliever of muscular pain and a stimulator of sexual pleasure. It was this second aspect that lost it its original approval by the early Christian Church and which, today, casts a shadow on this healing art because of its association with massage parlours. In the East, however, massage or therapeutic touch flourished during the T'ang dynasty in China (618–907CE), in eighth-century Japan, and in India, where regular lymphatic massage remains a valued aspect of total health care. Family massage is a regular event and includes all ages, from great-grandparents to young children, playing a similar role to the Sunday lunch of Western civilisation.

SWEDISH MASSAGE
Today's link between massage, Sweden and Swedish masseurs can be traced back to Henry Peter Ling, a student at the University of Stockholm during the early 19th century, who invented special stroking – this involved constant pressure while the hands glide over the skin – that has a sedating or relaxing effect on the main body muscles. Kneading, vibration and tapping or clapping techniques are aimed at stimulating and relaxing the body in whatever ways were desired.

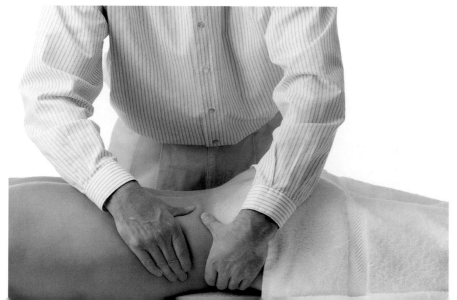

Massage techniques

There are four main techniques: effleurage, petrissage, friction and tapotement, as well as several others.

EFFLEURAGE
Light stroking, gentle and firm. Centripetal effleurage moves towards the heart and stimulates the circulation; rotary or spinal effleurage stimulates the smaller blood vessels in the skin. It is often used to start a massage session because gentle stroking relaxes the superficial muscles, giving the therapist access to the deeper tissues if required. Oil is often used, and aromatherapy often combined with this, adding, for example, a few drops of clary sage or chamomile which the patient inhales and absorbs through the skin, to induce a feeling of drowsiness and tranquillity.

PETRISSAGE
Deep and superficial firm, frictional stroking. The soft tissues are kneaded like dough, and it is particularly appropriate in cases of fibrositis, for example, when the toothache-like pain in small knotted clusters of fibrous tissue along the inner rim of the shoulder blades is relieved, perhaps for the first time in years.

FRICTION
Also known as frottage, this consists of small, circular movements against the bone, using a reasonable degree of pressure, and is aimed at the deeper tissues to relax muscular tension. This is also suitable for fibrositis.

TAPOTEMENT
This involves stimulatory hacking movements to improve muscle tone and strength. This is useful when a group of muscles has been out of action during an illness or following trauma.

Other techniques include:

SIMPLE TOUCH
Placing the hand so that it fits the curvature or other shape of a part of the body.

BRUSHING
Light fingertip contact performed slowly to spread rhythmic sensations over the body, and frequently employed as a finishing touch.

NERVE COMPRESSION
Firm pressure aimed at relieving knots or pain at nerve points.

RANGE OF MOTIONS
Passive exercising by rotating, extending and flexing the joints to maintain and improve flexibility and maximise the secretion of naturally formed joint lubricant fluid.

GENERAL COMPRESSION STROKES
Kneading or utilising friction, designed to improve the circulation and remove cellular waste.

PERCUSSION
This soothes the nerves, tones and invigorates the skin, and positively influences the vital organs and tissues.

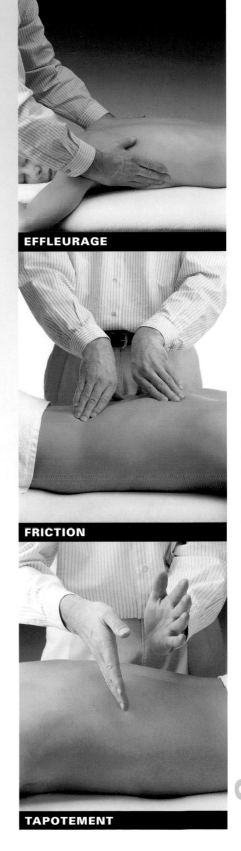

EFFLEURAGE

FRICTION

TAPOTEMENT

remedial massage

remedial massage

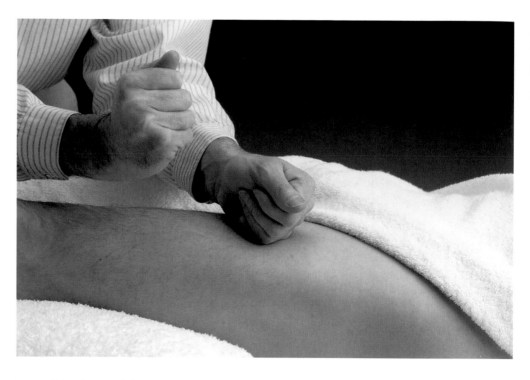

Right: Percussion is a massage technique developed to soothe nerves, and tone and invigorate the skin.

Far right: Neck and shoulder massages help release tension, which is often found between the shoulder blades.

Professional sportsmen and women have regular muscle massages to ensure that their bodies are in peak condition.

Peter Ling's special massage techniques quickly became extremely popular throughout Europe, and by the time Queen Victoria of England ascended to the throne in 1837, massage had become an essential aspect of health-care therapies of that time in the UK.

THEORY

Massaging the back (the most common area for which non-sports-related massage is sought) stimulates the sympathetic nervous system (one of the two main divisions of the autonomic nervous system): it speeds up the pulse, respiration and skin temperature, and elevates blood pressure (desirable in people who suffer from low blood pressure, chronic fatigue and depression). Gentle massage, on the other hand, stimulates the parasympathetic nervous system, lowering the heartbeat, encouraging the digestive processes, and freeing painful spasms and knots from tense muscles.

Correctly applied massage boosts the circulation of the blood without straining the heart. Safe aerobic exercise does this better, of course, and offers additional benefits such as normal weight maintenance, reduced levels of cholesterol in the blood, and improved functioning of heart and lungs. But there is no doubt of the benefits of massage, and therapeutic touch can be used after a debilitating

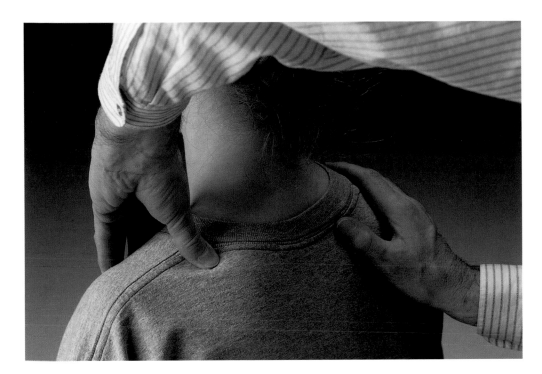

Baby benefits Babies, children and teenagers (if they will allow it) all benefit considerably from being massaged. It has been shown that babies who receive a regular massage put on weight more rapidly after birth than those who do not. Certainly, babies who are massaged seem to be more content and to suffer less from irritability and episodes of colic. (Look out for baby massage classes at your local gym or leisure centre – make sure that these are run by reputable massage therapists).

Physical bonding Massage can also improve the bonding process between a baby, its siblings and its parents, as physical contact is strengthened between them. Massage may help a baby or child develop a positive body image and help teenagers come to terms with their changing bodies. It will also help them to accept their body for what it is.

Stress relief Teenagers will also benefit from being massaged when they are going through stressful times at school or college – during the exam period, for example.

illness, for example, or for people with disabilities for whom a brisk walk or daily swim is not an option.

TREATMENT

Massage is frequently recommended as part of a wider detoxification programme. Skin-brushing (usually self-administered) consists of brushing your (dry) skin all over with a skinbrush or loofah, using firm but gentle sweeping strokes, starting in the area of the legs and feet and working up to the chest and shoulders and back of the neck. This encourages the skin's natural toxin-excreting function, and energises the lymphatic system (a major transport system for toxins from their site of origin to the exterior, from every area of the body).

In addition, as tight, knotted muscles are relieved of their spasm and their blood supply improved by professional therapeutic massage, excess tissue fluid containing the breakdown substances of metabolism (natural toxins) is absorbed and relieved of its toxic burden by the lymphatics, relieving bloating due to water retention. This invigorates the immune defence system (because it has less toxic waste to deal with), which is then free to combat inflammation, infection and any allergens to which the patient may be susceptible.

This cleansing effect is especially important to the chronically sick and disabled, who are unable to exercise; and to athletes who experience pain in overused muscles after a strenuous workout, due to a build-up of lactic acid following the metabolism of glycogen stored in the muscles and liver and utilised during exercise.

CAUTION

Massage should not be used on patients suffering from fever, or from acute inflammation such as that caused by infection or rheumatoid arthritis. Also postpone a massage session if you have recently had a heart attack or suffer from heart failure, deep vein thrombosis, an embolism and severe skin rash due to infection or any other cause.

remedial massage

The Alexander Technique is a health system aimed at correcting poor posture and body movement, with a view to combating physical and mental stress and their effects. It is given as a series of lessons by a qualified teacher, during which the client learns a new approach to skeletal, muscular and nerve function that will optimise health and well-being.

the alexander technique

KEY TO GOOD BREATHING

- Breathing should not be forced.
- Breathing through the nose ensures air is moist and warm before reaching the lungs.
- Deep breathing is linked to muscle toning.
- Breathing is affected by the relationship between the head, neck and back.

Using a full-length mirror you can see if your body posture is straight. Your spine should have a gentle 's' shape – neither over-arched nor flat.

THE FACTS

HISTORY AND THEORY

The Alexander Technique was devised by an Australian actor, Frederick Matthias Alexander, who experienced the relatively uncommon complaint *globus hystericus*, a form of voice loss. He found that he started to lose his voice when on stage – or when he even thought about reciting in public. *Globus hystericus* is actually a hysterical voice loss due to extreme performance anxiety, similar to a stammer, when the person gets 'stuck' with a word or syllable and, for an agonising few seconds, can get no further.

Alexander observed himself in a mirror when reciting, to see what happened. He noticed that he automatically pulled back his head and tightened his throat muscles, and, progressing to a three-way mirror, he further studied his posture, balance and movement. He corrected his head and neck position each time he was about to recite and, although the new, more relaxed stance felt odd, he persisted with it until he found his confidence (and performance voice) returning in leaps and bounds. His hoarseness disappeared, his weakened voice grew stronger, and he felt healthier and more clear-headed than he had done for a long time.

Alexander spent nine years studying himself and his movements, eventually observing and working with others. His observation that

people shorten their necks when startled led to the foundation of his theory and technique – that the head, neck and upper and lower back must be in dynamic equilibrium with each other for maximum lengthening of the spine and optimum energy and health. He developed a method of retraining the body to adopt healthier postures after years of inhibited movements and spinal contortions.

Alexander moved to London in 1904, establishing a progressive practice and later a training school for teachers of the Alexander Technique. He toured and taught in both England and the United States. Famous people whom Frederick Alexander treated (successfully) included George Bernard Shaw, Aldous Huxley and Archbishop William Temple.

Studies of his findings were later made by an American professor, Frank Jones, and an English doctor, Wilfred Barlow. The former used special photographic techniques and X-rays to capture the differences between observed, habitual movement, and movement under the training and guidance of Alexander's teaching. Dr Barlow examined the connections between misuse of the body (in poor

posture as defined by Alexander) and common medical disorders such as high blood pressure, rheumatism, arthritis, back pain and irritable bowel syndrome. Their findings supported Alexander's claims, and acceptance of his technique grew among the medical profession and the public. Today the Alexander technique is popular with performing artists, and is often included on drama courses.

BENEFITS

Always being aware of the position of your head, neck and spine.
Revealing bad habits.
Gaining freedom of movement with the correct use of the body.
Being aware of undue tension in the muscles.

If you do have to spend long hours working at a computer screen, ensure that your posture is straight.

the alexander technique

the alexander technique

Holding the neck in an awkward position for prolonged periods can lead to headaches, fatigue or even feeling faint.

TREATMENT

Treatment usually starts with the therapist taking a full medical history, noting past and present illnesses and/or injuries, family weaknesses, allergies, lifestyle, occupation and postures adopted during it (for example, sitting for hours in front of a computer), plus exercise and relaxation methods, if any. The therapist takes special note of the client's general posture and gait (how she carries herself while getting up, sitting down, etc.), signs of stress and tension, unconscious mannerisms, and overall appearance of health or lack of it.

The client may be asked to lie flat, with knees bent and head supported. The therapist will then make some adjustments to the client's position and help him to his feet in order to make him aware of what the optimum body position feels like. Many people feel vaguely uncomfortable when asked to lie on an examination or treatment couch for the first time, which manifests in arching the back and tensing torso muscles. All this is noted by the therapist, who may then discuss the subject of 'trust' and some

of our physical and emotional defence mechanisms for dealing with feeling vulnerable. The rest of the session will be spent standing or sitting while the therapist adjusts the client's posture and educates him/her to use the muscles with maximum efficiency and minimum effort.

Special emphasis is placed upon the person's usual head and neck positions: a common trait is to pull your head back and up before standing from a sitting position, and as a reflex when startled or feeling unsure of yourself. This places the cervical spine and upper part of the spinal cord in false positions relative to the brain above and the rest of the spinal cord and spinal nerves below. Headaches, fatigue, numbness, pins and needles and faintness can all result from an abnormally positioned neck. When correctly aligned, the neck feels and often looks longer (especially if shoulders were previously hunched), and minor symptoms are often relieved.

Patients may be asked during a treatment session to visualise how they would stand and walk if in peak physical and mental condition, using

During a treatment, the client may be asked to lie flat with head supported, knees bent and soles of feet planted flat on the ground.

this image to help generate new habits and provide a constant check to eradicate bad ones. Alternatively, they may be requested to see themselves as a puppet with invisible strings easing their head up into the right anatomical position, elongating their neck, freeing the top middle and lower end of the spine, and raising the hands and arms, leg muscles and feet, in equilibrium with the rest of the body, thereby renewing its energy and efficiency. The benefits of the process are unquestionably holistic, because they can be felt physically, emotionally and even spiritually (among other factors, self-esteem and confidence tend to rise when we 'walk tall').

USE

Conditions for which the Alexander Technique is sought include disorders of the bones, muscles and joints, which orthodox and perhaps some alternative therapists have been unable to relieve. Some clients just feel below par without knowing why exactly and, having heard of this therapy, seek a postural solution to their problem.

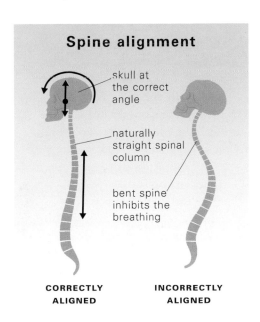

Spine alignment

skull at the correct angle

naturally straight spinal column

bent spine inhibits the breathing

CORRECTLY ALIGNED   **INCORRECTLY ALIGNED**

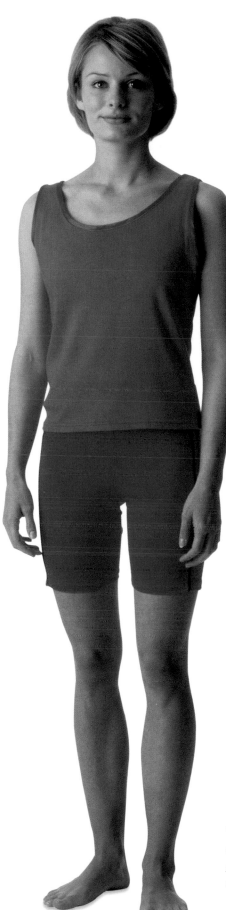

GOOD RESULTS

Specific medical disorders known to have responded to lessons in this technique include irritable bowel syndrome, chronic fatigue syndrome, diverticulitis, high blood pressure, asthma, trigeminal neuralgia (nerve pain in the side of the face), osteo- and rheumatoid arthritis, severe lethargy and lassitude, panic and anxiety attacks, pathological shyness or social phobia, tension headaches and migraine attacks, and chronic catarrh with or without sinusitis.

The correct alignment of the spinal column is an essential part of good posture. When we 'walk tall', our self-esteem and confidence improve.

the alexander technique

Applied kinesiology is both a diagnostic tool and a therapy based on human touch. Its practitioners believe that various forms of muscular weakness develop prior to the onset of (apparently unconnected) disorders, and also that what may appear to be muscular tension in one muscle group may in fact be weakness in its counterbalancing group.

applied kinesiology & touch for health

OTHER FORMS

Applied kinesiology is the most established form of the subject. There are many other, less orthodox forms, however, such as specialised, advanced and health kinesiology.

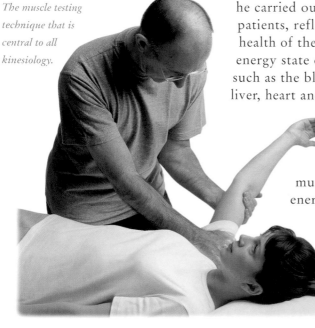

The muscle testing technique that is central to all kinesiology.

THE FACTS

HISTORY AND THEORY

The technique originated in 1968 from the findings of Dr George Goodheart, a US chiropractor. He discovered that standard tests for muscle tone and strength, which he carried out routinely on patients, reflected both the health of the muscle and the energy state of internal organs such as the bladder, kidneys, liver, heart and lungs. He postulated a functional connection between specific muscle groups and the energy channels represented by acupuncture meridians, and devised 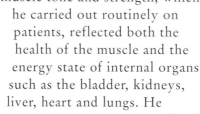 techniques for diagnosing and treating illnesses that drew upon the principles of both chiropractic and acupressure. He was able to identify joint malfunction, spinal lesions, internal disorders, psychological effects upon the functions of the body as a whole, nutritional deficiencies and allergies.

One of Dr Goodheart's pupils, Brian Butler, later introduced Touch for Health to the UK. This is essentially the same as applied kinesiology, but patients are taught to use it on themselves in order to detect and attempt to prevent disorders in the future. More recently, tests were introduced to demonstrate congestion of the lymphatic system (usually by uncleared toxins), and easy methods devised to help relieve poor circulation in the right and left lymphatic ducts (the two main pathways into which the network of lymph vessels drains on its way back to the chest). Some patients have reported improvement in conditions as diverse as lumpy breast tissue and hyperactivity. Applied kinesiology and Touch for Health have also been used for people with dyslexia.

TREATMENT

Disorders are viewed as malfunctioning energy pathways, and the appropriate muscle groups are tested with this in mind. Practitioners take a case history, including details of the current disorder, past medical history, family weaknesses, psychological and emotional state, nutrition and exercise, stress factors and the patient's response to these, and any known or suspected food or other allergies. Posture and muscle tone would be noted in great detail, as would areas of abnormal asymmetry, and instances of muscular tension and weakness.

As with all holistic therapies, treatment is directed at the underlying cause of the disorder, rather than simply relieving symptoms. Muscles are usually tested with the patient lying or sitting, the therapist examining first one side of the body and then the other. A group of muscles is initially tested, then the component muscles tested individually. The precise location of the muscular weakness shows where the illness is located. Muscular imbalances are corrected by the application of touch and pressure on relevant points, sometimes in combination with chiropractic manoeuvres.

Scientifically controlled clinical trials have been performed on applied kinesiology, involving hundreds of

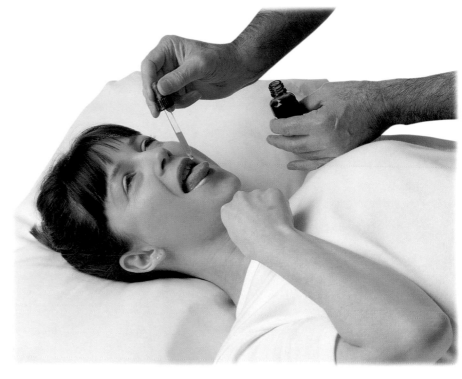

A therapist performs a muscle test on a patient.

patients over several years. Muscle testing has been shown to be extremely accurate with respect to the identification of various food allergies, and can detect specific problem foods in affected patients. Even 'hidden stressors' (foods with no apparent effect upon muscle strength) can now be identified in a test which, as Touch for Health, patients can be taught to perform for themselves.

Allergies to certain kinds of foods can be accurately identified by the process of muscle testing.

applied kinesiology & touch for health

Yoga is a movement therapy with origins in India dating back more than 5,000 years. It is also relatively new, in that little was heard of it in Britain until the 1960s, when the Beatles came into contact with the yogi Maharishi Mahesh. This section is concerned with the exercise aspect of yoga, known as hatha yoga.

yoga

PRECAUTIONS

- Do not practise the Headstand when pregnant or menstruating.
- Allow 3 hours to pass after eating a meal before practising yoga.
- Be wary of following a practice that does not seem to agree with your mind or body.

This asana is beneficial to people who are suffering from constipation or period problems.

THE FACTS

A HOLISTIC APPROACH

The slow, calm movement, the controlled breathing and the purpose behind the various postures (asanas) used in yoga bring balance and tranquillity to the body, mind and spirit. Most yoga teachers mention these holistic benefits as the basic aim of yoga, which in turn profoundly improve health and vitality. A huge attraction of yoga is its accessibility in some form to nearly everyone from young children to men and women in their seventies and eighties. Neither fitness nor strength is required in its practice, and most classes are suitable for people ranging from complete beginners to those who have mastered some of the more complicated asanas. You simply go at your own pace, following the teacher and doing the best you can, usually with plenty of help and encouragement from both teacher and other students.

BENEFITS

Yoga exercise improves both posture and breathing, which in turn benefits the circulation of the blood and the body's intake and utilisation of oxygen. Like most other movement therapies, it also increases the rate and efficiency with which waste material is excreted from the body via kidneys, bowel, skin, liver and lungs, thereby strengthening the immune defence system in its fight against infection, cancer and allergies. Certain asanas, such as the Corpse, the Fish and the Plough, aim specifically to improve bowel regularity, for

instance. All enhance breathing and improve blood supply to the kidneys and liver. Yoga also boosts the body's nervous and hormonal systems, and improves both flexibility and muscle tone by reintroducing the habits of stretching and bending after, perhaps, years of a sedentary lifestyle.

CLASSES
Unlike aerobic workouts and dance therapy sessions, you are extremely unlikely to hear music played during a yoga class. The target is to bring mind and body into harmony with one another and you have to concentrate to achieve this. A popular asana for beginners since practically everyone is capable of it is the Corpse (all asanas have Indian names and most also have Western equivalents). The name is suggestive of the shape your body assumes in following the asana; for example, Coil,

Cobra, Fish. For the Corpse, all you do is lie flat on your back, with your arms and hands by your sides and legs straight out in front, slightly parted at the ankles. This is normally chosen for both the beginning and the end of a yoga session, as it quietens the mind and helps focus your attention before you start and, at the end, allows you to relax fully before returning in mind and body to everyday affairs.

All the asanas are carried out slowly and smoothly, avoiding all rush and strain.

Yoga is a relatively new alternative therapy to the West, but it has been practised in India for over 5,000 years.

This asana is particularly useful to people with problems such as backache.

yoga

Each of the asanas is maintained for a few minutes (or however long feels comfortable), and then gently and slowly released and followed by a brief period of relaxation in a neutral position before the next asana is assumed. At all times, students are reminded of the importance of concentration, and shown how to breathe slowly, regularly and deeply in a way that coordinates with the type of asana(s) being used. There are also specific yoga breathing techniques to employ, such as 'alternate nostril breathing', which are usually taught as independent exercises.

The asanas are better demonstrated than described, and depending on how supple the student is, some are bound to be either impossible or uncomfortable initially, but it is surprising how quickly many aerobically unfit, stiff and overweight people become competent. A yoga instruction manual written 1,300 years ago states that an asana has been mastered when it can be followed naturally and effortlessly. Asanas are also combined by many practitioners with visualisation (a clear and deliberate image in the mind's eye of a thing or process you wish to bring about) and affirmations (positively phrased statements you

Performing the Corpse asana is one way to soothe away a headache.

wish to become true), particularly when healing benefits need to be directed at specific body areas or systems.

Health author Mark Bricklin, writing in *The Practical Encyclopaedia of Natural Healing* (Rodale Press), said of yoga: 'If you practise yoga postures, you are strengthening the body. If you control your breathing, you are creating a chemical and emotional balance. If you concentrate your mind in affirmations, you are practising the power of prayer. But if you synthesise all three, you are entering the most powerful mystery of healing: the basic harmony of life.'

USE
Common disorders successfully treated by yoga include the following with their corresponding asanas (each asana should be preceded and followed by deep breathing and relaxation).

For skin disorders, the Sun Salutation is recommended. This is a sequence of 12 postures.

For people suffering from insomnia, the Cobra asana might help.

yoga

The most useful yoga asanas and the ailments they can help

Corpse, Mountain, Complete Breath, Fish, Shoulder Stand, Locust, Plough, Twist, Cobra, Uddiyana, Knee to Chest, Yoga Mudra, Posterior Stretch, Sun Salutation, Grip, Kneeling Pose, Shoulder Roll, Lion, Knee in Chest, Neck and Eye Exercises

DEPRESSION
Yoga Mudra, Shoulder Stand, Plough, Corpse.

EYESTRAIN
Neck and Eye exercises.

FLATULENCE
Knee to chest.

HEADACHE
Corpse, Neck and Eye exercises, Shoulder Roll.

ASTHMA
Corpse, Mountain, Complete Breath, Fish, Shoulder Stand.

BACKACHE
Corpse, Plough, Locust, Knee to Chest.

CONSTIPATION
Corpse, Fish, Plough, Twist (loosens and flexes spine), Knee to Chest (reinvigorates liver, spleen and bowel), Posterior Stretch, Uddiyana, Yoga Mudra.

INDIGESTION
Corpse, Locust, Mountain, Plough, Twist, Cobra, Uddiyana.

INSOMNIA
Corpse, Mountain, Locust, Cobra, Posterior Stretch.

PERIOD PROBLEMS
Plough, Fish, Shoulder Stand, Cobra, Posterior Stretch.

RHEUMATISM
Twist, Mountain, Shoulder Stand, Knee in Chest.

SCIATICA
Shoulder Stand, Kneeling Pose, Twist, Grip, Knee in Chest.

SEXUAL PROBLEMS
Plough, Shoulder Stand, Twist, Complete Breath, Uddiyana.

SINUSITIS
Shoulder Stand, Corpse.

The Shoulder Stand can be used to relieve a range of ailments, including asthma, lethargy, piles and sexual problems.

EXHAUSTION AND LETHARGY
Mountain, Shoulder Stand, Corpse, Posterior Stretch.

OBESITY
Shoulder Stand, Locust, Posterior Stretch, Plough, Bow, Sun Salutation, Cobra.

PILES
Fish, Shoulder Stand, Plough.

PROSTATE GLAND
Kneeling Pose.

SKIN DISORDERS
Sun Salutation.

SORE THROAT
Lion.

VARICOSE VEINS
Shoulder Stand.

WRINKLES
Yoga Mudra, Shoulder Stand.

yoga

Relaxation and meditation are becoming increasingly valued as tools for stress management and for reducing the physical and mental effects of stress. Relaxation therapy consists mainly of simple breathing exercises and muscle relaxation techniques. Meditation is included in the practice of many religions as a means of achieving deep relaxation, inner harmony and focusing the mind. Both can be practised at home.

relaxation & meditation

RELAXATION BENEFITS

- Reduced blood pressure
- Better-balanced digestion and respiration processes
- Improved sleep patterns
- Relief from anxiety and depression

Relaxation tapes are often used to relax clients as part of a Quit Smoking programme.

THE FACTS

RELAXATION

Many people use a tape, of which there are two main types, for relaxation. The first plays soothing sounds such as spring rain, a waterfall or waves. You then just lie or sit back comfortably and listen to your chosen sound, and let it take over from your usual busy stream of thoughts, helping you relax your muscles until you experience true tranquillity.

The other sort of tape is the 'guided relaxation' kind often included in a Quit Smoking programme, or which a doctor may advise you to listen to to help you overcome insomnia, for example, or deal with severe stress reactions, phobias or panic attacks. You will be told to relax each muscle group in turn, until you are relaxed all over. Normally beginning with the muscles of the feet and calves, and working up the body to include the facial muscles, scalp and tongue, the pleasant and soothing voice makes it easy to relax.

Slow, regular breathing is central to successful relaxation. A common rhythm is 7–1, 7–1, involving inhaling to a count of seven, holding for a count of one, exhaling for a count of seven and pausing for a count of one before recommencing the cycle. When the breath and body are in quiet harmony the repetition of positive thoughts or intentions is most effective. You could start off saying slowly and repetitively, in harmony with your breathing: 'I enjoy a smoke-free healthy life' if, for instance, you were quitting smoking. Visualising your goal is another powerful tool; in this instance, picturing yourself inhaling fresh air, far from the fumes of cigarettes.

USE

Tension headaches, facial pain,
sinusitis, neck and shoulder pain,
even pain down the arm and into the
fingers, can arise from tension in the
shoulder girdle, upper back and neck.
Regular relaxation properly carried
out can have a real impact on the
physical level, and for general effects
of wear and tear it will appear to
work wonders.

MEDITATION

Like relaxation, meditation can
be approached in several ways.
Some authorities advocate sitting
comfortably in some quiet spot at the
same time twice daily for, say, 20 to
30 minutes. Here, the person relaxes
their muscle groups in turn, as
described above in the relaxation
section. It is necessary to breathe
calmly and regularly (either slowly in
and slowly out without pausing, or
breathing in for a certain count and
holding the breath, then exhaling
again to a certain count and pausing
before breathing in again). The third
element (besides patterned breathing
and physical relaxation), is
observation, which may come as a
surprise to the many people who
believe that, to meditate successfully,
you have to empty your mind
entirely of thought. Observation
actually helps the mind to relax
and enter the state of tranquillity
with which so much of yoga and
relaxation/meditation is concerned.
There are several different brain-
wave types functional in an active
brain, but during meditation
the brain produces high-
intensity alpha brain-
waves, the ones

associated with deep relaxation and
mental alertness. When the brain is
in an alpha state the body gradually
relaxes as the parasympathetic
division of the nervous system takes
over, reversing the body's fight-or-
flight response. Practised regularly,
meditation can induce the experience
of bliss, or, at the very least, provide
a healthful physical, mental and
spiritual rest from daily activities
and stresses.

*Relaxation tapes often feature
sounds associated with peace and
harmony, such as running water.*

*Regular meditation will promote a
wonderful sense of well-being and
internal harmony.*

relaxation & meditation

T'ai chi is a fulfilling holistic movement therapy which benefits the body, mind and spirit. Consisting of a series of essentially circular movements, it looks deceptively easy. But the smoothness and balance of the movements, controlled and regular breathing, and remembering how you progress from one part of a sequence to another, are highly demanding in terms of time, patience and memory.

t'ai chi & dance therapy

T'AI CHI PRINCIPLES

T'ai chi is based on three main principles: qi, the universal life force; Taoism; and the yin-yang principle. The most important of these is qi – stressing the internal power of a flexible body and calm mind.

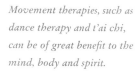

Movement therapies, such as dance therapy and t'ai chi, can be of great benefit to the mind, body and spirit.

THE FACTS

T'AI CHI

Thought to have been developed to help convalescing warriors regain their strength, and still recommended for this purpose today, t'ai chi is extensively practised in China and elsewhere as a system of preventive health care, since it is widely accepted that 20 minutes of practice daily over a period of years can prolong youthful vigour and rejuvenate the body. You can see people from all walks of life going through a particular movement sequence (generally out in the open) on the way to work, before lectures, in schools and during lunch breaks.

T'ai chi indisputably exercises every part of the body but the movements also conserve energy, because the sequences are economical, with no part of them being superfluous. The 108 basic movements are performed in a slow, calm and aware manner in one of two possible sequences, the first containing over 100 movement units, and the second containing between 30 and 40.

Watching a t'ai chi master demonstrating the sequences is similar to watching a perfectly learned and choreographed ballet solo. A lot of work is required to master any such physical activity and to overcome the tendency to stumble, jerk, make swift or superfluous movements or simply forget what to do next. However, you will not feel exhausted or frustrated after an hour's lesson (which is usually carried out in a class or group) but, rather, energised and balanced, less stressed and more confident than before, with improved breathing, digestion and bowel movements, steadier nerves and more resilience to stress.

Dance therapy is an excellent way of getting rid of inner conflicts and adverse stress reactions, and, like yoga, is suitable for people of all ages, regardless of their state of fitness and ability. It also offers many of the benefits of music therapy (see page 242).

Dance therapy can be taught on an individual basis, but is more often taught in a group.

DANCE THERAPY

Dance therapy exercises the body, improving posture, muscle control and, where aerobic, the function of the heart, lungs and circulation. It also releases repressed inner tensions and conflicts within people with mental and emotional problems, bringing them into conscious awareness and reducing their harmful influence.

With a little verbal encouragement and appropriate music, the most introverted person can usually be persuaded to express his inner turmoil, joys and sorrows by acting them out bodily in time to drums, percussion or military band music, for example. Doing so translates these emotions into something more tangible than thoughts and feelings, which cannot be expressed verbally. Most music therapy teachers keep classes small enough for each client's needs to be dealt with adequately, starting with limbering-up exercises and often grouping clients in a ring and holding hands. This emphasises intercommunication and being part of a whole at a physical level.

Total physical benefits are aimed at, with use being encouraged of every part of the body in whatever way the participants feel motivated. Suggestions may be made to jump up and down as you dance along, or curl up in a ball on the floor as soon as the music stops. Clients often elaborate these for their own self-expression, curling up in foetal distress, perhaps, or leaping up and down in rage, fear or joy.

Dance therapy can be a useful technique for people who have difficulties expressing themselves verbally.

t'ai chi & dance therapy

Feelings have been expressed in artistic form since the time of cave dwellers, but it was only in the 20th century that psychologists such as Freud, Jung and Klein ascribed symbolic meanings to the images and colours used in artwork. Colours themselves have always had symbolic meanings, and the impact of colour upon mood is widely acknowledged.

art & colour therapy

CAUTION

These therapies are of great value in treating certain psychological or emotional disorders. However, they should not be used as a form of self-help treatment for any psychological problem. Consult your doctor first.

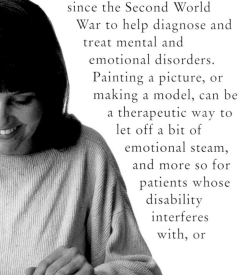

Aura-soma is mainly used to treat people with disorders related to stress and emotional problems.

THE FACTS

ART THERAPY

Art therapy is a combination of conventional and complementary medicine and has been used since the Second World War to help diagnose and treat mental and emotional disorders. Painting a picture, or making a model, can be a therapeutic way to let off a bit of emotional steam, and more so for patients whose disability interferes with, or prevents them from, communicating verbally. In this respect, music and art therapy share a common aim. A feeling of achievement and self-worth can be acquired or improved, simply by the act of creation, whatever its 'worth' in a wider, critical sense. Even more can be gained by patients from this in the healing sense, whenever it is possible to explore the symbolism of the work in order to gain insight into their inner conflicts.

The study by the therapist of a sequence of pictures or models produced by the same patient over time can prove enlightening and suggestive of progress or lack of progress in response to treatment. Assessing the 'meaning' of the work is generally down to the judgement of the therapist, aided by the patient. Art therapy is also used in prisons and hospitals for the criminally insane, where accurate assessment and analysis is vital.

Encouraging patients to try their hand at representative art (drawing or shaping things as they really appear to them) has the dual purpose of bringing them into closer contact with the world around them, and of revealing how close to, or separated from, reality they are. This is important in the cases of psychotic patients suffering from schizophrenia and phases of bipolar disorder (manic depression), where contact with reality is a direct gauge of their state of mental health.

COLOUR THERAPY

Many of us are familiar with colour therapy, through TV programmes on suitable colours for the home (to create mood in a room), and colour consultants who suggest suitable shades of clothes and make-up (assessed from the individual's colour type and expressed as spring, summer, autumn or winter). The effect of colours on the mood is also taken seriously in certain prisons and psychiatric hospitals, where a rosy pink hue serves to calm irritability and frayed tempers.

The therapeutic use of colour can be traced back to the ancient world, when the Chinese, Egyptians and Mesopotamians used it to cure the sick. Modern colour therapy dates from the 19th century and the discoveries made concerning the light spectrum and electromagnetic waves. Colour therapists believe that colours can be used to treat illness and improve physical, emotional and spiritual well-being. Each colour has its own vibrational frequency, which directly affects body organs and cells. A therapist will use different colours to correct vibrational imbalances in the body. Many practitioners also believe that the body emits its own energy field, or 'aura', the colours of which indicate a person's general state

of health. The psychological effects of this therapy are much more widely accepted than the physical.

AURA-SOMA

One variant of colour therapy, aura-soma, was invented by Vicky Wall, a pharmacist and chiropodist, in the mid-1980s. It combines elements of aromatherapy, herbal medicine and mineral supplementation with the use of colour. It originated from Wall's observation that mentally and emotionally disturbed people chose to buy cloudy rather than clear oil from an exhibition stand.

Wall could perceive people's auras and found that they tended to choose colours and sorts of oils to match their personal energy field. They selected oils comparable to themselves in terms of clarity or opaqueness, reflecting their need for its reinforcing effect upon their own aura. Wall used oils in balanced pairs to offer to patients, reading from their choices and the speed with which the oils settled after being shaken the patient's state of inner balance and physical and emotional needs.

Painting is a great way of expressing and releasing feelings of tension or emotional upset.

Wearing bright clothes will counteract depression, lack of self-confidence and low self esteem.

art & colour therapy

There is no doubting the powerfully emotive effect of music, which can marshal men to battle, soften rage into affection and romance, calm torment and, conversely, cause intense emotional suffering by means of its exquisite beauty. It has been used since time immemorial to induce all these states of mind; and also to heal disorders of the body, mind and spirit.

music therapy

ANCIENT THERAPY

Music has long been used as a healing remedy – there are accounts of the healing powers of music in the Bible. The Ancient Greeks also believed in music as a healer – Apollo was the god of music and healing.

THE FACTS

A THERAPY OF THE SOUL

Instances are recorded of the beneficial effects of certain types of music on anxiety and depression. It is often used with forms of therapy to induce a sensation of calm: for example, on relaxation tapes; and may be played in meditation. It plays an important part in dance therapy, where the combined effects of music and movement release inner turmoil and conflicts.

For people who find it difficult to communicate, music can provide a useful vehicle for self-expression.

In a way, music is a therapy of the soul, speaking to our spiritual faculties through the medium of our brains and sense of hearing. By reviving a despairing or lonely spirit, calming an overtaxed one or heartening a desolate and abandoned one, it lifts the mood and cognitive faculties and makes us feel physically and mentally better. In this way, it works in an opposite direction to many physically and emotionally directed therapies which first strengthen and balance the body before working upon our mental powers and our spiritual selves.

TREATMENT

There are not many trained music therapists in practice, considering the number of people in today's society who might be expected to benefit from their care. Those that do exist often have highly individual ideas about what music therapy is and how it should be practised; and often enjoy success in the easing of pent-up feelings, particularly in physically and mentally disabled people, encouraging them to respond to the music however they see fit. Many clients respond to the music by leaping up and down and/or screaming, running about in all directions, shouting, laughing or crying. Others prefer simply to lie down or sit quietly and comfortably while they absorb the music's healing qualities without feeling the need to demonstrate how it affects them.

USE

An alternative healing use for music is to encourage patients with verbal communication difficulties (such as autism, Asperger's syndrome or particular speech problems) to 'talk' through making musical notes, for example, on a piano, a recorder, or on drums, to express what they would like to say if they were able to do so.

Other disorders or situations in which music therapy has proved extremely helpful include asthma, dental nerves and painful childbirth. In a two-year experiment conducted during the 1960s in the United States, 30 asthmatic children between the ages of eight and 15 were encouraged to take up music when they entered junior or high school; 15 were given wind instruments, and the rest, other types of musical instrument. The 15 wind instrument players developed markedly improved physical and emotional health, especially in pulmonary function, and their disease progressed far less than that of the children who had learned to play non-wind instruments.

Other work has shown that women experiencing painful or prolonged labour will relax much more easily and require less analgesia (pain-killing gas and air, or other drugs) if tranquil and soothing music is played while they are in the labour room. The same benefits were found in a group of dental patients who were treated while they listened to cheerful and relaxing music.

Listening to classical music can have a calming effect. It can help when undergoing a painful or uncomfortable process, such as giving birth or dental treatment.

music therapy

Hypnotherapy is the use of trance to ease behavioural change or combat unwanted symptoms. It is now widely practised by GPs, lay therapists and medically qualified psychotherapists. While its occasional misuse in the form of stage hypnotism reflects adversely upon the whole question of trance induction, the general public are becoming increasingly aware of hypnotherapy's usefulness.

hypnotherapy

COMMON USES

Hypnosis is used most successfully in the treatment of addictions and phobias, but it can also provide effective pain relief for surgery, dentistry and childbirth. It also works very well as a relaxation technique.

Hypnotherapy has proved effective in helping smokers to give up.

THE FACTS

FINDING A THERAPIST

Most clients find themselves a hypnotherapist on personal recommendation or through local or national advertising. It's best to check on a therapist's credentials, and enquire how long they have practised and what sort of success they have achieved in treating your particular problem. In turn, you are likely to be asked about your general health, especially if you have sought help for physical rather than psychological symptoms. Usually, though, the therapist concentrates upon the client's mental and emotional state, enquiring about lifestyle, family and personal relationships, moods, stress factors, libido or sexual interest (if relevant), worries, fears and current symptoms, if present.

You should also be prepared to give at least an outline account of any past or present psychiatric diagnoses and treatment. Trance induction in the hands of an experienced professional can improve self-esteem, teach relaxation methods and help with the problems outlined above, but it is not generally considered suitable for the treatment of manic depression, schizophrenia and other psychotic illnesses, and personality disorders.

TREATMENT

Having assessed a client's suitability, the hypnotherapist then explores their attitude to treatment which, together with a genuine desire to get well, is more crucial to success than in any other therapy. The client needs to cooperate, practise self-hypnosis between sessions and show a reasonable degree of suggestibility (see below). The projected course of treatment would then be sketched out, and an idea given of the probable number of sessions required. Normally, patients attend once or twice a week for an hour; 3–4 sessions are generally sufficient to cure a habit such as smoking, provided no deep-seated neurotic reasons underlie the habit, but for long-standing depression or anxiety states, as many as 20 to 30 sessions may be required.

Suggestibility (ease of entering a trance) can be tested by getting the client as relaxed as possible, and suggesting, for example, that one of their arms is slowly rising from the chair arm or couch without any conscious effort. Arm levitation is a curious and impressive experience and augurs well for the success of treatment. An essential aspect of trance induction is the distraction of the client's conscious mind which houses the critical faculties. This may be done by getting the client to count backwards in sevens from, say, two hundred, while suggesting to his subconscious mind that he/she is becoming more and more relaxed.

IN A TRANCE

Unlike sleep, you remain, when in a trance, dimly aware of what is going on around you and can certainly snap out of it in an emergency, but you feel tranquil, drowsy and aware more than anything of the hypnotist's voice. You are also receptive to the therapeutic suggestions being made: for example, that cigarettes will taste more and more unpleasant from then on, gradually building up a deep distaste for smoking over perhaps 2–3

weeks. Self-hypnosis is usually taught as well, to enable the client to repeat the helpful suggestions to the subconscious between sessions. Post-hypnotic suggestions may also be planted during a trance, often to help with specific situations. An example in the case of someone with agoraphobia would be a sensation of relaxation and calmness coming over him/her while out shopping and encountering crowds.

Hypnotic trance cannot be used to compel a person to act contrary to his or her particular moral code, nor in a manner the person would normally find deeply shaming or embarrassing. The contrary appears true when you see volunteers emulating animals, for instance, on stage; but essentially they possess a strong (if latent) desire to perform in public, whatever they may claim after the event.

USES

Hypnotherapy has helped millions of people to stop smoking, for instance, and to overcome unwanted eating habits, panic attacks and phobic illnesses. Besides smoking, hypnotherapy works for some cases of heavy drinking and gambling, and long-standing depression, and it also may help people with obsessive-compulsive neurosis.

In a session, the hypnotherapist will ensure that the patient is in a trance before beginning treatment.

Hypnotherapy can be used to treat emotional states such as depression or anxiety, though a number of sessions may be required.

hypnotherapy

246

Some of us know about spiritual healing from documentaries about charismatic Christian leaders whose exhortations to sick members of the congregation are said to effect miraculous cures – returning mobility to stroke victims, for instance. Most spiritual healing, however, is done by ordinary people born with the healing touch, using their gift to relieve physical, mental or spiritual ailments.

spiritual healing

CAUTION

Healing is not a substitute for medical treatment. Consult a doctor if you are suffering from a medical condition before visiting a healer particularly if your disorder is emotional or psychiatric.

We all know the healing benefits of touch during periods of distress.

THE FACTS

POSITIVE HEALING ENERGY

Many practitioners discover their healing power accidentally, often as children. Obviously it helps them to develop their gift if parents and other family members have psychic interests or training, but some simply feel drawn to touch the weak or sick, perhaps from an innate desire to pass on to them some of their strength or well-being. If you consider the comfort of a loving arm around your shoulders, or even your hand held tightly, in moments of grief and distress, it is not hard to progress a stage to envisage the power of positive healing working in a similar way.

THEORY

Intrinsically holistic because of their view that harmony between body, mind and spirit is essential for good health, spiritual healers tend to recognise the 'life force' either as a personal god or as the 'creative intelligence' giving life and existence to all things. They revere its infinite healing capacity, and seek to re-establish its free-flow throughout their patient by linking the person with the 'god' or the intelligence, however this is conceived. The resultant triangle between healer, patient and 'god' liberates the healing energies from the divine source to flow into the sick person.

Interestingly, religious belief or faith on behalf of the patient is not essential for healing to occur. Although spiritual healing has occurred since time immemorial and is becoming increasingly accepted once more in the Western world, it is still misunderstood by many as a lot of meaningless ritual, or even as a trick to try to convert non-believers. For these reasons, spiritual healing is very often a last resort grasped in desperation by seriously ill people who seem to have tried everything else.

This is a pity, because although some maintain that miracles do occur, less energy channelling is required to correct bodily, mental or spiritual dysfunction in the early rather than the terminal stages of development. In addition, regardless of whether or not the hoped-for aim is achieved, nearly all sufferers can expect to experience greater calmness and tranquillity, and a lifting of the mood and spirits.

TREATMENT

Healers do not necessarily touch the body of the afflicted person. They work, instead, through the patient's 'aura' – the invisible but scientifically detectable electromagnetic field surrounding all living organisms rather like a biblical halo. Clairvoyants and psychics generally perceive the aura clearly, noting the jagged edges, discolouration and patchiness typical of a person or animal in distress. The aura extends around the body for up to 10 to 12 inches, and it is within this layer that most healers place their hands – perhaps over the part of the body stricken with illness – focusing their prayer, belief and healing energy where these are most needed.

The majority of spiritual healers refuse to charge for their services, although some permit donations to be given to cover their travelling costs, for example, or a simple meal if travelling long distances. The philosophy common to most is that the harmonious, simple life uncluttered by excessive materialistic

striving is the most conducive to health. They advocate simplicity and a natural approach to all things, from a wholefood, often vegetarian, diet to a lifestyle that respects the significance of all things – plants, animals and inanimate objects included – in the grand scheme of things. Patients may be gently reminded that, to receive, it is necessary first to give; and that hatred, resentment and rage inevitably cause pain, disorder and instability to the person nurturing them.

It should also be added that spiritual healers do not necessarily see success solely in terms of symptom removal. They strive also for the restoration of harmony and peace, and the granting of sufficient strength to face whatever the future may hold.

Faith healers are very popular and often have a dedicated following of people.

TYPES OF HEALING

Faith healing: This requires the patient to have faith in the healer's or the deity's powers.
Spiritual healing: Healers act as channels for a healing force. Different types include: Prayer healing; Aura healing; Psychic healing; Shamanistic healing; and Spiritualist healing.

spiritual healing

Studies into the effects of laughter have shown it to have significant health benefits. Giggling, roaring and snorting with mirth enhances the well-being of body, mind and spirit. It acts directly upon the brain and the endocrine glands, promoting the release of tension-breaking chemicals and reducing the effects of the stress hormones adrenaline and noradrenaline, transmitted into the bloodstream.

laughter therapy

USES

The health benefits of laughter therapy:
- Muscle relaxation
- Stress reduction
- Good aerobic exercise
- Anti-stress measure
- Treats depression
- Strengthens the immune system
- Natural painkiller
- Enhances confidence

Laughter therapy can be beneficial to people who are suffering from work-related stress.

THE FACTS

PHYSICAL EFFECTS

It is difficult, if not impossible, to roar with laughter while lying down flat. When our sense of humour is aroused, we tend to sit up, alternately tense and relax our limb and torso muscles, and inhale great gusts of air which we expel in short, or prolonged, noisy bursts. These actions combine to increase the pulse rate, increase the intake of oxygen by the lungs, raise the flow of oxygenated blood to the brain and, temporarily, elevate the pressure within the abdomen and pelvis. While the last-mentioned can lead to the involuntary loss of a few drops of urine in children, the elderly, post-menopausal women and anyone else with a weak bladder or urethra, the bonuses far outweigh the disadvantages.

Knots of muscular tension are released, reducing pain and stiffness. The immune defence system also receives a boost, creating extra T-cells to help fight infections and malignant cell change, and manufacturing antibodies against harmful foreign bodies and organisms. Mood-enhancing chemicals called endorphins are also released from deep within the brain, lifting the mood and promoting feelings of well-being, relaxation and content. These are the chemicals released during strenuous exercise, responsible for the so-called 'runner's high'; they boost a low mood and help to alleviate depression.

Linked closely with excessive stress factors, depression is associated with a reduction in the brain of the mood-elevating chemicals serotonin and noradrenaline (the latter plays numerous, mainly positive, roles within the body). The release of endorphins by laughter (or by exercise) can counteract the effect of this reduction, making a good

Laughter therapy can help people
of all ages, and works particularly
well with children.

belly-laugh the most natural and
accessible aid to mental health known
to humans.

Further benefits to the brain
(all linked directly or indirectly
with the increased flow of richly
oxygenated blood to that organ)
include enhanced creativity,
enhanced intellectual performance
and improved short-term memory.

TREATMENT AND USE

Assessed and confirmed in clinical
studies in the United States and
Europe, all these benefits encouraged
a growing awareness of laughter's
value. This led to the development of
'humourisme' therapy in France and
elsewhere, where comedians, amusing
videotapes and other sources of
humour are employed to help relieve
and cure the chronically sick.

Humourisme therapy has proved
especially popular in the treatment of
cancer patients, many of whom
understandably suffer from
depression, where it is combined with
orthodox medicine and a selection of
complementary therapies in an holistic
approach to the disease. It can greatly
enhance the effects of meditation and
visualisation, taught to patients with
cancer in a bid to help them boost
their immune defence systems.

Even where humour or laughter
therapy is not officially employed,
the usefulness of (non-frightening)
clowns in children's wards and
paediatric outpatient deparments,
for instance, has long been
recognised and sought. Laughter
therapy, including counselling and
taped material, is now available via
the Internet.

ANTI-STRESS

Laughter is one of the
best anti-stress measures
to practise. It is a great
muscle relaxant, it
expands the blood
vessels, and can reduce
the level of stress
hormones in the body.
It also strengthens the
immune system.

laughter therapy

glossary

abscess: a self-contained pocket of pus that results from a bacterial infection, and causes inflammation of the local area

acupoint: a point along a meridian at which the 'qi' is thought to be accessible in acupuncture. Acupoints are stimulated by the insertion of acupuncture needles

acute: something of sudden onset and brief duration

allergy: the body's abnormal response to a substance that in most people causes no response. Common allergies include hay fever, eczema and asthma

antacid: a remedy or medicine that reduces stomach acidity

antibiotic: used to treat infections caused by bacteria

asana: a body posture adopted in yoga

bacteria: microorganisms, some of which can cause disease

benign: of a tumour. Not cancerous and will not spread throughout the body

cardiac: pertaining to the heart

chronic: persisting for a long time; a state showing no change or very slow change

coagulant: an agent that acts to clot and thicken the blood

complementary: a term used to describe alternative forms of medical treatment – emphasising the fact that they support rather than replace orthodox medicine

compress: a pad usually soaked in hot or ice-cold water and applied to the body for relief of swelling and pain, or to produce localised pressure

cortisol: a steroid hormone produced by the adrenal glands which is important for the body's responses to stress

depression: a mental state characterised by a feeling of sadness or melancholy and a sense of reduced emotional well-being. This may be a normal response that deepens or persists or it may be a symptom of psychiatric illness

dermatitis: an inflammatory skin condition – a reaction in response to an allergen

discharge: an excretion or substance that is evacuated by the body

dysmenorrhoea: the severe pains that sometimes accompany the menstrual period

ECG: electrocardiogram – a recording of the electrical activity associated with the heartbeat

effleurage: slow, rhythmic massage

essential oil: a volatile and aromatic liquid that constitutes the odorous principles of a plant. This is obtained by a process of distillation from a botanical form or species. The pure concentrated essence is said to be the plant's life force

five elements: fire, water, wood, metal and earth – the system in Chinese medicine based on observations of the natural world

hernia: the protrusion of an organ or tissue out of the body cavity in which it normally lies

holistic: aiming to treat the individual as an entity, incorporating mind, body and spirit. From the Greek *holos*, meaning whole

hormone: a chemical transmitter substance produced by the body. This acts specifically on target cells to control their activity

hypertension: raised blood pressure

hypotension: low blood pressure, or a fall in blood pressure below the normal range

immunodeficiency: the failure of the immune system's defences to fight infection

infection: multiplication of pathogenic (disease-producing) microorganisms in the body

inflammation: the response of protective tissue to injury or the destruction of body cells, characterised by heat, swelling, redness and usually pain

inhalant: a remedy breathed in through the nose or mouth

laxative: a substance that provokes evacuation of the bowels

lesion: a structural or functional change in body tissues. Can be caused by disease or injury

meditation: exercising the mind in contemplation

melatonin: the hormone produced by the pineal gland that helps to regulate the sleep cycle

menopause: the normal cessation of menstruation; a life change in women

mucous membranes: the surface linings of the body, which secrete mucus

NSAIDs: non steroidal anti-inflammatory drugs which are used to bring down swelling and relieve pain

peptic: a term that is applied to gastric secretions and the areas that are affected by them

phobia: a persistant and severe fear, usually irrational, of a particular event or thing

pituitary gland: the 'master control' gland that is situated in the base of the brain. It produces many different hormones: for example, growth hormones and those that stimulate other endocrine glands to secrete hormones

poultice: the therapeutic application of a soft moist mass of fresh herbs to the skin to encourage local circulation and to relieve pain

qi (chi): the essential energy of the universe, which is fundamental to all elements of life. It runs through the whole body in channels or meridians

rhinitis: the inflammation (often chronic) of the mucous membranes lining the nasal passage

sebum: an oily, lubricating and protective substance secreted by the glands in the skin

sedative: an agent that reduces functional activity; calming

steroids: fat-soluble organic compounds that occur naturally throughout the plant and animal kingdoms and play many important functional roles

subluxation: the incomplete dislocation of any two bones where they meet at a joint

TIA: transient ischemic attack; a mild form of stroke

tonic: restores tone to the systems, balances, nourishes and promotes well-being; strengthens and enlivens the body

topical: the local application of cream, ointment or tincture, or other medicine

trauma: a physical injury or wound, also an unpleasant and disturbing experience causing psychological upset

ulcer: a slow-healing sore that can occur internally or externally

ultrasound: extremely high frequency sound waves, inaudible to the human ear. They are used to break up kidney stones and produce images of the interior of the human body

vitamin: a small group of substances that are needed for healthy growth. They are essential constituents of the diet

X-rays: electromagnetic radiation with great penetrating power

bibliography

Acupuncture by Peter Mole, Health Essentials series
publ. Vega Books; new edition April 2002.

Aromatherapy: An A – Z by Patricia Davis and Sarah Budd
(illustrator), publ. The C W Daniel Company Ltd., 1995.

The Beginner's Guide To Mind, Body and Spirit by Rosalind
Widdowson, publ. Regency House Publishing Ltd., 2001.

The Complete Medicinal Herbal by Penelope Ody,
publ. Dorling Kindersley, August 2000.

Earl Mindell's Vitamin Bible For The 21st. Century publ. Warner
Books, May 1999.

*The Family Guide to Homeopathy: Symptoms and Natural
Solutions*, by Dr. Andrew Lockie, publ. Simon and Schuster
Books, reprint 1993.

*How To Lower High Blood Pressure – The Natural Four Point Plan
To Reduce Hypertension* by Dr. Caroline Shreeve, publ. Thorsons
(Harper Collins), revised edition 2001 (originally plubl. 1989).

The Raw Energy Bible by Leslie Kenton, publ. Vermilion,
January 2001.

Yoga, Tantra and Meditation in Daily Life by Swami Janakananda
Saraswati, publ. Samuel Weiser 1992.

further reading

The Alternative Dictionary of Symptoms and Cures by
Dr. Caroline M Shreeve, publ. Century Hutchinson, 1986.

The Green Witch by Barbara Griggs,
publ. Vermilion Books, 2000.

Naturopathic Medicine by Roger Newman Turner,
publ. Thorsons, 1984.

useful addresses and websites

Aromatherapy Organizations Council

PO Box 19834, London SE25 6WS

Tel: 020 8251 7912

Association of Reflexologists

27 Old Gloucester Street,

London WC1N 3XX

Tel: 0870 5673320

www.aor.org.uk/

Bach Flower Therapy

The Dr Edward Bach Centre,

Mount Vernon, Sotwell,

Wallingford, Oxfordshire OX10 OPZ

Tel: 01491 834678 Fax: 01491 825022

www.bachcentre.com/

**British Association of Counselling
and Psychotherapy**

1 Regent Place, Rugby,

Warwickshire CV21 2PJ

Tel: 01788 550899 Fax: 01788 562189

www.bacp.co.uk/

British Chiropractic Association

Blagrave Street, Reading, Berks RG1 1QB

Tel: 0118 950 5950 Fax: 0118 958 8946

www.chiropractic-uk.co.uk/

British Homeopathic Association

15 Clerkenwell Close,

London EC1R 0AA

Tel: 020 7566 7800 Fax: 020 7566 7815

www.trusthomeopathy.org/

British Medical Acupuncture Society

12 Marbury House, Higher Whitley,

Warrington, Cheshire, WA4 4QW

Tel: 01925 730727 Fax: 01925 730492

www.medical-acupuncture.co.uk/

British Osteopathic Association

Langham House East, Luton,

Bedfordshire LU1 2NA

Tel: 01582 488455 Fax. 01582 481533

www.osteopathy.org/

British Reflexology Association

Monks Orchard, Whitbourne,

Worcester, WR6 5RB

Tel: 01886 821207 Fax: 01886 822017

www.britreflex.co.uk/

British Society of Hypnotherapists

37 Orbain Road, London SW16 7JZ

Tel: 020 7385 1166

www.bsch.org.uk/

**Institute for Complementary
Medicine**

PO Box 194, London SE16 7QZ

Tel: 020 7237 5165 Fax:020 7237 5175

www.icmedicine.co.uk/

International Association of Colour

46 Cottenham Road, Histon,

Cambridge CB4 9ES, UK

Tel: 01223 563403

**International Federation of
Aromatherapists**

182 Chiswick High Road,

London W4 1PP

Tel: 020 8742 2605

www.int-fed-aromatherapy.co.uk/

**National Federation of Spiritual
Healers (NFSH)**

Old Manor Farm Studio,

Church Street, Sunbury-on-Thames,

Middlesex TW16 6RG

Tel: 01932 783164

www.nfsh.org.uk/

**National Institute for Medical
Herbalists**

56 Longbrook Street, Exeter EX4 6AH

Tel: 01392 426022

Psychosynthesis and Education Trust

92–94 Tooley Street, London SE1 2TH

Tel: 020 7403 2100

www.psychosynthesis.edu/

**UK Homeopathic Medical
Association**

6 Livingstone Road, Gravesend,

Kent DA12 5DZ

Tel: 01474 560336

www.homoeopathy.org/

index